Dr Jenni Nuttall was an academic who taught and researched medieval literature at the University of Oxford for the last twenty years, and who had a lot of practice at making old words interesting. She had a DPhil from Oxford, completed the University of East Anglia's MA in Creative Writing and was the author of a reader's guide to Geoffrey Chaucer's *Troilus and Criseyde* with Cambridge University Press. *Mother Tongue* was her book first for the general reader. She died in 2024.

Praise for *Mother Tongue*

'Fascinating, intriguing, witty, a gem of a book' Kate Mosse

'Full of interesting observations ... Entertaining' Philip Hensher, *Spectator*

'Wonderful' *Daily Telegraph*

'Jenni Nuttall's *Mother Tongue* will easily be one of the wittiest and most insightful books of the year' *Buzz Magazine*

'A fresh, informative perspective on women's lives through the centuries' *Kirkus*

'A great book on the history of women's words in the English language' *New European*

'An eye-opening survey ... This is required reading for logophiles, feminists, and history buffs' *Publishers Weekly*

T0349112

'Incisively scholarly, affectionately humorous (and sometimes quietly furious) . . . this superb book teems with historical marvels and their 21st century resonances' Rebecca Wragg Sykes, author of *Kindred*

'What a revelatory delight of a book. It is richly scholarly, wry and funny, healthily grounded in women's bodily experiences . . . There is a nugget of joy and wisdom on every single page' Victoria Whitworth, author of *Daughter of the Wolf*

'[Jenni Nuttall] minutely details the shifts of language and meaning over the centuries through the lens of women's experiences' *Observer*

MOTHER TONGUE

THE SURPRISING
— HISTORY OF —
WOMEN'S WORDS

JENNI NUTTALL

virago

VIRAGO

First published in Great Britain in 2023 by Virago Press
This paperback edition published in 2024 by Virago Press

3 5 7 9 10 8 6 4

Copyright © Jenni Nuttall 2023

The moral right of the author has been asserted.

All rights reserved.
No part of this publication may be reproduced, stored in a
retrieval system, or transmitted, in any form or by any means, without
the prior permission in writing of the publisher, nor be otherwise circulated
in any form of binding or cover other than that in which it is published
and without a similar condition including this condition being
imposed on the subsequent purchaser.

A CIP catalogue record for this book
is available from the British Library.

ISBN 978-0-349-01531-6

Typeset in Goudy by M Rules
Printed and bound in Great Britain by Clays Ltd, Elcograf S.p.A.

Papers used by Virago are from well-managed forests
and other responsible sources.

Virago Press
An imprint of
Little, Brown Book Group
Carmelite House
50 Victoria Embankment
London EC4Y 0DZ

An Hachette UK Company
www.hachette.co.uk

www.virago.co.uk

For my daughter,
whom I love more than words

Contents

Introduction

Women's words

—

As a tutor at the University of Oxford, I teach the history of the English language as well as Anglo-Saxon and medieval literature. Each term my students and I explore English in its infancy and adolescence. I love the urgent, need-to-know queries about vocabulary that get fired at me without warning. Often young feminists want to know more about the history of words relating to women's lives and experience. Does the first syllable of *woman* come from *womb* or from another root? one undergraduate asks. Is a *maiden* always a virgin? demands another, and is a *maiden* always a girl? What do *spinsters* have to do with spinning? How can *rape* and *rapture* derive from the same etymological origins?

Sometimes I know the answer off the top of my head but often I have to look things up. And the questions don't stop there. At home in the last decade or so, bringing up a daughter who is, like so many children, fascinated by the origins and meanings of words, I've answered many queries about names and terms. Now she's a teenager, we search for the right words to tackle trickier topics. What is the best vocabulary with which to talk about the practicalities of puberty? What do I tell her about the myths and realities of love and sex, those new voyages on which she might soon embark, their dreams and their nightmares? In my teaching room or seated around the kitchen table, I've often turned to my dictionaries for help and encouragement.

The history of women's words, it turns out, is full of surprises, of things which aren't necessarily what you'd expect. Even our basics have unfamiliar beginnings. In Old English, the very first version of the language brought to the British Isles by fifth- and sixth-century migrants, *mann* or *mon* (as it was then spelled) meant not 'man' or 'male' but 'human' or 'person' (so *mankind* was once not quite as default male as it sounds to modern ears). Though the oldest English writings are hard to date precisely and the survival of texts very patchy, the first illustrative quotation in the *Oxford English Dictionary*'s entry for our modern word *man*, taken from one of the oldest medical books in English copied at the end of the tenth century, in fact describes a woman being treated for heavy periods. The book advises that a doctor should place horse dung on a hot coal and let it smoke between the thighs so that 'se mon swæte swiþe [so that the person sweats a lot]'. Not a pleasant-sounding treatment, but rather marvellous that this dictionary's first person is female.

Likewise, the etymology of *woman* itself is not a simple story. Some Renaissance language experts thought its origin must indeed be 'womb-man', with *woman* meaning 'that kynde of man [i.e. human] that is wombed' (so says Richard Verstegan in a 1605 book). But *woman* in truth comes from the Old English compound *wifman*. You might think that a *wifman* was a person who is, or is destined to be, a married woman: a limited, patriarchal definition. But that's not exactly right either. *Wif* and *wer*, in the oldest English, mean 'woman' and 'man', regardless of marital status. So a *wifman* is a woman-human. Scholars have not been able to agree on the etymological roots of that single syllable *wif*. Something to do with weaving, they speculate, or waving to and fro (perhaps our swaying hips or our busy multitasking?), or something about our private parts. No one really knows.

As I've been fielding questions at work and at home, I've realised that many of our current words for women's lives and experiences are relative newcomers into English, at least when viewed from the perspective of someone who spends most of her time paddling around in English's very beginnings. While words like *wife* and *man* have the deepest roots, many others appear much more recently, inventions of what linguists call Modern English, the version of the language which has evolved from the beginning of the eighteenth century to our present day. But what about the English that came before: the thousand and more years spanning Anglo-Saxon Old English, medieval Middle English and the Early Modern English of the sixteenth and seventeenth centuries? Was there just radio silence, gaps and voids of meaning ready and waiting to be filled with words not yet coined? Or did women have useful terms within reach before this more recent set of inventions? There might, I realised, be a lost history of women's words.

With the aid of dictionaries and glossaries, I trekked back into the first thousand years of the English language to find the beginnings of women's words, our now-forgotten vocabulary, like an explorer going far inland to locate the origin of some mighty river. There's something perverse, I know, about turning away from a vast flood to find the soggy patch in a field or the unimpressive spring bubbling through a rock which marks its source, but there's a certain satisfaction in knowing a word's history and a certain magic in finding the very first articulation of a particular idea or experience. There's no need to fall for what linguists call the 'etymological fallacy', the idea that a word's initial sense or its etymological origins must determine its current meaning. English today is many Englishes, a global ocean system of different varieties and local currents, and when words flow out into their wide oceans, as millions of speakers use and abuse them, their meanings broaden and change. This book will map out some of these evolutions. From time to time words get lost along the way and this book rediscovers them too.

These early English words for aspects of women's lives have so much to offer us today. It's clear that working women, for example, aren't a recent invention of modernity but a long-established workforce who were as proud of their labours as we are of our own jobs nowadays. Paying attention to the first vocabularies of caring, motherhood and maternity shows that these three words are not exact synonyms which demand that all women be maternal and motherly. The histories of words for the ages and stages of female life cycles explain some of the pigeonholes into which society still wants to post us. The origins of the terms we use today for violence targeted at girls and women expose the deep-dug foundations on which perpetrators build their excuses and justifications. But, as well as showing us what we're up against in a patriarchal world, these words might also inspire us. Any lingering sense of shame we might feel about menstruation, for example, is dispelled by the past's enthusiastic and fluent discussion of this topic. In old words we can find surprising new thoughts about our bodies' capacities for desire, for pregnancy and for much, much more.

These old words might also embolden us to find as many new words as we need to express exactly what we think and feel. And there's nothing to stop us finding fresh purposes for aged terms. As women have slowly made progress towards equality, we've paradoxically lost some of the most expressive and eloquent bits of English vocabulary for describing our lives and experiences. Like vintage tools laid out for sale at a flea market, we can pick up these older words, puzzle out their purposes, compare them with today's language and see if we have any use for them, decorative or practical.

Heading back upstream, this book explores women's words in the English spoken in Anglo-Saxon, medieval and Early Modern Britain up to around the year 1800, as well as casting some glimpses overseas as the horizons of this language were expanded through exploration and colonisation. My mother tongue's history begins with Old English, the language brought to England's shores in the 400s and 500s by migrants from Germany, Denmark and the Netherlands, some of whom were from tribes called the *Angles* or *Engles*. By the year 600, written records use *Englisc* to name both some of the people living in England and the language that they spoke. This name *Englisc* gains currency rather quickly, so you might think that other languages like Late Spoken Latin and Brittonic were rapidly swept away. Yet the arrival of English didn't bring about wholesale and immediate ethnic and linguistic cleansing. On the ground there was a mix of cultures and plenty of multilingual speakers for many decades until English dominated in the ninth century. In this book I use the modern adjective *Anglo-Saxon* to describe the people and cultures of England between the arrival of these migrants and the Norman Conquest in 1066, but this is a shorthand label for a much more diverse situation. English found its way to dominance amid the fusions brought about by waves of immigration as well as amalgamation with the native Romano-British population. Over several centuries English was transformed from immigrant language to a *vernacular*, the name given to the language spoken by most people in a country as a matter of course (as opposed to languages learned and used for specialised purposes by a smaller elite).

When William I and his Norman followers conquered

England in 1066 and took over its lands and institutions, English was demoted to a third-class language below Latin and French. It was now the *vulgar tongue* (from *vulgus*, Latin for the 'general public' or the 'common people'). *Vulgar* as an adjective first meant 'commonly understood' or 'widely known' before its meaning gradually grew ever more negative: first 'unlearned', then 'ordinary' or 'coarse', and finally 'rude'. This subordination below other languages dramatically transformed English, its grammar changing markedly and its vocabulary supplemented with words borrowed from French. In the following centuries, Middle English, as scholars call medieval English, was a kind of linguistic Wild West. Without dictionaries or grammar books to keep it in check, Middle English ran riot with different dialects, rebellious spellings and experimental, unregulated vocabulary. From the thirteenth century, English gradually regained its former role as a language for literature and for officialdom and institutions as the French influence weakened over time. Things settled down a bit with Early Modern English, the language which evolved across the centuries between 1500 and 1700. Little by little, driven by the need for mutual intelligibility and by the wider circulation of texts which served as models to imitate, English's variation was reduced, and its wildness reined in by dictionaries, grammars and the teaching of the language in schools.

These changes in English's status altered how people felt about their mother tongue. The phrase *lingua materna* appears first in the early twelfth century when scholars unfavourably compared this domestic language, the speech you learned among the women who looked after you as a small child, with Latin, the language of the fathers. Not literally the language of your father necessarily but clerical or academic 'fathers' who taught in schools and universities. Only when reformers demanded that the Bible and other aspects of Christian worship be available in English from the fourteenth century onward did the mother tongue begin to be described more approvingly as a familiar and homely kind of communication. In the eighteenth century, the *mother tongue* was represented by some philosophers as the language in which you could express yourself most intimately and authentically. Scaled up, this same logic argued that there were discrete 'nations', ethnically and linguistically distinctive groups ('the English' or 'the Germans', for example), whose characteristics were supposedly reflected by the particular qualities of their different vernaculars. Proponents of these nationalistic views used the phrase *mother tongue* to hint that there were some natural, biological underpinnings to their theories.

These days we're more suspicious of simplistic equations made between language and identity. The language in which you feel most comfortable may not be your own mother's first language. Like Anglo-Saxon, medieval and Renaissance societies, we take multilingualism for granted as a familiar part of our world. Today, as a result of Britain's ignoble history of colonisation and empire, English is a mother tongue for some speakers but a second or third language for many more. In 1578, the Anglo-Italian dictionary-maker John Florio said that English was 'a language that wyl do you good in England, but passe Dover, it is woorth nothing'. Speaking English well was a real advantage in Britain, says Florio, but once you set out from its borders, sailing across the Channel, heading out toward the wider world, it was pretty useless. Not true, of course, today. Now about 1.35 billion people speak English across the globe, of whom 1 billion speak it as a second or additional language.

It's almost impossible to conceptualise today's variety of world Englishes, the different seas and rivers through which the English language's numerous currents flow. So this book concentrates on the English that I study in the writings of the past and the words that I hear in my own small world. In these chapters, I work by snippets and excerpts, assembling a patch-work quilt of dictionary entries and quotations, each phrase or sentence making up my larger textile. More often my discoveries are the oldest words used about women by men, for most of the words in the mouths of women in the past were never recorded. But sometimes my patches are the words of women themselves, some of them the first women to write and publish on particu-lar subjects.

Many of the terms used by and about women went the way of natural wastage, lost from view as newer words were invented. But words can also be suppressed by more deliberate attempts to restrict speech. It's easy to think of knowledge and language marching on in lockstep, leaving behind myths and ignorance and heading toward clarity and openness. But society goes backward as well as forward, sometimes getting worse rather than better at talking about certain topics. In the 1390s, for example, the medieval poet Geoffrey Chaucer included frank descriptions of parts of a woman's body in one of his *Canterbury Tales*. In the *Miller's Tale*, a woman called Alison takes revenge on Absolom, the obsessive parish clerk who's getting in the way while she has a fling with her lodger, an Oxford student called Nicholas. Offering her admirer-cum-stalker a kiss through the window, Alison puts out her 'hole', her anus, and he kisses her 'ers', her arse. Feeling something scratchy with his lips, Absolom recoils because, as he says, women don't generally have a beard. Chaucer is having some fun here because pubic hair was called the *nether beard* in medieval English, the beard down below.

Almost exactly four hundred years later, an anonymous author published a modernised version of Chaucer's *Miller's Tale*. For Georgian readers, Chaucer's language, especially his frank realism about a woman's body, was a much more sensitive

matter, even though they took pride in the literary history of
their mother tongue. While Chaucer's original audience enjoyed
the thrill of rude words, Georgian readers weren't so keen. The
updated 1791 version replaces 'hole' and 'ers' with 'buttock'
and 'bum', making this outrageous kiss somewhat less precisely
located. Chaucer's description of Alison's pubes, 'rough and
long y-herd [long-haired]', becomes something 'rougher than the
down on ladies cheeks'. Medieval and Georgian bodies have just
the same bits, the 'limbs which few see, but all know to exist',
as this anonymous Georgian moderniser describes them. Yet
the eighteenth-century fashion for decorum dictated that such
knowledge had to be modestly veiled in language.

By 1835, when Charles Cowden Clarke published his *Riches of
Chaucer*, an anthology of the medieval poet's greatest works, he
left out words, phrases and entire tales, supposedly 'impurities'
which 'modern refinement' did not require. In Clarke's collection the *Miller's Tale* was omitted completely. Such censorship,
Clarke explained, was to ensure that this anthology of Chaucer
was suitable to be read by the 'young women of England'. Those
subjects which a culture feels to be taboo, often matters related
to our bodies, to sexuality and to human reproduction, are
pushed out of sight and out of direct language. In the nineteenth
century, taboos about talking or reading about sexuality and
fleshiness got ever stronger, especially for girls and women. Our
vocabulary today still bears the consequences of this general
shushing of women and their words.

This is in part because, despite the fashion for politeness and
prudery, scientists and doctors in these centuries, predominantly
men of course, had professional licence to carry on their sexist
speculations about women's physiology, anatomy, sexuality
and psychology. Their freedom to speak was something more
ideologically inflected than mere hypocrisy. In the eighteenth
and nineteenth centuries, claims for universal rights for every

human had grown ever more purposeful and insistent. Enslaved people demanded liberation, social reformers agitated for better conditions and political representation for the poor, and women had begun voicing their claims for equal treatment in society. Yet spooked by revolutions and radical upheavals, those who preferred the status quo kept culture's brakes firmly jammed on against rapid change.

One way to resist reform was to promote 'science' (however inaccurate or misconstrued) that divided humans into biologically distinct 'races' or which supposedly 'proved' the lower classes to be somehow naturally degenerate. Likewise, it was claimed that new scientific discoveries confirmed earlier philosophical and religious prejudices that women were (in various immortal phrases) the *gentler, weaker, fairer, softer* or *frailer sex*. Aspects of femininity which we would now call gendered stereotypes were presented as essential attributes of womanhood. Much of the key vocabulary we use today for aspects of women's bodies, lives and experiences comes from this period when certain parts of society dug in to resist change.

It turns out that before Georgian and Victorian fashions for modesty dampened down discussion, there was a glut of lively, unruly and often startlingly vivid women's words. There was plenty of sexist thinking, of course, but always voices ready to challenge misogyny and sexism. Good reason then to leapfrog over the last two centuries of English, going further back to rediscover our language's first thousand or so years. The openness of the distant past reminds me strongly of our own current commitment to candour. Today we talk much more plainly and urgently about experiences of menstruation and menopause, pregnancy and childbirth, and about other aspects of women's health across our life cycles. We're also speaking far and wide about the consequences of living in a gendered society. Women are challenging the sexist thinking embedded in medical science and psychology. We're calling out the culture which enables the sexual and physical violence some men target at women. We can now, in theory, narrate our life stories in any register or genre with whatever vocabulary we like. But we might nonetheless still want to have women's words to hand. Though laws have granted equality on paper for some of us, statistics show we're not yet there in practice. Gendered socialisation still tries to set us off on different paths through life. The work of caring falls disproportionately on women's shoulders, as does the housework, both of which have to be juggled with work outside the home.

The subjects of this book's chapters – the language of the distinctive parts of female anatomy, of menstruation, of sexuality, of pregnancy and childbirth, of caring, of working, of the stages of our life cycle, of male violence aimed at women and of patriarchy and inequality – may not be relevant to every one of us. Not every woman's body works in exactly the same way. Some of us won't ever be pregnant. Some do a great deal of the work of caring and some of us not so much. Some of us will be fortunate to feel relatively immune from violence directed at women, but many of us do not. Some won't feel that the sexist lineaments of the past have much influence on our lives, but many of us do. Some of these words we share with transgender and non-binary people who wouldn't classify themselves as women. Each individual takes what they need from the common word-stock.

The first woman to author a work in English whose name we know, the medieval mystic Julian of Norwich, said that she wrote about her Christian faith 'al in general and nothing in special'. By this, she meant she didn't presume to tell individual readers that they were either damned or saved. Likewise, she didn't claim any special authority or virtue for herself. Just so the women's words I've chosen are relevant *in general* but not necessarily *in special* for every reader. But I hope my grammar of *us* and *we* can stretch to include whomsoever might know something of the experiences each chapter describes. Linguists in the eighteenth century once decided that it was supposedly more correct to use the generic *he*, *him* and *his* when referring to mixed-sex categories of people. This default setting makes it seem as if men are central and usual and women the exception. Turning the tables, I hope those readers who don't have first-hand knowledge of the particular experiences whose vocabulary I explore will forgive me the use of a generic *we* and *us*.

Language, the Harvard linguist Dwight Bolinger once said, cheerfully mixing his metaphors, is 'a stage built over a graveyard from which fossils rise and dance at night'.[1] Not skeletons, you note, but something more primeval, ancient creatures halfway to alien. Thanks to the long continuity of our words, history doesn't rest quietly dead but stays on to haunt us. Words used by and about women are particularly afflicted by the outdated ideas and backstories that our language drags along behind us. Our vocabulary bears plenty of traces of the sexism of the past when experts and authorities were mostly male. Yet I think it's still worth bothering with. For all its lagging prejudices, knowing more about this vocabulary can help us root ourselves more firmly in the footings of our culture and of our thoughts. We can take these fossils for another spin around the stage, altering the choreography as we go.

One

CORS

Words for Female Anatomy

—

We'll begin our journey into English's past with the set of words which name what the Georgian moderniser of Chaucer's *Miller's Tale* called the *particulars* distinguishing male and female anatomy. Worrying that his readers might take offence at even his sanitised version of Chaucer's tale, he points out that the 'most mincing prude', the most refined of ladies, knows, as he so elegantly puts it, that 'the structure of her body differs in some particulars from that of her brother's body'. There's no getting away from the importance of this vocabulary in the history of women's lives. Female physiology has in the past been the supposed grounds on which certain humans were allocated subordinate roles in patriarchal societies. Those of us in the female category were once limited in our life choices: under-educated, kept out of most professions and hobbled by the law. Women's paths through the world, whether they liked it or not, were predetermined and constricted because they had been selected for certain treatment on the basis of their particular reproductive anatomy.

Nothing about the fact of being female itself, of course,

inevitably invites this subordination. Nothing about the part we might be assumed to play in the two-by-two process of mammalian reproduction demands or deserves or justifies these limitations. Yet it is no accident that those parts of us needed to make new members of our species emerged as the sorting mechanism and were often cited as part of the faux-logic 'explanation'. The restriction of a chunk of humanity wasn't based on some arbitrary feature (maybe your eye colour, the length of your big toe, or whether your belly button sank in or popped out). Rather it targeted exactly those things which families and institutions found advantageous to control and exploit: lineage and inheritance, for example, and child-rearing and other kinds of reproductive labour which make and sustain human life.

The anatomical words which name female sex characteristics have been much on my mind recently. I hear myself pronouncing them carefully out loud as I seek to give my daughter plain facts and accurate explanations rather than squeamish euphemisms about the physical changes of puberty. They've also rung in my ears as I've chewed over the recent trend for the phrasing in some public health campaigns, marketing and journalism which replaces words like *women* or *females* with terminology laser-focused on physiology and anatomy such as *people with a uterus* or *menstruators*. Some of us find this body-centred language helpfully inclusive, a neat substitution which acknowledges those with female anatomy who would not categorise themselves as women, but others find it dehumanising, reducing an entire person to a body part. Whatever our view on this new linguistic impulse, if we're to be referred to as *vulva-owners* or *cervix-havers*, we'd better be up to speed on these words' backstories.

As fancy-pants, barely digested Latin – *labia, clitoris, vagina, uterus* and *ovaries*, for example – their etymologies are mysterious to most of us. Newly curious, I looked them up in the *Oxford English Dictionary*. In doing so, I was struck by how relatively late-arriving they are in the history of English. *Vulva* makes its debut in vernacular books written by medieval surgeons and doctors around the year 1400, but the rest don't appear in English until the seventeenth century, when the discoveries of Renaissance anatomy were described for English readers. Their belated arrival is surprising because most of the words for parts of the human body, our *cors* (as you might call your physical form in medieval English), are much more long-serving than this, present and correct in the first English spoken by the immigrants who brought their language to Britain's shores. They're still hard at work today, though their spellings and sounds have altered in a language which has been spoken for nearly a millennium and a half. Old English *hnecca*, for example, is the foremother of *neck*; *earm* becomes *arm*; *fot* and *hond* turn into *foot* and *hand*. A few names are borrowed from other languages. *Leg* and *calf*, for example, are added from Old Norse, the speech of the Scandinavians who settled in Britain at the end of the ninth century.

What, I wondered, explained this difference between these unisex body words and our names for female sex characteristics? Was it that these primary and secondary sex characteristics were not yet named? Perhaps it was all a blur, an unmapped land? Were Anglo-Saxon and medieval experts just too prim and proper to write down names which were used in private speech? Or were there earlier terms which didn't make it into our contemporary English? I set about my dictionaries and glossaries to investigate. And, after some searching, it turns out that there are some earlier words. This chapter reveals what was once and what might have been, the first, now-forgotten words used in English for female sexual and reproductive organs before Latinate labels became the standard terms. It also tells the story of words like *womb* and *breast* whose meanings have evolved over time, as well as body-based words such as *hysteria* and *hysterical* which have often been used to justify women's subordination in society.

Just before we get to the words for particular parts of our anatomy, what about the history of words which describe us together as a type or group such as *womankind* or *sex*? In Old English, *cynd* or *gecynd*, the ancestors of our modern word *kind*, described something's nature, its innate character or condition. As a suffix, *kind* imports into the word *womankind* the false logic of biological essentialism, the idea that female anatomy brings with it some fixed, innate essence, predetermined modes in which women naturally think, feel or behave. This essentialist thinking has for centuries been offered up as the fake justification for why women supposedly deserved a subordinate, limited place in the world. Today we reject it from top to bottom. In theory at least (though the hard-wired realities of a long-gendered society still make many things difficult in practice), a woman might have any personality, appearance or behaviour and follow any path in life. There is no single kind of woman.

But *kind*, strangely, might also be the best word we have to recognise both our similarities and our differences. *Kind*, in the sense of 'type' or 'sort', is also the term used by today's biologists to take account both of the vast variation of the natural world and also the explanatory and predictive connections they observe within this diversity. The philosopher Alison Stone borrows this concept of a *kind* to define femaleness.[1] Members of a biological *kind*, Stone explains, share clusters of properties, features which aren't coincidental or random but related and typically co-occurring, though an individual member of a kind may have some but not all of the cluster. Certain properties can often predict or explain other features shared by many but not all members of that kind. Females, likewise, typically share co-occurring and related features though individuals may not have identical bodies or experiences. We are a kind of *kind*.

Alongside *kind*, *cynn* was another Old English word for a group of individuals who share some qualities though aren't necessarily identical. In its modern spelling, *kin* specifies our family, our relationships, but in Old English the word described all manner of categories or groupings. It was used not only for families but for nations, tribes and races, as well as naming a species, class or sort. In a book of Anglo-Saxon herbal medicine, for example, it described two types of the same plant, female and male. In a Bible explainer written by Abbot Ælfric of Eynsham around the year 1000, *cynn* also named the two sorts of humans God created in Genesis, able to continue their species by themselves without any further input from the Creator. By the beginning of the sixteenth century, *kin* gives us that useful adjective *akin*, formed from the phrase *of kin*. Things *of kin*, things *akin*, are related but not exactly the same. Just as the notion of *sisterhood* expresses feminist solidarity between women while acknowledging other inequalities which might make our lives very different, *wif-cynn* – *woman-kin* as we might modernise it – holds space for differences.

Compared to *kind* and *kin*, *sex* is a more narrowly focused term, used particularly to label the two types of humans needed for sexual reproduction. This word, an Englishing of the Latin word *sexus* and the French *sexe*, was brought into the mother tongue by fourteenth-century translators. In the first book of the Bible, God instructs Noah to take two members of each species into the ark to ensure nature's continuation after the flood. God clarifies, in case anyone was to misunderstand him, that he means a pair of 'masculini sexus et feminini'. Medieval English translations of this verse opt for phrases like 'male sex and female' or 'of male kynde and female'. At about the same time, Geoffrey Chaucer, when he wasn't inventing his much

racier *Canterbury Tales*, translated a book of Christian philosophy written by the Roman politician Boethius. As proof of
God's divine forward-planning of the universe, Boethius points
out how nature reproduces itself by the workings 'of sedes [seeds]
and of sexes'. Chaucer adds a helpful gloss for *sexes*, a word which
might be unfamiliar to readers without any Latin, 'that is to seyn
[say], male and femele'. *Male* and *female* now seem a matching
pair of words but, as you can see from Chaucer's spelling, they
come from different roots. *Male* stems from Latin *mas*, 'male,
masculine', via *masculus*, 'a male'. Medieval English males could
be spelled *madles*, *masles* and *mascles*, variants which sound
more like country nicknames for creepy-crawlies, before the
spelling settles down. *Female* comes from Latin *femella* meaning
'girl' or 'woman', the diminutive form of *femina*, 'woman'.

The past didn't need to know about gametes or chromosomes
to bifurcate humans in this way. An understanding of how
plants and animals reproduced themselves by the workings
of seeds and sexes, plus observations about typical differences
between male and female humans, did the job just fine. A collection of medical advice written around the year 850 says that
a doctor should, when diagnosing and treating, pay attention to
the 'micel gedal', the considerable difference, between the bodies
of male and female patients (not something that medical science
always remembered in the following centuries and a fact which
researchers still sometimes forget today). A medieval guide to
gynaecology lists five 'diversites', the general differences between
adult men and women. Men often go bald while women do so
only rarely, men have beards and they have nipples like women
but not breasts. Their different genitals come fourth on the list
and the fifth difference is that a woman typically has 'a vessyll
that no man hath', the vessel in question being the womb.

Medical authorities did also understand, as we do now,
that some women have variations or differences of sexual

development (also called *intersex variations* or *conditions* by some organisations and campaign groups). When faced with atypical bodies such as these, the Church and the law were mainly concerned to fit them neatly back into the norms of sexuality and gender. Some medieval surgeons described methods by which they might be able to normalise unusual bodies, probably more as theory than in actual practice. Terms now considered outmoded like *hermaphrodite* and *androgyne* arrived in English as these surgical textbooks were translated into the vernacular in the fourteenth century. But awareness of these variations didn't call the logic of the overall categorisation into question. The sorting of humans on the basis of sex carried on apace. Its knowledge base might be incomplete by our standards, its explanations and theories sometimes rebuilt and renovated according to new scientific discoveries and changing cultural pressures, but the categorising of humans on the basis of femaleness and maleness was never doubted.

The first English words for female reproductive anatomy appear rather tentative, not always precise or straightforward. Of all the European vernaculars, English has some of the oldest medical guides written not in Latin, the common language of scholarship, but in the mother tongue. In the ninth century, a man named Bald, perhaps a layman earning his living as a physician, asked a scribe to compile and copy out medical information, not just local knowledge but wisdom which can be traced back to North African, Byzantine, Greek and Roman experts too. This Old English text is usually now called Bald's *leechbook* (a *læce-boc* being the book of a *læce*, a doctor or healer). The contents list tells us that Chapter 60 of Book II, now infuriatingly missing from the twelve-hundred-year-old manuscript, had forty-one cures for gynaecological and obstetric problems.

Another leechbook has one chapter on pregnancy and another on menstrual difficulties. Anglo-Saxon medics were expected to offer expert advice on obstetric and gynaecological matters.

In these first English medical books, the words for female sex organs are general rather than specific, leaving the reader to pin down exactly what's meant from the context. Such vagueness might betray uncertainties among male experts about the exact configuration of the female anatomy. Genitals, whether male or female, are called our *gecynd*, another use for the ancestor of that all-purpose word *kind*. *Gecynd-lim*, the 'kind-limb' or 'kind-part', was used collectively for those body parts which indicated, in the sorting of humans according to the mechanics of sexual reproduction, what *kind* your body was. Another word, *cwiþ* or *cwiþa*, names both the womb and the vagina. That strange letter called a *thorn*, like a *p* whose lobe has become a little less pert and perky, is one of the runes used in the writing of Old English, pronounced like *th*. About *cwiþ*, which leaves no trace of itself in later English, I can tell you almost nothing – except how very ancient it is. Linguists can reconstruct an ancestor of *cwiþ* in Proto-Germanic, the language spoken first perhaps around 500 BC in parts of Germany, Denmark and the Norwegian and Swedish coasts. This mother language (in the matrilineal metaphors of historical linguistics) gave birth to daughters, the three sister languages of West, East and North Germanic; English is her great-granddaughter.

After the Norman invasion of 1066, the French speech of the new ruling elite brought new vocabulary into English. The unspecific Old English *kind-parts* were joined by newer medieval euphemisms, fuzzy words which verbally pixilate those body parts considered socially tabooed. Genitals might be called *privites* (i.e. 'private parts') or the *privy member* (i.e. the 'secret limb'). Even blurrier were the phrases *privy thing* (i.e. 'secret thing') and its French equivalent, *bele chose* (i.e. 'pretty thing'), used for vulva and/or vagina. But don't assume from these delicate phrases that medieval society didn't want to think about human genitals. Those same courtly readers also enjoyed French *fabliaux*, outrageous stories about sexual escapades told in very explicit language. Chaucer's *Miller's Tale*, with its pubic hair and arsehole kisses, is an English version of this popular French genre.

This love of risqué narratives might also explain the literary appeal of a middle-aged middle-class woman with a captive audience talking about genitalia. No, not me, but Alison, the Wife of Bath, who is for many readers the most memorable of Chaucer's pilgrims in the *Canterbury Tales*. Chaucer presents her for the titillation of his posh audience of court nobles and city clerks. Her speech might appear to be the perfect place to find the words women used for their own private parts but it turns out she's not quite what she seems. Before Alison narrates her entry for the pilgrims' storytelling competition, she recounts her life story: five marriages, first as the much younger wife of older men (having started as a child-bride of twelve), and now as a kind of medieval cougar who, aged forty, has wed an Oxford academic twenty years her junior. Arguing that she is much better suited to marriage than celibacy, Alison points out boldly that our genitals were 'nat maad for noght', not made for nothing, but made for various purposes: urination, procreation and sexuation (that is, for the purpose of distinguishing the sexes).

Strangely though, many of the words Chaucer gives to Alison for what we would call genitals are unisex: 'oure bothe thynges smale', our 'harneys' (a word like our modern *tackle* or *gear*). If she marries again, she'll use what she calls her rather phallic-sounding 'instrument' just as generously as God has given it to her. Perhaps Alison is imagined to be so sexually dominant as to become somehow masculine. What's more, when referring to her own female genitals more directly, she's not as explicit as she might be. Reliving for the pilgrims how she ranted at her older husbands, she remembers that she told them not to be possessive when she was out and about with her friends because they'd have plenty of 'queinte' at home. Later on, she over-shares that each of her husbands said she had 'the beste quoniam' there could be. *Queinte*, a word meaning 'a trick', is a near-miss for *cunt*; *quoniam*, Latin for 'in as much as', puns on the French word *conin* meaning 'rabbit' which echoes the French *con* meaning 'vagina', from Latin *cunnus*. Are you keeping up? By means of these substitutions, like the mincing of oaths which turns *damn* into *dang*, Chaucer sidesteps the word *cunt*, but we know what he means. The Wife of Bath talks candidly, but her genitals are unisex and she sounds at times like some punning intellectual. She's more a product of men's imagination than a reliable guide to how medieval women discussed their sex lives and private parts.

Chaucer's last-minute swerves are all the stranger because *cunt* was alive and well in other registers of early English. It appears fairly often in place names, for example. A tenth-century legal document mentions somewhere in Hampshire towards the 'cuntan heale', the cuntish hollow. Other medieval place names use this uncompromising syllable to identify narrow wooded valleys or clefted hills (including the magnificent *Cuntewellewang*, 'cunt-spring-land', near a now-deserted medieval village in Lincolnshire). From the thirteenth century to the sixteenth, twenty or so streets around England were called Gropecunt Lane, a nickname which spread from one Oxford alleyway where university students bought sex to many other towns. Perhaps, you might think, *cunt* was just for student banter and nudge-wink names for dingles and dells, but it also appears in academic writing too. *Cunt* glosses *vulva* in Latin learners' vocab lists and turns up in medical textbooks translated into English for surgeons and doctors. One copy of a late medieval guide to treating women's gynaecological problems hedges its bets, using both this bluntest of words and its fancier synonym. Women, it says, have 'an openynge callid a cunte or privyte of the wombe'. The *C-word*, which Britain's Ofcom Broadcasting code still today says 'requires exceptional justification' to be uttered on late-night TV because of its 'potential to cause widespread offence', was in the Middle Ages a word for academics and experts, even if Chaucer and his high-class audience felt funny-peculiar about it.

While *cunt* was in use in some registers of medieval English, it wasn't necessarily the most precise word. Does the medieval gynaecological guide's 'openynge' mean the vagina or the vulva or both at once? Such imprecision isn't unusual in this early vocabulary, as we'll see in the first words in English for ovaries, wombs, vaginas and vulvas. Before Renaissance anatomists could provide more accurate descriptions and labelled diagrams for interested readers based on their own dissections of human cadavers, medieval medical texts gave female sex organs sometimes confusing and overlapping names, often relaying ancient observations whose accuracy had got baggily out of shape as they passed from one language to another. Sometimes female body parts didn't even have their own words. Testicles and ovaries shared a single name in medieval English, both called 'stones' due to their pebbly shapes. In the 1370s, a retired herbalist called Henry Daniel wrote a guide to uroscopy, the diagnosing of illnesses from patients' urine, its colour, consistency and the specks that floated in it. This method of diagnosis, holding a sample in a jar to the light, would suit those who like poring over paint names and shades: Daniel's textbook suggests colours like *subcitrinish*, *subrubecund*, *prassine* (a kind of leekish green) and *rockish*. Digressing from the liquid in hand, he explains that on each side of the womb are 'two stones [i.e. ovaries] schapen like ballok stones of a man [shaped like a man's testicles]', parts which are called in English 'the moder ballokes stones', the mother bollocks stones.

The *moder* or *mother*, translating Latin *matrix*, is one of the medieval names for the uterus, so these are the womb's bollocks or balls. A strange turn of phrase to modern ears, but one which makes sense for an age not yet fully up to speed about ova and sperm. The idea that reproduction needed a sperm and an egg came later, suggested by studies of other creatures and plants. An English version of a Dutch medical dictionary published in 1684 explains this newer name: 'The Testicles of Women breed Eggs, and therefore they are rightly called Ovaria', ovaries. Human *ova* were not observed until 1827; the first crystal-clear images of ovulation, the egg squeezing out from an ovary's follicle, were only captured in 2008. It's worth a Google: you see a golden globule setting forth on its own odyssey, its future as yet uncertain, rather than the more usual artist's impression of a ponderous grey planet dwarfing a plucky sperm-onaut at the moment of fertilisation.

Because of unisex names like *stones* and *testicles*, some historians, most famously Thomas W. Laqueur in his 1990 book called *Making Sex*, have claimed that vernacular languages didn't have separate labels for women's private bits before Renaissance anatomists named these particular parts in their Latin treatises. Laqueur's book argued that, before a shift in thinking in the eighteenth century, expert opinion considered male and female reproductive anatomy as evidence not of two sexes but of one sex in two different forms. This older framework was supposedly derived from the Greek physician Galen and his second-century AD writings on anatomy. At times Galen did seem to imagine human genitalia to be as invertible as a rubber glove. Perhaps he meant that male and female sex organs were essentially the same: a womb was an inverted scrotum, a vagina was a penis that had not been extruded like a sausage, ovaries and testicles were the same, merely positioned differently. Drawing in older Aristotelian theories about digestion, nutrition and circulation, some experts-of-their-day believed that sexed bodies were the products of different extremes of one physiology, males much 'hotter', females much 'colder' (not literally warmer or cooler in body temperature but stronger and weaker in terms of what we might call metabolism). Female genitals remained inside because the body that owned them was supposedly under-cooked, a near-miss rather than a fully finished creation: a might-have-been-a-male.

Yet, as we'll see in the next three chapters, ancient medicine's fascination with menstruation and the workings of the womb reveals that classical and medieval medics were entirely aware of sexuate differences (that is, the typical anatomical differences in female and male bodies needed for human reproduction). And there are other reasons to be sceptical of Laqueur's suspiciously all-encompassing thesis. Galen's homologies might in fact be analogies, not *the same* but *a bit like*, methods for male physicians to visualise what was hidden in female bodies (and perhaps to cover over their own ignorance). And rather than being a conceptual framework stretching from classical antiquity to the Renaissance, there's little evidence that the sections of Galen's works that imagined genitals as innies or outies were read in medieval Europe at all.[2]

Rather, when his entire works were translated into Latin and printed in 1490, Galen's homologies, ignored for many centuries, roared briefly back into fashion as a trendy theory. But by the mid-sixteenth century, Galen's homologies had run into trouble as anatomists made hands-on investigations of bodily forms and functions. Testicles and ovaries might seem vaguely interchangeable but was it the uterus or the clitoris which was the inverted penis? And what about the breasts? Male bodies don't have chest indents equivalent to female breasts popped inwards. Like lots of super-fashionable theories, Galen's logic of blister-pack bodies was quickly undermined by sceptical re-examination. Continental anatomists called the homologies ridiculous in the 1500s. In England these ideas turned up like a late-arriving train around the year 1600 only to be swiftly dismissed as utterly absurd.[3] But once a racy idea is out of the traps and set running, it's hard to catch it and put it back in its kennel. Galen's inside-out thinking popped up for a century or two after experts started making fun of it, side by side with accounts of sexuate differences.

So, Laqueur was wrong about a dramatic paradigm shift from one sex to opposite sexes and wrong about the supposed lack of vocabulary too. In the Middle Ages and Renaissance, English borrowed words in this semantic field from Latin and French, these transliterated terms taking their place alongside vernacular nicknames like *cunt* or the multi-purpose *stones*. I'll save the clitoris and its strange early English names – the *kiker*, the *hayward of corpse's dale* – for my chapter on the language of sex where, as an organ devoted to pleasure, it best belongs. For now, we'll track the evolution across the centuries of the rest of the terminology for uterus, vagina and vulva, following its twists and turns.

In classical Latin, *vulva* usually meant the womb, but its meaning was redesignated deep in the not-in-fact-very-Dark Ages. In the 620s, the Bishop of Seville, one Isidore, compiled a *summa*, an everything-you-need-to-know book. Being a work which helped you blag any subject under heaven, it became widely popular across Europe with academics and churchmen. As well as fast facts, this encyclopaedia offered easy-to-remember explanations of word origins, giving it its title: the *Etymologies*. The *vulva*, Isidore speculates, perhaps took its name from *valva*, a word for doors which fold or doors which open and close in matching pairs. Seventh-century etymology like this was mostly guesswork.

Isidore's verbal retrofit gives the labia, the crinkles of skin and flesh on either side of the vagina, a job to do: stay together or open up, admit or protect, let out or keep in. Perhaps not exactly folding doors, but at least those fabric partitions that sometimes get stretched across church halls, concertinaed, pleated and plush.

Scholars today, on the other hand, think the best explanation of the origin of *vulva* may be a derivation from the verb *volvere*, 'to go round, to roll', because the womb goes around the foetus. *Vulva* appears in a few medieval English translations of medical textbooks, caught halfway between English and Latin in free-style spellings like *wulve*, *vlve* and *wlve*. There were other English names for this part of the body too. Henry Daniel, the friar who wrote a textbook on uroscopy, says that the vulva is also called the *womb-gate*. My favourite medieval term for the vulva is *wicket*, a name for a smaller gate, especially one that opens in a larger door or gateway. Thinking of them as gates, or Isidore's curtains or doors, resists the feeling that our vulvas should be as 'neat, petite and discreet' as possible. That phrase was coined by the broadcaster and sex educator Alix Fox to highlight the unrealistic expectations about female bodies that plague us today. Ideas about how vulvas should look have teamed up with the other ideals of beauty that encircle us, their messages easy to internalise though it's harder to say who exactly promotes these standards and why they do so. Even their names, *majora* on the outside and *minora* nearer the vagina, can make us feel abnormal. *Major* and *minor* sound as if they should be concentric, the smaller neatly fitting inside the bigger, when for many of us the opposite is true, the inner overspilling the outer like petals escaping a bud.

As the *labia majora* and *minora* show, the names chosen by physicians and scientists are not always a good fit for every female body. The terminology brought into English by sixteenth-century anatomists, though more precisely descriptive than medieval medical textbooks, nonetheless imposed certain assumptions. Rather than being a long-standing anatomical word, *vagina* began life as the Latin word for a sword's scabbard. It started its journey towards being the standard English term for the stretchy, muscly tube that joins vulva to womb as a mere rhetorical flourish. An Italian called Realdo Colombo, who had trained under the most famous Renaissance anatomist of them all, Andreas Vesalius, completed a textbook on human dissection just before his death in 1559. Colombo wanted to illuminate what Vesalius had called the *fabrica*, the structure and materials of the human body. For readers who might not themselves have squinted down at human innards from the teetering tiers of an anatomy theatre, comparison and imagery were key. Colombo therefore described the part into which the penis is thrust 'tamquam in vaginam', as if into a sheath. It's a throwaway metaphor, an intuition about the coevolution of penis and vagina for sexual reproduction. But for those in the know about its etymology, the word figures the penis as dagger, the vagina as mere receptacle. How convenient for propping up some of those shall-we-call-them *phallusies* which kept women pinned in their subordinate place: masculine action, feminine passivity, as well as the idea that vaginas are designed solely for heterosex.

Not many of us can resist a new buzzword, though, whatever its built-in faults, so *vagina* caught on as a name for this body part in the seventeenth century. The word was taken up by French medical writers, including Madame Louise Bourgeois, author of a manual on gynaecology and obstetrics published in 1609 and midwife to the French Queen Marie de Médicis, and surgeons such as Jacques Guillemeau, who published his own guide hot on Bourgeois's heels a few months later. *Vagina* arrived in English in a 1612 translation of Guillemeau's handbook. Following Guillemeau's terminology, the translator describes the anatomy of 'the entrance or Vagina of the wombe' or, going in the other direction, the 'outward necke, or Vagina'. That older synonym explains why we've ended up with *cervix* – the Latin for 'neck' – as the name for the part where womb meets vagina. Medieval surgeons used *neck* not only for the thing balancing our heads but also for bits of the body where something broader met something slimmer. Like a bottle or a vase, wider at the base and narrower near the top, the womb (looked at from the perspective of its owner) has a neck, tipped up, leading out. As the word *vagina* became the standard term thanks to the writings of Renaissance anatomists, *cervix* shrank back to name only the strong cylinder that opens and closes at the bottom of the womb. *Cervix* is a rather dull word for something so animate – it changes texture and position across the menstrual cycle, tailoring day by day the mucus it makes in its infoldings.

The translator of Guillemeau's textbook thus gave his reader both the newish word *vagina* and some helpful glossing in plainer English. As English medical writers translated works by Continental experts, they not only brought new Latin terms into English but also sometimes gave a descriptive gloss or recorded or invented a replacement English term. Some of the best alternative names and descriptions come from pages which might have been lost for ever if the medical authorities of the day had had their way. Helkiah Crooke was a physician trained first at Cambridge and then at the University of Leiden with its state-of-the-art physic garden and dissection theatre. While working in London in the 1610s, he pitched a book on anatomy to a publisher, an anatomical treatise which would open up the secrets of every part of the body, including the genitals of both sexes. But the Bishop of London, whose job it was to inspect and grant licences to books on sensitive subjects, brought Crooke's plan to the attention of the College of Physicians. While the bishop sought to suppress obscenity, the College were worried about their monopoly over anatomical knowledge. They thus told Crooke that certain illustrations and descriptions of genitalia should be left out of his proposed edition.

Crooke ignored these attempts to tell him what to publish, so next the College tried and failed to buy off the printer. Crooke and his backers stalled while the book went to press, sending Jane Jaggard, the printer's wife, to appear before the Fellows of the College to listen patiently to their objections. I hope she had fun wasting their time. Having fended off this interference, her husband, William Jaggard, published Crooke's *Mikrokosmographia* in 1615. Crooke was, let's be clear, no feminist. His views on women and their bodies would see him cancelled today. But he was more of a friend to women than the surgeon John Banister, who refused to describe female sex organs on the grounds of 'indecencie' in his own book of anatomy, the *Historie of Man*, printed thirty-odd years earlier. Though fearful of readers with dubious or erotic intentions, Crooke thought that everyone should find every inch of their anatomy in his pages, so that 'those who are sober minded might knowe themselves, that is, their owne bodies'.

What else can Crooke tell us about knowing ourselves and our own bodies? With his anatomist's eye for form and function, Crooke calls the outer labia *wings* and the inner labia *nymphae*, 'nymphs'. *Wings* is Crooke's Englishing of equivalent words in Greek, Latin and French which are used metaphorically to describe parts of human anatomy resembling birds' wings; and *nympha* means 'clitoris' in some ancient Greek medical writing – a meaning revived centuries later in the medico-misogynist diagnosis of *nymphomania* – and 'labia' in others. *Labia* itself means 'lips' in Latin. By extension, *labia* was first used for the edges of a wound and then for the folds of skin around the vagina, appearing initially in English in the latter sense (as far as the *Oxford English Dictionary* can tell) in a surgeon's anatomy book in 1634. I rather wish Crooke's *nymphs*, used twenty years before *labia* arrived on the scene in English, had caught on instead.

Our nymphs, explains Crooke, supposedly guide urine neatly away, giving them a job a bit like the classical spirits who watch over springs and fountains. If that were true, al fresco weeing when caught short might be easier for women. But it's encouraging to think of our labia as a kind of tutelary spirit, watching benevolently over our plumbing. It wouldn't be the first time that they've protected precious places. *Sheela na gigs* are guardian talismans in the form of female figures which were carved high up, often almost out of sight, on British and Irish churches and castles from the twelfth century to the sixteenth. They hold open their super-sized labia as a *paso doble* dancer holds up her skirts. For those of us not brave enough for such exhibitionism, whether in reality or just in private thought, perhaps we could consider them our protective *wings*, gently clasping as a bird folding its feathers around itself.

Crooke's mission to describe anatomy and its variations for his readers puts into words what is often left out of side-sliced sex-ed diagrams these days. The gap between these neatly clinical schematics and our natural reality can make us feel that our own private parts are somehow grotesque. I wish we could talk about (or at least think about) these parts of us with as much relish as a Renaissance anatomy expert. Crooke writes that labia sometimes 'grow to so great a length on one side, more rarely on both' and that the inner nymphs 'do hang sometimes a little foorth', blossoming beyond 'the lips of the lap', another of Crooke's names for the vulva. They're 'partly fleshy, partly membranous, soft and fungous'. *Fungous* meaning spongy like a mushroom: labia won't meet any demand that flesh be taut, smooth and symmetrical. If you consult the Labia Library or Vulva Gallery online, or the artist Jamie McCartney's 'Great Wall of Vagina' (panelled with plaster casts of four hundred vulvas – perhaps the pun of its title excuses its anatomical inaccuracy), you'll see that vulvas are biomorphic not geometric, living forms of nature rather than mathematical figures, as organic in shape as coral colonies in a reef.[4]

Like the whorls and loops of fingerprints, or the unique patterns of our eyes' irises, labia declare our individual thisness, our *haecceity*, as a medieval philosopher would have called it. So too do the different forms of the ever-changing cervix. Go if you dare to the website of the Beautiful Cervix Project, where you can find photographs of what a mid-sixteenth-century physician, Thomas Raynalde, called our 'kernelly snout', a fleshy bulge or 'nose' which 'bosseth [i.e. thrusts] downward' but touches 'no side nor part' of the vagina.[5] It's hard to think of the cervix as beautiful, or even as lively as Raynalde's animal-like organ, when more often we encounter it as a potentially life-threatening body part which needs regular surveillance. I confess that something about the word *smear* itself makes me shilly-shally about booking my appointment just as much as the invasive nature of this particular health check. *Smear* describes the spreading of a specimen across a glass slide so it can be viewed under a microscope rather than describing the test itself which is more scrape and scour than smear and blear. As a name for a procedure its connotations make me feel queasy, leaving the prospect even less appealing.

Raynalde, as you can see, had quite the way with words describing female innards, a talent he put to good use in writing a book which combined new anatomical knowledge with the latest thinking about pregnancy and childbirth. Seventy years before Helkiah Crooke defied the College of Physicians to publish his descriptions of genitalia, Raynalde had already communicated some of this information to English readers. In 1540, a headteacher called Richard Jonas had translated into

English, via a Latin intermediary, a German anatomical and gynaecological manual for midwives in training. Five years later, Raynalde revised Jonas's book and added his own summary of Vesalius's literally cutting-edge research into the anatomy of our sex organs. This was popular-science writing at its finest, speeding this new knowledge from a deluxe Latin volume to a cheap-and-cheerful English guide in a couple of years. Raynalde also gave *The Birth of Mankind* a new subtitle, *The Womans Booke*, showing his desire to empower his readers 'the better to understand how everything cometh to pass within your bodies' during pregnancy and labour. *The Womans Booke* was a best-seller, reprinted thirteen times in the next one hundred years, the *What to Expect When You're Expecting* of its day.

In a Latin preface to a later edition, Raynalde confesses that he would have written his book differently if he hadn't been distracted by '*necessariis curis familiaribus* [unavoidable domestic cares]'. Perhaps he was busy doing his fair share of housework and childcare at home – I'd like to think so. But he did find the time to make this subject matter 'speake Englysshe', as he says in his introduction, an English that rejected technical terms in favour of concrete simplicity. He labels the vulva the 'passage port', because it's the 'port gate or entrance of that passage or way into the womb or matrix'. You can see he had a teacher's zeal for spelling things out *very* carefully. What we would call the vagina, he called the 'womb passage' or the 'privy passage'. The cervix is a second *port*, 'the womb port'. A *port* is a gateway, like those thickset stone arches for accessing and defending cities. Raynalde set out not so much to give doctors new terminology for these body parts but to give women all the information he could about their reproductive anatomy. And perhaps he succeeded. A copy of *The Womans Booke* now in the Cambridge University Library has a seventeenth-century inscription which reads 'Elizabeth

King her scillful boock'. Whether midwife or mother, and however dreadful her untutored spelling, Elizabeth found this book
skilful in the sense of 'knowledgeable' or 'clever'.

In order to reassure his pregnant readers, Raynalde had every
incentive to make the way out of the womb seem as substantial and
spacious as possible. His descriptions are better than Colombo's
penis-sheath vagina, but for some of us these city plans of ports
and passages don't apply. Bodies vary and change as much as the
names for things and the meanings of words. One in five British
women will have a hysterectomy at some point in their lives. One
in every five thousand women is born with MRKH syndrome,
giving them typically no uterus and a shortened vagina. Those
of us with a womb pre-installed might think it a gift-gadget never
asked for but often demanding maintenance: menstruation, contraception, abortion. Or we might be happy to have it ready and
waiting for pregnancy, crossing our fingers that it'll work when the
time comes. Or some uncertain mishmash of both of those.

At least the words *uterus* and *womb* give us a technical term
for scientific best and an everyday name for the rest of us. If
only every one of these anatomical words had a straightforward
vernacular label to sit alongside their Latinate name. *Womb*, in
its early days, was a capacious word, meaning 'belly' and 'stomach' as well as 'uterus'. There are plenty of men with wombs full
or empty, big or small in medieval English. When the Green
Knight interrupts King Arthur, Sir Gawain and the rest of
Camelot one Christmas, this romance's author says that, despite
being very tall and very green, the Green Knight's 'wombe', his
abdomen, was very trim. Likewise Old English's *hrif*, a syllable
which survives in our modern word *mid-riff*, meant both 'belly'
and 'womb'. Not till the seventeenth century does *womb*'s usual
sense become that of the uterus.

Were it not for two extra wombish words, *hysterical* and *hysteria*, we could move swiftly on to the mammary language of the breasts. Those troublesome words have had considerable impact on medical experts' treatment of women's physical and mental health across the centuries. Like Gawain's opponent, these words remain evergreen, springing to the lips of those not keen to listen to what we say. *Hysterical* writes off our arguments as emotional, agitated, driven by passion not reason. They are notably lopsided, without a male equivalent, though *testerical*, meaning 'driven by testes and/or testosterone' has been proposed. Words which begin with *hyster-* derive from the ancient Greek word for 'womb', which comes ultimately from the same Indo-European base as *uterus*, the two individual words appearing because two different suffixes were attached to the same root. *Uterus* is first recorded in an English text in Crooke's 1615 *Mikrokosmographia*, a straightforward borrowing of the medical name of the womb from Greek via Latin. *Uterine* is even older, used in medieval English to describe two children who share a mother but not necessarily a father.

The histories of *hysteria* and *hysterical*, and the illnesses which they have labelled in the past, are, by contrast with *uterus* and *uterine*, more complicated and more full of misconceptions.[6] It's a myth to think that a Greek doctor called Hippocrates coined the term *hysteria* in the fourth or fifth century BC, just as it's an oversimplification to say that everyone in the past thought that the womb wandered round the body like a wild animal. There's no Hippocrates the author, but rather a bunch of anonymous textbooks attributed to a famous doctor. It's like allocating ideas to the Mr York or Mr Spark who wrote those helpful Notes. The best-known account of the rambling uterus wasn't even written by a doctor but by a fifth-century BC philosopher, Plato, who described the female body's animal instincts to procreate as a restless creature which, if thwarted, could block the flow of air within the body. By the second century AD, some medics were already highly sceptical that the womb literally moved, not least because anatomists saw it firmly tethered by its ligaments. Perhaps Plato's description was more metaphorical than literal. Plus the noun *hysteria* wasn't used in ancient Greek at all.

Yet there *was* in ancient medical texts a set of symptoms often labelled as *hysterical*, i.e. uterine. Women experiencing these symptoms felt a kind of 'suffocation', perhaps a spasm or a fit, a feeling of choking or numbness. *Why* the womb was to blame differed depending on which expert, Arabic, Greek or Roman, you consulted: it rose because it was 'hot' and in need of cooling, or it retained stuff it should spit out and thus became too 'cool', poisoning other parts with noxious fumes. Or it moved (so said those happy to skip over anatomical reality) or at least somehow moved its *influence* to other organs, causing stifling, paralysing sensations. All this explains why we get the adjective *hysterical* first in English in 1603, well before the noun *hysteria* appears first in medical Latin in the later seventeenth century and then, in 1757, in English. Uterine suffocation came first, mutating into *hysteria* as scientists and doctors diagnosed and treated hysterical women.

The first person to use *hysterical* in English, a doctor called Edward Jorden, was an expert witness who testified in 1602 that a girl called Mary Glover had not been bewitched by one Elizabeth Jackson, but had instead been laid low by this 'suffocation of the womb'. Jorden was sceptical about the validity of accusations of witchcraft, but much less critical about this medical diagnosis. Writing up his opinions in a souvenir pamphlet published in 1603, he was vague on what caused hysteria: 'some unkind humor', he said, some unnatural fluid which the womb can't or won't expel. Not all his medical colleagues were so incurious. Seventeenth-century doctors noticed the similarities between the symptoms of hysterical women and those men suffering from hypochondriasis, a diagnosis for physical aches and mental gloom caused, it was thought, by organs of the upper abdomen, the liver and spleen. In 1681 Thomas Sydenham informed a fellow doctor who had written asking for advice that in men the symptoms are 'called hypochondria, but this disease is as like hysteria as one egg is like another'. As eggs is eggs, the womb couldn't be the cause. Sydenham thought instead that lack of activity explained why sedentary women and studious men (in the sexist logic which presented men's inactivity positively and women's negatively) often suffered from such similar afflictions.

The writer Lady Mary Wortley Montagu, in a 1758 letter to her friend Sir James Steuart, recommended Sydenham's work even as she sympathised with the hysterical torments of Sir James's wife. Sydenham, thought Lady Mary, convincingly demonstrated how men's 'wise honourable spleen', the emotional sensitivity so fashionable in Georgian Britain, was exactly 'the same disorder and arises from the same cause' as hysteria. She also pointed out that not only had men monopolised 'learning, power, and authority', but they had also imagined themselves to be superior in terms of mental strength, although the overlap of *hysteria* and *hypochondria* showed this to be untrue. Faced with such scepticism, the word *hysteria* might have died out, becoming as archaic as earlier medical diagnoses like *splenetic* or *distempered* which have worn down over time into old-fashioned descriptions of different temperaments. But the convenient *phallusies* bound up in the idea of *hysteria*, justifying women's restricted place in the world, were a hard habit to kick. Despite scientific scepticism and counter-evidence, despite the craze for gender-neutral attacks of 'nerves' and fits of the 'vapours', older ideas kept trundling along. Doctors diagnosed far more women than men with hysteria; those who said that men were hysterics nevertheless thought that women were much more susceptible to this disease.

Then came what Mark S. Micale, in his 2008 book *Hysterical Men*, calls the 'Great Victorian Eclipse', a sudden amnesia on the part of nineteenth-century doctors about the previous century's insights about hysteria. Certain parts of society, contemplating the unpredictable consequences of revolutions in America and France, had a vested interest in keeping things just as they had always been, even in the face of progressive arguments for equal rights for every human. Much of Victorian science and medicine thus promoted knowledge and theories which emphasised differences between the sexes and saw those differences as natural or inevitable. Older theories and evidence which challenged such essentialist thinking were downplayed, forgotten or discredited. If the two sexes were, in their fundamental nature, a binary of superior and inferior, women's subordination could continue apace even as Enlightenment philosophy encouraged claims for equal treatment. On both sides of the Atlantic, physicians grew certain once again that hysteria was 'peculiar to females', as a chapter summary in Thomas Laycock's 1840 book on hysteria had it, blaming body parts (especially ovaries), physiology or sexuality (too much, not enough, can't win either way). Or their more sedentary lifestyles were at fault (in the case of privileged women who did little unpaid or paid work) or their tendency to manipulate and mislead doctors. We've reached I-can't-even.

But it didn't stop there. Trained by a French neurologist who specialised in hysteria, Sigmund Freud blamed not bodies but psychologies, giving this diagnosis new life in the twentieth century. For Freud, it was triggered by childhood sexual trauma, with women especially vulnerable to having suppressed memories transform themselves into bodily hysteria because of their supposed passivity. While the womb has never wandered, what *has* scurried to and fro, evading any attempt to pin it down, is the dodgy sexist 'logic' which kept the diagnosis of hysteria alive and well. As the cultural historian Heather

Meek concludes, *hysterical* has always been the 'catch-all that explained everything that was wrong with women'.[7] Now this catch-all has become a verbal trap which exposes men's sexist views of forceful women, a word swiftly challenged when it slips out in the heat of the moment. Former Trump campaign chief spokesman Jason Miller called then-Senator Kamala Harris's questioning of Jeff Sessions in a 2017 Senate committee 'hysterical', before being swiftly quizzed on his choice of words by CNN's political analyst Kirsten Powers. Veteran Australian broadcaster Steve Price accused a female journalist, Van Badham, who challenged him during a TV debate on domestic violence in 2016, of 'being hysterical', later saying that he had been 'verballed by an aggressive woman'. Both men were taken to task in the media for their choice of adjective. Perhaps such blowback will finally kill off this word.

If the loaded legacy of *hysterical* enrages us, perhaps the first English vocabulary of the breast can soothe. The *breost* in Old English wasn't only a body-part word for the front of the torso, but also named the place where your thoughts, beliefs and feelings lived. English's earliest vocabulary revealed humans to be something more than a soul within a meat-sack. As well as the mortal body and the eternal spirit, humans possessed two further not-body components: the first you might call our 'life force' and the second the *mod*, the mind, our emotions, memories and thoughts. The first poems written down in English suggest that our mind isn't in the head but lives in the chest, the breast. Our *breost-sefa*, the 'breast-mind', held our innermost thoughts, what we might today call our *heart of hearts*. As Professor Leslie Lockett explains, when you think or remember or feel in Old English poetry, your breast-mind seethes, swells, constricts or relaxes, heating or cooling depending on the particular trigger.[8]

Mind and physiology are inseparable. Only when medical writing based on some of Galen's theories arrived in England in the eleventh century did the mind uncouple from the body to take up residence in the brain.

So our breast was, at least to start with, a place of thought and feeling, and everyone had breasts *plural* in Old English, thanks to the torso's symmetrical halves. At the same time, *breost* also named those body parts, built of lobules and ducts that cluster like chrysanthemum petals, which we would call breasts today. Two hundred and fifty years after they were made around the year 700, the Lindisfarne Gospels, an intricately illuminated manuscript of the four books of the Bible which tell the life of Christ, were updated with a running gloss in one of English's earliest regional dialects. In the blank space left between the Latin lines with their plump and tidy letters cheek by jowl, a word-by-word Northumbrian translation was added in a smaller but livelier script. Given the hand-trembling job of adding glosses to this holiest of books was a tenth-century priest called Aldred, whose dad was Alfred and whose unnamed mum was (as he tells us in a little note) a *til wif*, a 'good woman'. Perhaps he was thinking of her when he glossed a verse from Luke's gospel. Seeing Christ performing miracles, a woman shouts from the crowd that the womb that birthed him and the breasts that fed him are truly blessed. Aldred glosses *ubera*, 'teats', not only with *breosto* but with *titto*, an early version of our *tit*.

Tit, for me, is the least-worst of mammary words. Talking about *my breasts* out loud sounds a bit formal, as if I'm using my posh telephone voice. I like the jollity of *boobs*, but a *boob* is a fool and a *booby trap* snares the hare-brained. All three of those words probably derive from the sort of affectionate nonsense – *bubby*, *bub*, *boo-boo* and the like – which parents and carers often burble at babies. To be *busty* sounds like you might be broken, or headless, or just particularly big-breasted. *Bosom* is a lovely word, originally naming the comforting, hugging circle which the arms and chest can make. But maybe my bosom doesn't want to be a pillow for all and sundry. Other nicknames for breasts – *baps, melons, fun-bags* – make them appear like inflatable pillows that might pop without warning. Slang words for breasts are sniggering metaphors: *jugs, knockers, puppies, rack.* Early English does at least have a better set of synonyms. The glossary section of a 'how to learn French' book published in 1530 translates *mamelle* with four English words: 'Tete, pappe, or dugge, a womans breest'.

Tete becomes our modern word 'teat' with its uddery connotations, its spelling shifting a bit from the Old English *tytto*, Though more often allocated to women, these parts can be found in men's bodies too: knights in medieval romances, for example, were sliced or hacked *to the pappes*, 'up to the breasts'. In one of the mystery plays staged at York in the fifteenth century, dozy travellers who don't realise they're talking to the resurrected Jesus gossip about a soldier piercing Christ's side with the point of a spear 'atte the pappe' as he hung on the Cross. And around the year 1160, Ailred, abbot of a Yorkshire monastery, wrote some spiritual guidelines in Latin for his sister who lived as a religious recluse. Translated into English a couple of centuries later, the guide suggests that she have in her cell a crucifix with Jesus's 'tetys ... al naked' so that she can imagine being fed by his sweet milk.

English takes a while to find the words to describe the breast all the way from torso to nip, like a toddler learning how to stack cups into a tower. In a vocabulary list written down for learning or teaching Latin in the mid-tenth century, *mamilla* ('breast') is glossed by *titt* while *papilla* ('nipple') gets the gloss of *forweard titt*. It's logical at least: the nipple, whether flat, inverted or protruding, is generally forward of the tit on which it sits. In the Middle Ages, the same idea gives us *pappe hede*, the top of the breast. By the sixteenth century, *nipple* prods forth, though its spelling – *neble*, *nibble*, *neaple* – takes a while to settle down. Lastly, the *areola* arrives, always muddled up in my mind with *aureole*, the golden crown or ring of light illuminating the head of a saint or angel. But *areola* just means 'little area', a boring word for a ring so sensitive and so varied in its colours and sizes. *Areola* edges into English as a technical term added by the publisher John Kersey in 1706 to an updated edition of an older diction-ary, Edward Phillips's *New World of Words*. Kersey glosses *areola papillaris* as 'the Circle about a Nipple', but I wish another of his definitions had caught on instead of *areola*. Though *areolae* aren't *aureoles*, perhaps the similarity of these words had made some connection between the two things. *Halo*, Phillips writes, means both the fuzz of light around the sun, moon or stars and also the 'Spot or Circle of Flesh which encompasses each Nipple in the Breasts of Women'.

In truth, it's not the names of the parts but the slew of thoughts and words that get attached to our boobs which clutters up how we might feel about them. In the 1650s, a Yorkshire schoolteacher called Joshua Poole compiled a one-stop-shop book for the would-be poet. The *English Parnassus* had everything a junior versifier might need: lists of rhymes and illustrative passages from famous poems, plus 'apposite epithets', suggestions of words you could add to any given noun if you got stuck in your composition. *Breast* gets the following jumble of adjectives:

> uberous ['milk-giving'], fluent, sagging, tender, stressed [perhaps 'oppressed'], swelling, milkie, hanging, flagging, lolling, dimpled, veinie, streaked, spicie ['aromatic'], delicious, flowing, luxuriant, warme, coursing, azure, streaked

Quite the confusion, but Poole's list is better than the clichés of love poetry: the greengrocery of strawberries and apples or the geography of orbs, hemispheres and globes. Geometry too can't fully capture our breasts' negotiation between body and gravity. The algebra of bra sizes – 34A, 42HH – only approximates our shapely varieties, bulbiform, campanulate as a bell, or gibbous like the moon between semicircle and full. Poole's pick-your-own buffet shows how many paradoxical things can be thought and said about breasts. They're almost holy yet stubbornly fleshy, desirable and dissatisfactory, functional and erotic. Among the noise, it's hard to work out what *I* might think or feel about them.

In the third century AD, a Roman magistrate tortured a Sicilian teenager, Agatha, for her religious faith. As her legend tells, this magistrate Quintianus was so angry that she would neither marry him nor renounce her Christianity that he ordered her breasts be cut off. In medieval and Renaissance paintings, Agatha often appears holding her two breasts on a platter, two jellified and cherry-topped desserts. It makes me shudder and daydream. What if we *could* just take them off? We could keep them in a bedside drawer, ready to be suctioned on when wanted for a particular purpose. No need to strap them down to exercise; nothing to be stared at or groped. No bras to constrict. No need to bear the weight which leaves bra-strap grooves in the shoulders and pain in the backs of women with the largest breasts. No need to check them anxiously for lumps and dimples.

With one in seven British women and one in eight American women diagnosed with breast cancer over their lifetime, many of us will need a mastectomy, no martyrdom or silly thought-experiment of mine but a vital treatment. Some will have breast reconstruction, others will choose to 'live flat' or be a 'uni boober' (as members of post-mastectomy support groups sometimes say). We thus need words for breast-less-ness as well. Perhaps we might borrow a term or two from the warrior women who supposedly cut off one tit to make firing their bows and arrows easier. That's myth rather than history, made up to colour an old legend because *Amazon* sounds like it might derive from Greek *a-mastos* ('without a breast'). Yet explorers of the Americas did sometimes think they had met the Amazons (and named a river and a region after them). More sceptically, the London vicar and geography fan Samuel Purchas, who published an anthology of travel writing in 1625, noted that though there were 'warlike wives' in the New World, there was no sign of any 'unimammians' (a word for Amazons preserved for posterity by Isidore of Seville's *Etymologies*), no 'one-breasted Nation'. The one-breasted and no-breasted nations aren't hiding in the rainforest but are right here, dealing as best they can with the after-effects of surgery.

Inventing our own words and phrases like *uni boober* or *living flat* helps us grapple with what might happen to our bodies, but it's harder to replace or rewrite the standard vocabulary for our anatomy. We're generally stuck with the dancing fossils we've inherited from the past. Over the centuries, most of the vernacular alternatives have slipped by the wayside. *Cunt*'s fall from grace is the most dramatic. In 1611, John Florio's multi-lingual dictionary *Queen Anna's New World of Words*, which he dedicated to the Danish wife of James I, could explain the meaning of an Italian word by the definition 'a womans cunt or quaint'. But by the end of the eighteenth century, this word was considerably less acceptable. The near-perfectly named Francis Grose, a literary hack who packaged his research on everyday slang into a *Classical Dictionary of the Vulgar Tongue* in 1785, called what he printed as C**T 'a nasty name for a nasty thing'. Grose's turn of paraphrase shares with the word itself the misogynistic snarl *cunt* can still have today. It's a slur beyond rehabilitation for some of us. For others, it can be reclaimed: one of Eve (now V) Ensler's *Vagina Monologues*, a collection of dramatic pieces tackling different aspects of women's lives first performed in 1996, repeats *cunt* over and over until its taboo energy is spent.

As for the rest of our body-part vocabulary, Latinate terms won out over most of their medieval predecessors and over the alternative vernacular names and glosses which enliven English books of anatomy. Latin names take up their official positions in medical guides, encyclopaedias and dictionaries, especially those that give the meanings and etymologies of less-familiar technical words which were popular in the years after 1700. But as time went on even those antiseptic medical words could attract disapproval. As the fashion for propriety and purity which censored Chaucer's *Miller's Tale* grew ever stronger, words for reproductive anatomy and sexual activity were increasingly taboo in non-specialist settings. By the 1760s, makers of newer dictionaries criticised the older etymological dictionaries for having included 'the most obscene Terms our Language is acquainted with'. Their more modern dictionaries were advertised as being cleansed of 'Terms that carry any Indecency in their Meaning'.

In particular, moralists thought that women and children were vulnerable to the supposed dangers of rude words. The *General and Complete Dictionary of the English Language* published in 1785 recommended itself as entirely suitable for 'female readers' who can 'consult it without a possibility of offence to delicacy' because such terms had been omitted. And so, while nineteenth-century doctors and psychologists were free to develop their theories of women's malfunctioning privates when talking among themselves, these words were pushed out of bounds for public discussion, erased from general dictionaries into which anyone might dip. These Georgian and Victorian taboos against public mention of sexual activity and reproductive anatomy lingered on into the twentieth century, taking many decades of education and activism to undo.

Does it really matter if today's words for female sex organs are dressed in the white coat and stethoscope of scientific Latin? I think it does, though there's no easy way to scrap them and start afresh. For all their anatomical precision, technical-sounding words make our minds glaze over and forget. We get easily muddled when asked about them. A 2019 survey of Britons found that 45 per cent of women couldn't label the vagina on a diagram, while 43 per cent of women questioned were unable to name the labia or urethra. A 2020 poll of American women found similar uncertainties: 59 per cent misidentified the uterus on a diagram, 46 per cent could not locate the cervix and a quarter could not find the vagina.

Something seems to go awry when we learn about our biology in this language. Diagrams of a body sliced in half, internal bits neatly packed together like a tidy underwear drawer, are not much help. The alternative is contortionist self-exploration and inspection, and even then it's difficult to match up anatomical labels with what we can see, upside-down or mirror-image, or what we can feel with our fingers. 'Which hole is which?' girls ask themselves. As for what's inside, we've to take on trust what we're taught, or can teach ourselves, about an already plumbed-in system we can't see. Were these parts' names more user-friendly, we might feel a little more at home with them and a little less ashamed. If only we could turn back the clock and revive the single-syllabled simplicity of *wings*, *gates*, *ports*, *tits* and *nips*.

Two

FLUX

Menstrual Language

—

'*Period*,' my daughter said one day while musing about menstruation, 'is not a very nice word.' I agree: it's an empty, evasive name. A period is a blank, a square on a school timetable – *free period, second period* – or the jump on a calendar from one date to another. As a description of a bodily function, it's pretty minimalist, suggesting that what matters most is nothing more than time and timing. Periods, it proposes, are like clocks or trains, stopping or starting, regular or running fast or slow. What's more, *period*, like our modern-day words for the female sex organs, is a late arrival as a name for the shedding of the lining of the uterus. Though *period* has meant a quantity of time since the Middle Ages, only at the end of the seventeenth century does the phrase *monthly period* appear in medical books as a name for menstruation. From there, *period* becomes what it is today, an almost silent term, a pale and polite label thrown over a bloodier reality. Like *time of the month* (first recorded referring to menstruation in 1931 according to the *Oxford English Dictionary*), *monthly period* is a prissy kind of diary description. Accurate to a degree, but not a phrase which conveys anywhere near enough about its realities.

Why do our modern words for periods have to be so limited and unappealing? We're caught between the clinically scientific and the Gothic horror of slang (*Code Red, on the rag*), with not much more than *period* left in the middle. Yet it wasn't always this way. Monthly bleeds had other names for many centuries before the word *period* appeared on the scene. This chapter tells the story of English's first words for menstrual bleeding, the physical symptoms which sometimes accompany it and the methods which were used to deal with it. Such language was often more expressive than our bland contemporary terms.

Let's start at the very beginning, or at least the beginning of written references to menstruation in English. At the end of the sixth century, Pope Gregory I sent missionaries to pagan Britain to convert King Æthelberht and his Kentish subjects to Christianity. Leading the mission was a monk called Augustine, who, having baptised the king and converted ten thousand English men and women, became the first Archbishop of Canterbury. Perhaps paving the way for this mission's success was Æthelberht's Christian wife Bertha, a Frankish princess from the continent whose marriage, years before Augustine turned up, was agreed on the understanding that she could keep her faith and have her own bishop close at hand. Gregory had encouraged Bertha to persuade her husband to be baptized. With the conversion achieved, Augustine wrote a letter back to Gregory in Rome asking questions about how to run this new English Church. The *Libellus responsionum*, 'the little book of answers', is the name of the letter that the pope sent back to him.

One of Augustine's questions concerned whether a menstruating woman should go to church or take communion. You might think that what a woman could and couldn't do was none of Augustine or Gregory's business, but the Book of Leviticus in the Old Testament sets out instructions as to which bodily emissions, whether semen or menstrual blood, rendered a man or woman 'unclean' and hence temporarily excluded from religious worship. That Augustine asked Gregory about the matter suggests some debate over whether archaic decrees about ritual purity still applied to Anglo-Saxon Christians. Perhaps forward-thinking sixth-century women like Queen Bertha wanted these questions decided by someone with a hotline to the man at the top in Rome. Answering Augustine, Gregory reassures him that a menstruating woman can indeed go to church because her periods are part of her physical make-up rather than being a sign of sinfulness or impurity. Gregory's answers were recorded for posterity in the Northumbrian monk Bede's history of the English Church which he completed in 731. Bede's *Historia* was translated into Old English between about 883 and 930, putting Gregory's Latin, and his word for menstruating, into the written record of the mother tongue. *Monað-aðl*, the compound chosen by the translator to render Latin *menstruus* into English, is literally 'month-disease', *aðl* or *adl* meaning 'sickness' or 'ailment'.

The word making up the first part of this compound, *monað*, comes ultimately from *moon*, a connection left over from measuring time not by months of different lengths making up three hundred and sixty-five days of the solar year, but according to the moon's changing phases of twenty-nine and a bit days. Etymologically at least, periods are *moon-th-lies* as well as *month-lies*. These moon months were sometimes called *lunations*, a more elegant word than *period*. *Lunation* was indeed briefly used as a polite term for menstruation in an 1822 medical textbook, but it didn't catch on. Nowadays researchers have disproved any synchronisation between the moon's cycles and the revolutions of our own bodies.[1] Periods run to our own internal clock rather than any public timetable, the endometrium building up and then shedding. Some of us feel the *sine* waves of our hormones rising and dipping, or track our periods on our phones, rather like astronomers plotting lunar phases. But just as the moon, thanks to my own ignorance of its cycle, often surprises me when I glimpse it late at night or early one morning, full or new, close or far, so I'm often caught unawares by my own body when I lose track of menstrual time.

The other part of that Old English translator's compound, *aðl*, implies that to menstruate is to suffer with a disease or a disorder. Classical and medieval medicine thought of menstruation wrong-headedly as the discharging of some superfluous fluid or the result of incompletely digested food, yet in doing so they did at least acknowledge that it was a natural bodily process. The translation of Gregory's Latin letter answering Augustine speaks of a woman's 'oferflownis ... gecyndes', which we might translate as her natural overflow. But however natural they are, periods do often bring the *dis-ease* of cramps or backache, or bleeding that is too heavy or goes on too long. Anglo-Saxon medical treatments may be stomach-turning to modern eyes, but these earliest English physicians dealt openly with issues that until very recently were often hidden behind the vague phrase *women's troubles*. In one set of remedies copied out in the first half of the tenth century, gynaecological treatments sit alongside cures for lice, cancer, paralysis and sore knees. If a period is delayed, the healer should prescribe nice-sounding things: herbs in ale to drink, a hot bath and a warm poultice applied to the lower parts of her belly. For this cure to work, it should be given when the woman expects her period. That timing is something a doctor can't know – it runs to no external calendar of months or moons. It belongs to the individual. 'Ahsa þæs æt þam wife', says the author of this ancient medical handbook: ask the woman about this.

In giving treatment for periods which are somehow blocked or stoppered, Anglo-Saxon cures recognised that periods are in essence a process of flowing. I like the fluidity of words like *oferflownis*, *period* being too static a word to capture an experience which is, in all senses, liquid, beginning and ending with streaks and spots, flowing heavily and lightly. Another Old English word for menstrual bleeding, *flewsa*, is a relative of the Latin *flux*, 'flowing'. In medieval medicine, a *flux* is a running-out of liquid from the body, whether semen, blood or the product of illness or disease. The dysentery that killed Henry V and hundreds of his victorious army on campaign in France in 1422 was called the 'bloody flux', a name that makes the grim reality of its blood-filled diarrhoea all too plain. Though some fluxes could be fatal, a medieval English translation of a fourteenth-century Latin surgical handbook is careful to say that 'alle fluxe of blode' is unnatural and should be treated immediately *except* for 'the mesurable menstrues': the monthly period. Medieval physicians knew that period blood was to be expected: a flux unlike other much more dangerous bleeding.

I'd rather have a *flux* than a period, I think. At least nouns like *flux* and *flow* can be turned into usable verbs: our bodies *flux* and *flow*, discharging like a battery and then recharging. Flux in physics measures the rate at which liquid or matter or energy flows out from or over something. Doc Brown's flux capacitor in *Back to the Future* stores energy and releases it in a burst to fire the DeLorean through time. But the word *period* can't easily be converted into an action. Nobody says *I'm perioding*, and *I'm menstruating* sounds absurdly formal when said out loud. *I'm on my period*, we hiss under our breath, or, more dramatically, *I'm bleeding*. The latter is somehow right and wrong: it is undoubtedly blood but not the sort of blood that should panic you, at least once you get used to it.

Words like *flux* and *menstrues* arrived in English as barely changed Latin – this is the jargon of academics, doctors and surgeons writing in technical terms. Yet laypeople too were curious about knowledge of all kinds and wanted to read about

it in a language they could understand. At the end of the fourteenth century, a priest called John Trevisa translated a kind
of medieval *Encyclopaedia Britannica* with the encouragement
of a Gloucestershire nobleman named Thomas, Lord Berkeley
for whom Trevisa worked as a private family chaplain. Medieval
readers like Thomas (and his daughter Elizabeth, who also
commissioned translations) wanted to explore philosophy, medicine, religion and history in their own mother tongue. They
also wanted to read about the workings of their own bodies.
Prompted by words like *flux* and *superfluitas* in his Latin source
which describe how the body discharges various bodily fluids,
Trevisa calls menstruation 'such a rennyng as women have'.

Rennyng is our modern word *running*: in medieval English
menstrual blood ran just as water or paint runs. This feels spot-
on to me: to menstruate is to learn the irresistible properties of
liquid, its irrepressible flow that soaks and stains. For something
that is supposed to be measurable in dinky amounts – teaspoons
and eggcups – period blood always seems so plentiful. Those
who menstruate are experts in the fluid physics of capillarity
and sorptivity, the rates at which fluid moves and absorbs. We
divide our menstruating days and nights by what volume of
liquid a tampon or a pad can hold for how much time. We worry,
perhaps obsessively, about failing in our calculations and leaking
over clothes, chairs or bedding. We make menstruating a magic
trick, the one where you pour water into a paper bag and then –
pouf! – make it vanish. Period blood flows freely yet is hardly ever
seen by anyone but us: we take great care to make it invisible.

Such worries can never be put fully aside because period
blood is not some universal, predictable constant, so many milli-
litres per minute, but a rate that varies from hour to hour and
from person to person. A medieval guide to gynaecology and
obstetrics from the beginning of the fifteenth century captures
the endless variety: 'summe women have it [their period] many

dayes and sume but fewe dayes, summe surfetously and summe lytill while and esyly'. Some bleed without much trouble for only a little while, some flow *surfetously*, excessively. Its author warns off any curious man who might poke his nose into this book and tell its contents to the world. Women who might be in need of the information, he says, have the same bodies and the problems as those pious women who are saints in heaven. He points out that holy women, the most revered in medieval Christianity, saints, martyrs, mystics and even the Virgin Mary herself, suffer these troubles, and so there is no shame to be felt.

This medical author therefore pushes back against medieval theologians who argued themselves out of the idea that the Blessed Virgin herself had periods. Piety and purity, they thought, seemed incompatible with normal bodily functions. Medieval mystics and recluses sometimes severely restricted their food intake in what has been called holy anorexia, a state of saintly perfection in which very little entered or left their bodies. One fifteenth-century Norfolk woman, Joan the Meatless (*meat* in the sense of 'food', as in *mincemeat*, 'chopped food'), reputedly survived for fifteen years on nothing more than weekly Eucharistic wine and wafers. The stopping of such women's periods brought about by their lack of nutrition could be taken as a sign of saintliness. In contrast to such thinking, this medical author wanted to reassure his readers that even heavenly woman shared their bodily reality.

Flowing *surfetously* is nowadays called *flooding*, menstrual flow so heavy that it soaks quickly through whatever protection you use. For those of us who do have it relatively easy, it can be hard to wrap your mind around just how excessively blood can flow. Until my mid-thirties, I'd no real idea what flooding was: I thought naively it was an exaggeration, a hyperbolic way of describing super-heavy flow. *I* could manage my periods, so why couldn't women who flooded manage theirs? How wrong I was.

Once, when my daughter was a toddler at playgroup or in the library – I forget the place but the sensation is stubbornly vivid – I stood up and felt a sudden deluge, blood running fast from some hidden, unknown reservoir. Everything soaked through, knock-kneed and stricken, I shuffled first to the toilets and then, self-consciously, home. Since then, I've never underestimated the fluxing, flowing powers of menstruation.

Like the fabrics which absorb blood so enthusiastically, English itself is porous, sucking in words from other languages whenever it makes contact with them. Thanks to the Norman Conquest, medieval England was a multilingual nation – for the elite at least. Nuns in their convents spoke English and French, as did noblewomen and noblemen. Professional men in the universities, the Church, government and the law spoke Latin, French and English. With languages rubbing up against each other in bilingual and trilingual minds, it's no surprise that Middle English gained more words for menstruation. One new word, *flowers*, comes to English from French, but was a common way to describe periods in many tongues. The *Trotula* are a set of popular and widely translated medical texts which took their name and authority from a twelfth-century healer, Trota of Salerno. Historian Monica H. Green has discovered that fourteen of the twenty-two languages into which the *Trotula* texts were translated used their word for 'flowers' in place of the Latin word *menses*.[2]

One *Trotula* text explains how this name came about: just as trees cannot bear fruit without blossoming first, so women who don't menstruate can't bear children. Though ovulation's part in the menstrual cycle was not fully understood until the early twentieth century, medieval medical experts knew that regular menstruation was linked to fertility. English medical books describe how to treat a woman 'in tyme of flourys' or 'whan she has her flours'; they advise on how to start 'the flode of her flowres' for those women seeking to increase their fertility. It's hard to think of periods as flowery or floral, though blood does bloom and blossom unexpectedly on gussets and bedsheets. But maybe we could reclaim the word as the best that English has to offer. *I'm on my flowers*, you might say, or *it's flower time*. It would be a euphemism, a polite substitution which covers reality like a new throw over an old sofa. Better than peculiar phrases like *the curse, on the blob* or *Aunt Flo* which dictionaries dutifully record as alternative names. I don't think anyone uses parabolic, don't-say-what-you-mean expressions like these any more.

In the sixteenth century, as the Middle Ages somehow became the Renaissance without anyone noticing, English was turbo-charged by the new technology of printing. Presses poured forth translations not just from French and Latin but Italian and Spanish too. Along with these came everything that might be needed for education and for making the most of both English and all the other languages taught and studied in Britain: dictionaries, grammars and guides to rhetoric and poetry. Sir Thomas Elyot, a self-taught Oxfordshire gentleman, retired to Cambridgeshire and compiled a Latin–English dictionary after years of avoiding the bear traps of a career as a civil servant and diplomat in Henry VIII's government. His dictionary was not the first such work but far more comprehensive than anything that had come before. Unlike earlier Latin–English dictionaries which left out this subject, Latin words for menstruation, *menstruum* and *muliebria*, are defined matter-of-factly by Thomas as 'a womans naturall purgation called floures' and 'naturall evacuations, which women have, called their floures'.

While Elyot has one everyday English term for periods, another dictionary written sixty years later gives plenty more to choose from. In 1598, John Florio dedicated the first edition of his English–Italian dictionary, the *Worlde of Wordes*, to three aristocratic patrons, one of whom was a woman, Lucy, Countess of Bedford. In Florio's dictionary, the Italian word *menstruo* gets a gush of words in its English definition: 'a womans monethly termes or flowres or fluxes or issues'. In his second, 1611 edition, Florio adds yet another synonym: 'a womans monethly termes, issues, fluxes, sheddings or flowers'. Renaissance Englishwomen had a wealth of words for their periods, each deemed perfectly suitable for dictionary definitions. *Sheddings* and *issues* are, like *flux*, words describing the flowing of liquid and the discharge of bodily fluids.

Terms, like our more recent word *period*, measures menstruation in calendar time rather than liquid flow. Thomas Raynalde explains in his 1545 *Womans Booke* that 'In Englysh they [i.e. periods] be named termes' because they return 'at certane seasons, times and termes'. Raynalde understands that he can't specify their timings, for they have a rhythm of their own, not governed by clock time nor necessarily perfectly regular. Even now, period trackers predict, but bodies do their own thing. As we saw in Chapter One, Raynalde had no truck with outdated ideas about women's bodies. In his section on the womb, he says it's utterly wrong to think that periods are the purging or cleansing of some waste matter a female body can't process. He challenged the logic found in Elyot's dictionary definition, resisting the idea that periods are 'evacuations' or 'purgations' of waste matter, however natural. This is blood, says Raynalde, as 'pure and holsum' as any other blood. How could it not be, he argues, because in pregnancy it nurtures that most precious of things, a human life. Menstrual blood replenishes itself every cycle like a 'natural source, spryng, fountayne, or wel' – why use one word when four can surge forth liquidly? – ever fresh and ready in case a baby is conceived.

Even more progressively, Raynalde won't even countenance

the 'dreames and playne dotage', the fantasies and stupidity, of those who claim that period blood is dangerous. Though he says he won't waste paper and ink repeating them, he means the widely circulating superstitions that menstruating women could render mirrors cloudy or spotted, or wither flowers or blight fruit in an orchard, or exhibit some other menstrual superpower. One Tudor 'book of secrets' (a popular 'how-to' genre of recipes and do-it-yourself tips) advises that if you wanted to clear your garden of 'lise [lice] and other small beastes', you could simply get a menstruating woman to walk around it and 'all the vermine will fall doune deade'. I wish this were true – it would make gardening much more entertaining. Just as we read about scientific cutting-edge research one minute and surf dubious blogposts about the benefits of apple cider vinegar the next, so Tudor readers devoured both Raynalde's progressive views and all the old delusions about menstruation.

If Raynalde could write so enthusiastically about the wonders of menstrual blood in his mid-sixteenth-century *Womans Booke*, it seems indefensible that we're nowadays rather more reticent about discussing the experience of menstruating, even though our scientific understanding of it is much more detailed. Apart from sex education and biology lessons in schools, menstruation has until very recently been largely taboo, something which feels inappropriate for public discussion, more so perhaps than sex, or toilet habits, or dying, or any of the other topics that embarrassment or fear leads us to hide or cloak in euphemism. Something experienced on any given day by more than 300 million women worldwide is submerged, silenced.[3] I'm not sure I've ever talked about them at any length to anyone. Many conversations about periods are semi-wordless, with ellipses dangling – 'my ...', 'I'm ...' – and the rest completed by a grimace or a gesture.

Looking back into the English language of the past, the experience of menstruation, if not exactly front and centre, was at least part of the public world of the inquisitive and interested. Though earlier English speakers didn't have our scientific answers, they had just as much curiosity about nature and the workings of the human body and didn't necessarily share our sense that periods are taboo. Classical and medieval collections of *problemata*, 'problems' which needed answers, were still going strong in the Renaissance. Each problem began with a question about the causes of things which could be observed in the world around us: 'Why have we one nose and two eyes?', 'Why doe not fish make a sound?', 'Why hath a man hands, and an ape also which is like unto a man?' The answers are generally a mix of superstition, speculation and whatever some ancient authority has written, but you can't deny that these are good questions. (Why *are* fish silent?) Make no mistake, the *problemata* are full of sexism and misogyny, written as much to entertain as to educate and without Thomas Raynalde's progressive zeal for new science and better knowledge. Yet they are undoubtedly as interested in periods as they are in everything else that might puzzle the curious. The chapter on menstruation in a collection of problems printed in Edinburgh in 1595 contains twenty questions. Why does the female body have periods, for example, what makes the blood flow out, and why don't younger girls and women over fifty have them?

Some of the questions peer inquisitively into individual experiences, showing a fascination with menstruation which wouldn't be on show in a modern book of curious facts or puzzling trivia. 'Why doe they runne longer time in some, then in other some?' Why do some women's periods last longer than others? Another *problema* asks, 'Why have women paine and griefe in the running of their flowers?' Why is menstrual bleeding sometimes painful? To a question about where menstrual blood is held in the body comes the reply that some say the womb but Ibn Rushd, a twelfth-century Muslim polymath known to the West as Averroes, writes that menstrual blood comes from veins near the spine. Ibn Rushd's physiology may be wide of the mark but, in the science quoted in this *problema*, he has a firm grasp of the physical symptoms: 'women at that time have great griefe in their backe, by reason of expelling the flowers'. These *problemata* are fascinated by variation: how long menstruation lasts, how fast it flows, what kind of pain it brings. Raynalde's up-to-the-minute gynaecological guide also pays attention to individual differences. Some women have a period lasting three days with 'lytell or no paynes', he writes, while others suffer 'great effeoblysshment [considerable impairment] and stronge paynes in the backe' and have periods that last up to eight days. Menstrual *effeoblysshments*, one of those anarchic Renaissance words that doesn't even make it into the dictionary, come in many varieties. Once when I was a teenager, my cramps getting stronger and stronger through each dismal minute of a school assembly, the world in front of my eyes turned gingham and then went black. I came to on a narrow bed in the nurse's room. What a muscle the uterus must be to clamp itself so powerfully and painfully to the point of unconsciousness.

Like menstrual blood, we mostly keep these cramps hidden from the wider world nowadays. Yet menstrual pain, or at least a woman *pretending* to have such pain, appears early on in the Old Testament. Towards the end of the Book of Genesis, the patriarch Jacob, father of the twelve sons who head the twelve tribes of Israel, decides to take his children and his two wives, Rachel and Leah, back to Canaan, his homeland. Before they leave, Rachel steals her father Laban's *teraphim*, mysterious objects which might be statues of 'household gods' or ancestors. No one is quite sure why she does this strange, impulsive thing: to save Laban from idolatry perhaps, to have a memento of her

old life, as a Plan B in case Jacob's God fails him, or just as plain
rebellion. Laban comes looking for the stolen objects and Jacob,
unaware of Rachel's theft, challenges him to search for them in
their tents. Improvising frantically, Rachel hides the *teraphim*
under something to do with a camel (a camel's saddle, or its
straw, or a cushion made of camel hair – words are slippery and
translations vary) and sits on it. When her father approaches her
perched atop the camel-related item, she apologises for the fact
that she can't stand up. It's her time of the month, she tells him.
This ingenious excuse works both bodily and culturally: having
her period makes her ritually impure and thus it's inconceivable
to Laban that she could be so close to his objects of devotion.
To a disobedient daughter bold enough to exploit it, the stigma
of supposed impurity could come in useful.

Any scholar who sat down to make an English version of the
Bible would thus quite quickly encounter a woman pretending
to have her period. Rachel's words, admittedly, are euphemistic: talking to her father she apologises for being 'in the way
of women'. We know what she means though, even if it's not
spelled out. But sometimes scholars did tease out what they
thought was happening. By the 1540s, every parish church had
a Bible in an authorised English translation which any literate
churchgoer could read. As Tudor readers eagerly explored scrip-
ture in their mother tongue, they had questions which needed
answers. Up stepped a clergyman called Andrew Willet, a man
who didn't do anything by halves. He had written a vast history
of the arguments between the Catholic Church and Protestant
reformers which, by its final edition, was 1,300 pages long. He
had eighteen children and ran his household to a strict timetable
with notices and rules pinned on the walls. He also set about
writing commentaries explaining every detail of every verse of
the Bible, managing seven of its books before he died in 1621.

In his guide to every inch of the Book of Genesis, Willet

explains Rachel's tricking of Laban for an Elizabethan readership less bothered by concepts of Old Testament ritual purity and more interested in matters of biology:

> Not that women while their monethly custome is upon them are not able to rise by many times they are beside that infirmity troubled with the head-ake and are stomacke-sicke and not fit to be disquiete.

It's not, he reassures his quizzical readers, that menstruating women can't stand up at all (for if that were the case, how would they manage eighteen kids plus the housework?) but that they also have headaches and stomach aches and should not be troubled unduly.

Rachel's excuse made perfect sense to sixteenth-century minds fascinated with well-being and self-regulation. The health of the menstruating body was a matter not reserved for specialists but covered alongside all of the other functions of the human body. Medical texts, flying off the printing presses, offered guidance on how to reduce excessive bleeding, regulate timing and flow, and ease period pain. Some of the treatments are gruesome – leeches and pessaries – but others sound like well-intentioned fuss and care: herbal drinks, poultices, rest and hot baths. If you'd enough money to afford treatments, you'd have no trouble getting a doctor to pay attention. I'm sure some of this was the Tudor equivalent of mansplaining – male physicians muscling in on territory that women had themselves been managing for centuries – but at least they were keen to help.

Those who couldn't afford a medical consultation might try self-treatment at home. Having talked his way out of an austere life as a Carthusian monk and travelled throughout Europe studying medicine at the best universities, Andrew Boord wrote a *Breviarie of Health* in 1547, organised into brief chapters for those with short attention spans. Boord's chapter on menstruation for dummies lists four colours of vaginal discharge: 'there be foure kindes of womans flours red tauny [i.e. tawny, yellowish] whyte and blackish'. For the purposes of quick at-home diagnosis, he reassures readers that 'the red is naturall, and the other be unnaturall'. Menstruation that looked like blood is as expected, while other kinds of discharge are symptoms which need treatment. Periods were thus often called *the reds* in Early Modern English to distinguish them from discharges collectively known as *the whites*. *The reds* is not a bad name, for period blood is never one standard paint job like postboxes or telephone boxes, always plural rather than singular in its shades of red: strawberry, burgundy and rusted dark brown, clots that are almost black. Young girls expecting the bright scarlet of a cut finger (or even the mystery blue liquid once beloved of TV adverts) are surprised to find darker hues in their knickers. Perhaps we need a neatly labelled menstrual colour chart, with names like the titles of Rothko's murals in the Tate: *Red on Maroon, Light Red over Black, Black on Maroon*. I've always loved those vast hypnotic canvases, shades of red and black, one block of colour laid over another. Maybe gazing into their dark insides returns us temporarily to a foetal view, contemplating the deep red room of the womb.

The canvases for our impromptu paintings are pads and tampons, much smaller than Rothko's huge screens. Pablo Picasso's ruddy Rose Period lasted for a couple of years, but our Red Period persists for thirty or forty, though the results are rarely exhibited in public. Even when they are blank and unused, we hide pads and tampons up sleeves, deep in pockets, safely zipped in bags. So too many of the collective names for these *feminine hygiene products* or *sanitary protection* are euphemistic – even the word *menstrual* is often hidden from view when referring to the practicalities of managing periods. Of course, we're lucky to have these portable, disposable modern inventions which make life so much easier, but the euphemisms don't just keep a bodily process out of mind. They intimate that menstruation is somehow *un*hygienic or *in*sanitary, an echo of ancient ideas of ritual impurity. At least *period pants* and *menstrual cups* are names that look you straight in the eye. Recently, a New Zealand supermarket chain called Countdown claimed to be the first in the world to replace the usual euphemisms on its signage with plain-speaking references to *period products*. It's taken a long time to get here.

With the majority of medieval and Renaissance texts having been written by men, they're silent on the practicalities of managing menstruation month in, month out. On this subject, they've no advice to give, no new science to impart. In past centuries, women fashioned home-made solutions themselves. Some made pads of cloth or spare rags; many bled into their clothes in what we'd now call *free bleeding*. Before the convenience of tampons and sanitary towels, I wonder if period blood appeared more regularly on skirts, on the ground, on seats or fingers or streaked down the insides of legs. Even with washing machines on hand, period blood fights to be seen, clinging on after soaking, faded to brown or khaki. Dark-coloured clothes keep the secrets of these stains for us, as they have throughout history. Yet the historian Sara Read points out a peculiar paradox.[4] Though the practicalities of what women did are barely recorded, sanitary protection had a much higher profile than it has today and hence we can find some early terminology, but not necessarily where you might expect it to be.

This is because the ancient equivalent of sanitary protection makes several appearances in the Old Testament and thus quickly makes its way into early English. There it is in Isaiah 64, the *pannus* (as it appears in the standard Latin Bible called the

Vulgate), the cloth or rags for menstruation. In this chapter, a
prophet confesses the Jewish people's sinfulness so as to appeal
to God for help. He goes further: even the Jews' righteous deeds,
their pious devotions and good works, are nothing more than
the fabric women use to soak up their period blood. Be in no
doubt that this image is chosen to shock as something impure,
to be thrown away or burned. The unauthorised but very popular medieval Bible translations called this 'the cloth of the
womman' used for 'uncleene' blood. Miles Coverdale's Bible, the
first printing of an entire English translation made in Antwerp
in 1535, translates this phrase as 'the clothes stayned with the
floures of a woman'. These translations, even as they peddle
taboos (the rags are not only literally stained but also supposedly
polluted or defiled), give us the words which English speakers
used for the things that helped women deal with menstruating:
rags, *cloths* or *clouts*. A clout is a rag which can be chucked away
or burned, as well as being a dismissive word for clothes in general (as in *ne'r cast a clout . . .*).

Sixteenth-century book buyers had an enormous appetite
for collections of prayers, hymns, pious songs, and saintly stories. One Tudor bestseller was *The Monument of Matrones*, a
massive book of 1,500 pages published between 1582 and 1584,
stuffed with prayers and devotions for women, the matrons of
its title. Its second section offers the first anthology of writing
by women in English, including works by Elizabeth I, Lady Jane
Grey, Katherine Parr and others. Anyone who thinks that our
Renaissance foremothers (at least the ones wealthy enough to
buy the *Monument*, and there must have been enough of those
to make it commercially viable) weren't literate needs to bump
their head against this colossal volume. Perhaps it was sometimes bought by husbands to read to their wives, hopeful that
they would be inspired by biblical examples to be devout and
quietly obedient. Yet its contents are tailored, emphasising the

experiences which shaped many women's lives in this century: marriage, childbirth and widowhood.

If an image like Isaiah's menstrual rags was good enough for the Bible, it was good enough for Tudor Christians. One of the *Monument*'s devotions teaches its readers that because of Adam and Eve's Original Sin, humanity's 'giltie [guilty] and polluted nature' is 'like the foule and menstruous cloath of a woman'. In the heady (and sometimes frankly crazy) world of Protestant piety, the devout were encouraged to imagine their own nature as used menstrual products, their own deeds as nothing more than bloodied rags. Another religious guide borrows the image from Isaiah to say that at the Last Judgement, even good deeds will seem like 'a cloth bespotted with the flowers of a woman' and that the devout should ask for God's mercy rather than feel any certainty that their own virtue will be sufficient for salvation. I wonder how the *Monument*'s matrons felt seeing the imagery of menstruation flung about like a used sanitary towel chucked around by schoolboys.

By the middle of the seventeenth century, menstrual rhetoric could even become political. Britain had executed a king and descended into civil war; the Church was split between those who thought local congregations should be free to organise autonomously and those who thought some centralised control was needed. Into the fray jumped a clergyman called Thomas Edwards, determined to demonstrate the dangers of such Independent churches by cataloguing the hundreds of heresies and errors which he thought they encouraged. After Edwards had published his first volume of accusations, a score of Independents retaliated in their own pamphlets, the Civil War equivalent of the instant hot take. One Independent preacher, John Goodwin, complained that Edwards invented far more heresies than he had successfully detected. Goodwin says that 'before the course of his menstruous or monethly labour comes upon him', before Edwards's next *period* of writing, he'll supply him with many heresies to be corrected from Edwards's own book. Further on in the same reply, Goodwin hopes that Edwards will rectify an earlier mistake 'in the next return of his monethly course upon him'. Edwards's writings, his self-righteousness, are not menstrual rags but period blood itself: he is menstruating words (not a metaphor you could imagine the commentariat using today given our general squeamishness about periods). Edwards is very offended by this, arguing in his second instalment that it's hypocritical of Goodwin to tone-police him about other things when Goodwin himself 'speaks of monthly courses etc. more than once'. He calls Goodwin's menstrual metaphors 'expressions most immodest and uncivill'.

For some commentators, menstrual language was fair game for the cut and thrust of religious argument but for others this subject matter was offensive. In his guide to a happy marriage published in 1617 with the not-as-sexy-as-it-now-sounds title of *A Bride-Bush*, William Whately, a Puritan preacher, felt it was his duty to explain to newly married couples that period sex was not allowed in the Church's eyes. He says he must therefore make reference to what women call 'their flowers or terms' in his own 'plaine, but modest speeches' in order to make this clear to his readers. Whately's self-justification shows he feared that some readers might be offended. Seventeenth-century letters and diaries refer to periods obliquely as 'them' or 'those' or use codes like 'm.d.' (for *monthly* or *menstrual disease*), suggesting growing squeamishness about this topic even in private.[5] We can also find the beginnings of euphemism, the desire to have pretty, witty or polite phrases to avoid naming menstruation directly. An anthology of proverbs published in 1650 says that 'when a woman hath her flowers', the French say 'the Harbenger of the

Moon hath mark'd the lodging'. A harbinger travels ahead of a sovereign to find them somewhere to stay, showing the chosen house with a dab of paint. A 1611 French–English dictionary glosses '*Son Calendrier est rubriché* [i.e. 'her calendar is full of rubrics']' with 'said of a woman that hath her monthlie disease' or 'hath her Tearmes'. Religious festivals were rubricated, that is printed in red, on calendars – hence 'red letter day' for a special occasion.

In the eighteenth century, the vocabulary of menstruation became more scientific as well as yet more euphemistic. The everyday language of *flowers* and *terms* weathered away as medicine became increasingly professionalised. Man-midwives, who from the 1720s onwards offered their services as an alternative to traditional female birth attendants, set themselves up as experts not only on matters of obstetrics but also on menstruation, long before the full details of ovulation and hormone cycles were fully understood. Two doctors who in 1776 published the texts of their lectures for aspiring man-midwives cheerfully admitted that the workings of the menstrual cycle were more a matter of God's 'arcana', God's divine mysteries, than a fully understood process. But this lack of knowledge didn't stop such experts intimating that menstruation was less a normal part of life and more a health problem which required constant vigilance.

A century later menstruation became paradoxically both even more taboo and discussed more keenly, with sexual and reproductive anatomy remaining a hot topic for Victorian physicians and scientists. These researchers were keen to find new scientific justification for women's supposedly inferior physiology yet these same subjects were excluded from acceptable public speech. The Victorian scholars who published the first editions of Old English writings primly camouflaged Anglo-Saxon references to menstruation by glossing Old English words like *monað-að1* with Latin *menses* or Greek *catamenia*: terms a less educated reader might not be able to understand. God forbid that some layman or, more importantly, laywoman, might happen on a more forthright Anglo-Saxon description of period problems.

At the same time, as gynaecology became established as a medical specialty in the mid-nineteenth century, menstruation was used by experts as evidence of women's supposedly weaker constitution. Menstruation could be cited as proof to confirm doctors' prior assumptions that women were mostly perpetual invalids, disqualified from full participation in education, government and the professions by their unruly bodies. The American doctor Edward Clarke argued in his 1870 bestseller, *Sex in Education*, that girls needed different education during adolescence to prevent the impairment of their fertility and well-being as blood needed in their nether regions was diverted by study to their brains. Campaigners fought back hard against such nonsense. The Medical Women's Federation, founded in 1917 to promote the interests of women doctors and female patients, published an article called 'The Hygiene of Menstruation: An Authoritative Statement' in the *Lancet* in 1925. Its opening sentence was indeed authoritative and clear: 'Menstruation is a natural function; it is not an illness, and girls should therefore continue their ordinary work and play during the period.'

Nearly a hundred years on from the plain-speaking of the Medical Women's Federation, menstrual language and imagery are currently super-fashionable. Pantone, famous for its standardised colour-matching system, launched a shade called 'Period' in 2020, 'an energizing and dynamic warm red shade encouraging period positivity'. It's not quite clear what you might paint or print in that colour – perhaps a feature wall in a bathroom or wallpaper for your very own version of Jane Eyre's red-room? You can even say you're on your period without a word. In 2019, the Unicode Consortium approved a 'drop of blood' emoji which could be used to symbolise menstruation. There are energetic campaigns to tackle *period poverty* and promote *period dignity*, the idea that periods should not feel like something shameful. The floodgates of menstrual language have reopened.

Yet surprisingly it's still hard to overcome what Professor Clare Chambers has named *shametenance*, the work we do to keep menstruation and other bodily functions which we feel embarrassed about out of sight. On the back of the toilet door in my local supermarket is a sign saying that, if caught short, you can ask for free period products at the front desk. Yet it also gives you a code: you can 'ask for a package left by Sandy' if you don't want to say what you need directly. My daughter and her friends do talk about menstruation, and teachers give straightforward health education, but I'm not brave enough to email her judo coach to ask for help with the practical challenges of training year-round in a brilliant-white sports kit. Instead she manages. We've come a long way but there are still impediments. To use the punning language of activists and campaigners: it's about bloody time this natural function was part of everyday life.

Three

Lust

Sex and its Terms

＿

Of all the items of vocabulary whose roots and origins I've traced, many of the words which name and describe sexual activity are very recent arrivals into English, the product of supposedly scientific investigations by nineteenth- and twentieth-century sexologists and psychologists during the decades in which women's own words on these subjects were generally hushed by ideas of modesty and decorum. Words like *orgasm*, as we'll see, took on their modern meanings as new science reinforced old prejudices. The notion of bodies having *erogenous zones*, for example, comes into English from nineteenth-century French studies of women supposedly suffering from hysteria. These female patients were supposedly so highly strung, so mentally disturbed, that they might orgasm from the merest touch of one of these mapped-out areas.

Justification then to push these more recent words aside for a bit and grope further back into the earliest centuries of my mother tongue. What words were there in the first thousand years and more of English to describe women's sex lives, to name masturbation or cunnilingus, for example, or to denote the act of women having sex with other women? Does the past have anything better to offer than Victorian values and vocabulary? Or is much of this older language likewise contaminated with *phallusies* invented by religious and medical experts to justify women's subordination? The English of the past was rather more explicit about women and their pleasures than we might imagine at first thought, though often with an ulterior motive close at hand.

In a chapter about the language of sexual desire and enjoyment, it's right to start with the clitoris, that body part whose main duty is the giving of pleasure. It's a part whose role is often minimised and underplayed. Those front-on sex-ed diagrams which label only the small button of the glans as the 'clitoris' would fail a test in what the conceptual artist Sophia Wallace, whose works celebrate the clitoris's distinctive alien-craft-ready-to-take-flight form, calls *cliteracy*. *Cliteracy*, a portmanteau word fusing *clitoris* and *literacy*, is the accurate and informed understanding of the clitoris's anatomy and function. The clitoris isn't one chickpea nub but a multi-part organ shaped like the wishbone of a roast chicken. Its hypersensitive glans is a concentrated nerve centre, swaddled by its protecting hood, but a much larger clitoral body runs backwards up and over, splitting into two anchoring 'legs' and two engorging 'bulbs'. Both the legs and bulbs swell and stiffen with arousal, embracing the vagina like a blood-pressure cuff.

The history of the word *clitoris* shows us that its function was more or less understood from antiquity, though medical men were not always able to put their finger quite on the part itself. According to a dictionary of rare Greek words made by a grammarian in Alexandria in the fifth century AD, *kleitoris* referred to the skin covering female genitals – roughly in the right area if not exactly on the spot. It's from this noun, this list-maker says, that Greek gets the verb *kleitoriazein* meaning 'to rub' or 'to touch'. Not any old touching, you understand, but pleasurable touch by yourself or someone else. Not a bad start in terms of accuracy, but male experts were unwilling to stick with simple pleasures. Unable to conceive of a part that had no role beyond enjoyment itself, the tidy minds of ancient medicine gave the female orgasm a job to do. In the past, female orgasms were thought to play a key part in human reproduction. Before the truths of cyclical ovulation were discovered, medical experts filled in the blanks of their understanding by philosophical or medical guesswork.

Hippocratic texts from Greek antiquity thus said that the two halves needed for the reproductive whole were supplied by two 'seeds', one the semen and the other, more mysteriously, a female 'seed'. Both male and female orgasm were needed for conception (so the theorising went) and so our shudders and shakes of pleasure were the release mechanism. Various fluids were thought to be this 'seed': cervical mucus, the vagina's self-cleaning moisture or the wetness of arousal. That line of thinking firmly yokes sex and fertility together, but it did legitimise pleasure for some, especially if you combined this science with the medieval Church's view that the only sex which wasn't sinful was baby-making marital sex. Fingers crossed that plenty of earnest medieval and Renaissance husbands thus took their wives' sexual pleasure very seriously.

This tidy-minded theory also meant that medical experts needed to show some knowledge of female arousal and orgasm, however theoretical. The first stirrings of English names for the clitoris, found in the words of medieval surgeons translating Latin textbooks into their mother tongue for a wider readership, are approximate rather than accurate, though they give some lively English nicknames for this body part. In Latin it was named the *tentigo*, a word meaning 'tenseness' which could describe both an erect penis and the arousal of the clitoris. One translation of a French surgeon's guide calls the *tentigo* 'the hay-ward of corpse's dale'. If the vulva is the body's *dale*, its wooded, shady valley, then the clitoris is its *heie-ward* or overseer, the manager in charge of hedges, fields and harvests on a medieval farming estate. I like the idea of the clitoris as big boss, coordi-nating arousal across the whole landscape of the body. Even if this name also links pleasure with fertility, at least it's the female body in charge.

Our herbalist-turned-friar Henry Daniel, writing at about the same date, was more confused in terms of anatomy, calling the *tentigo* the vulva's 'wall' or 'tongue' to start with, whatever they might be, and then confusing it with the hymen. Maybe he had more practical experience with flower beds than lady gardens? But he also records that in some regional dialects of English the *tentigo* is called 'the kiker in the cunt'. How punkish that sounds. The etymology of *kiker* is mysterious, not related to kicking, I'm afraid, but perhaps instead to the action of tilting upwards, akin to the erection of a penis.

In the sixteenth century, as anatomists made their own obser-vations through dissection of corpses rather than relying on hand-me-down ancient knowledge, the location of the clitoris was identified more precisely and its ancient name more accu-rately pinned on a particular body part. The Italian anatomist Gabriele Falloppio (he of the tubes) said that he had found the clitoris in his dissections, a part which he claimed other anato-mists had ignored or failed to find. In the chapters of the 1615 anatomy guide which the College of Physicians had tried to sup-press, Helkiah Crooke brought the word into English. Turning the Greek dictionary's etymology on its head, Crooke said that the noun *clitoris* came from a verb, 'an obscoene worde signify-ing contrectation'. *Contrectation*, as a mid-seventeenth-century glossary defines it, is the 'wanton handling of a woman'. *Wanton* is a flexible old adjective which can mean 'reckless', 'ungoverned' and 'playful' as well as 'sexual'. Despite his reticence, Crooke knew exactly what the clitoris was for. It was, he said, 'of most exquisite sense', exceptionally sensitive, being 'the especiall seat of delight' in what he delicately calls sexual 'imbracements'. No dismissal of the clitoris in favour of vaginal orgasms here.

Thanks to the theory erroneously linking orgasm and ovulation, Crooke thought that when women's genitals were touched 'lustfull imaginations' were sent up the wires from the clitoris to the ovaries which then fired out their seed on demand. A 1668 anatomy book was yet more mechanical: 'by the rubbing thereof, the Seed is brought away'. But in the first textbook about obstetrics written in English by a midwife rather than a doctor, female pleasure is rather more expansive and language more expressive. Jane Sharp, about whom we know almost nothing except that she worked as a midwife for thirty years, published in 1671 her *Midwives Book*, written to better inform her 'sisters, the Midwives of England'. Perhaps because she, unlike the great parade of medical authorities before and after, was in possession of insider information, her book is eloquent about female rapture as she explains women's reproductive anatomy.

Not only is the clitoris 'the chief pleasure of loves delight', says Sharp, but the labia and the 'many round folds and plaights [i.e. pleats]' of skin inside the vagina also 'cause the more pleasure'. She also renames the bump of flesh that sits over our pubic bone on this basis, labelling it not the *mons veneris* or the *mons pubis* (i.e. the 'mount of Venus' or 'mount of the *pubes*', Latin names first used in English around the time that Sharp herself is writing), but 'a little bank called a mountain of pleasure'. If only women had been allowed to name their own anatomy, perhaps all our terminology would be as evocative and shameless as Sharp's topography of gratification.

Compared to Sharp's language of *many* and *more*, her descriptions of pleats and folds and little banks which can make mountains of pleasure, slang over the centuries has been much more timid about the clitoris and its delights: a mere twenty-eight entries in Jonathon Green's *Dictionary of Slang*, while the penis has more than a thousand nicknames. There are a few playful inventions – *the little man in the boat, the bean, the pearl* or, rather charmingly, the *lickerish allsort* – but no informal words or euphemisms that have caught on widely. If we're stuck with *clitoris*, it's not the ugliest word, I suppose, but it does little justice to this part and its functions. When abbreviated, *clit* sounds like a lock clicking shut on a Tupperware box. If it were really such a small thing, an on-off switch hidden inaccessibly round the back of a printer that you feel for with your fingertips, then a little word might do. But to fully flesh out the qualities of the *chief pleasure of loves delight*, I prefer the connotations of these older names, their kicking, bracing and bossing energy.

Although Helkiah Crooke primly explains the origin of the word *clitoris* as 'contrectation', what we might call *manual stimulation* by another party, he's less forthcoming about women handling themselves for their own pleasure. This is a set of early vocabulary that's hard to find. Generally words for solitary self-pleasuring are slow to form in English. And when they do, we learn these words not from anyone writing about their own self-delight, but from disapproving discourses about sin and wickedness, expressed in the vague and overlapping terminology of the medieval Church. Categories like *lechery* or *sodomy* could include masturbation as one of the sex acts which religious doctrine labelled 'unnatural'. Male masturbation was more obviously singled out for condemnation as 'unnatural' because semen ended up nowhere near a fertile womb. Perhaps experts' uncertainty about whether women even had 'seed' made it easier to sweep women's masturbation under the mental rug.

The first descriptions I've found of female self-pleasuring in English are both disapproving and very vague. Women who devoted their lives to God as nuns and recluses, unmarried and with much daily privacy, aroused equal doses of suspicion and fantasy on this front. In his twelfth-century Latin book of advice, translated into English a couple of centuries later, the Cistercian monk Ailred of Rievaulx urged his recluse sister not to think that a woman 'withoute a man' couldn't sin. Women, like men, can act 'unnaturally' (in the Church's logic) in ways which 'schal not be sayd', which mustn't be put into words. He may here be hinting at women loving women, whose vocabulary we'll get to further along in this chapter. What's more, he said that solitary religious women might spontaneously combust with desire without even a touch, or a self-touch. If she's not careful, he warns, his sister might be so greatly tempted, and feel such inner burning and rapture, that she could lose her virginity without any of what the translator calls *fleshly doing*. By that logic, most teenagers need never worry about remaining virgins.

Some men found it impossible to believe that many of us would be just fine with a nice hot drink and a psalm or two. In the spring of 1395, a group of religious reformers nailed a list of their 'conclusions', their self-evident truths, to the front doors of London cathedrals. The Church called them heretics for their ideas about the Eucharist; in everyday English they gained the nickname of the Lollards. Many of their ideas anticipated those of the Protestant Reformation, but, like some of today's progressive men, their reforming ideas didn't extend quite as far as women. They argued against celibacy for nuns because, according to long-standing sexist thinking, women are fickle and their bodies defective and incomplete. They therefore couldn't possibly stick to the vows of celibacy they had taken, said the Lollards, so these women must be busy 'knowing with hemself'.

Knowing can mean 'to have sex with' (as in 'carnal

knowledge'), while that pronoun *hemself* can mean either 'with themself' in the singular or 'among themselves' in the plural. Whichever it is, maybe that's what goes on when the *himselves* are out of the picture? The Lollard reformers also targeted vowesses, usually middle-class widows in later life who took an oath before a bishop to remain chaste and devote themselves to God though still living in their communities. The life of a vowess sounds lovely to me, if you could rustle up enough piety and cash – all that time to think in peace. The Lollard listicle said that vowesses should remarry because they too would commit 'prive synnes', secret transgressions. Without husbands, women's desires supposedly ran riot.

Maybe it's nicer if what we *fleshly do* when we are *knowing with ourselves* stays fuzzy and private, as indistinct as this medieval rumour-mongering, hidden away from language, labels and stigma. It's a soliloquy that needs no words, something that's nobody's business but yours. The vocab of self-pleasuring often only comes sharply into focus when somebody chooses to make it shameful. Such preoccupations are much more modern than medieval. From Latin via French, the word *masturbate* appeared in English in the early seventeenth century, as did *mastuprate*, referring to the same thing. Both are inspired by the same Latin verb, *masturbari*, the altered spelling of *mastuprate* reflecting an assumption that this Latin verb might ultimately derive from *stuprare*, meaning 'to defile'. To *mastuprate* was defined in Henry Cockeram's 1623 *English Dictionarie* as 'dishonestly [i.e. shamefully] to touch ones privities'. After about 1650, clergymen singled out masturbation as a specific vice rather than bundling it up vaguely with other acts.

Then, thanks to an eighteenth-century bestselling book called *Onania*, first published in 1716 but running into many editions and selling perhaps fifty thousand copies, masturbation took on a starring role as a cause of social, mental and physical problems. *Onanism* is the sin of Onan as described in Chapter 38 of the Book of Genesis, this being most likely *coitus interruptus* even though his name was later associated with solo endeavours. *Onania*'s frothing subtitle – 'the heinous sin of self-pollution, and all its frightful consequences' – gives you the general idea. In fact, its anonymous author may have been a doctor keen to flog lotions and potions, a writer with an incentive to position masturbation as an illness which required treatment.

For women, who, apart from secretive vowesses, self-knowing nuns and self-combusting recluses, had been mostly left out of the conversation up to this point, *Onania* turned masturbation into an equal-opportunity character flaw. Though one might think, says *Onania*'s author, that women are modest by nature, such a view is mistaken. Any such difference between men and women's behaviour comes merely from 'Custom and Education'. This rejection of essentialism (the idea that a particular category of person has a fixed, innate way of being) oh-so-nearly pulls off the flimsy loincloth hiding patriarchy's nether regions but can't or won't connect the dots. If women knew more about self-pollution, implied this author, they'd do it just as much as men (and maybe they already did, I'd wager, but just kept it quiet). The writer of *Onania* thus suggested that children should be told nothing about it. The narrative that masturbation was sinful, harmful and best left unmentioned dominated for the next couple of centuries and beyond.

With this baggage-train trailing behind them, *masturbate* and *masturbation* are words that are hard to love. The etymology of the Latin verb *masturbari* is itself unclear: perhaps it comes from *manus* ('hand') and *stuprare* ('to defile'), with its spelling gradually shifting closer to the verb *turbare*, 'to disturb'. It's difficult to feel shameless about self-pleasuring when these words echo verbs like *disturb* and *perturb* which, like *turbare*, derive from the Latin noun *turba* meaning 'commotion, upheaval'. There are plenty of slang words for masturbating which we might use instead, but much of it feels male-dominated, describing a different set of physical actions. One early eighteenth-century writer calls masturbation *manufriction* (from Latin *manus*, 'the hand') which seems a more neutral description – I wish that had become the standard term. In John Cleland's pornographic novel *Fanny Hill* (1748), the heroine, an orphan who's ended up in a brothel, makes her own 'vain attempts at digitation' before she loses her virginity with a man. For Cleland, fingers are a poor substitute for a penis, but many of us feel that not all *digitation* is in vain.

Skilful *digitation* or *manufriction* will bring us, with luck, to the peak of sexual excitement. There must be earlier words for the mountain-top of sexual activity, for *orgasm* and *climax* are both late arrivals into English's sexual glossary. *Orgasm* first meant any kind of violent spasm, emotional excitement or rage: orgasms can happen in poetry, in the blood or elsewhere in the innards. Then the word became sexual, naming in the eighteenth century what biologists would now call *oestrus*, that part of an animal's hormone cycle when she's on heat. Linguistically at least, the first orgasmic urges belonged to the females of various species. Finally, in the mid-nineteenth century, it shifted towards its modern meaning when medical experts pathologised in the formal language of science many aspects of sexuality which we would now think of as entirely normal. A *climax* started off naming the peak of an ascending series, whether that be rhetorical figures or a musical scale. It too gained its sexual sense in English in the nineteenth century as researchers set about measuring and investigating the what-and-how of sex and sexuality.

Before these words arrived in our language, early English described the peak of sexual pleasure through verbs – *going*, *coming, spending* – as well as vaguer terms like *pleasure* and *bliss*. There was also *enjoy* and its noun *enjoyment*, modelled on the sexual sense of the French word *jouissance*. We can see this noun being used fairly candidly by a spy and writer born in 1640 who probably started her life as plain old Eaffrey Johnson from Kent. Via spells in the English colony of Surinam in South America and in the Netherlands, and after marriage to a German merchant, Eaffrey reinvented herself as Aphra Behn, playwright and celebrity. Her play *The Amorous Prince*, staged in 1671, opens with Frederick, the prince of the title, having spent a passionate night with a woman called Cloris. As he explains in the next scene, he's had to promise her marriage – what else is a posh chap who's 'all on fire, and dies for an enjoyment' to do? An *enjoyment*, Behn calls it, that indefinite article suggesting at least sex and perhaps more particularly orgasm.

Another English word used to translate French *jouissance* was the Latinate 'fruition' (from the verb *frui* meaning 'to enjoy, to have the pleasurable possession or enjoyment of something or someone'). We know it means 'orgasm' because the seventeenth century hatched a minor fashion for poems written 'against fruition', poetry making the argument that delaying sex, or orgasm specifically, was a good thing to do, especially for men. The logic was sometimes that of health (the old idea that this 'little death' weakened the male body), or that the chase is better than the catch, or just plain sexism. Once *enjoyed*, said one of these poems, women become as dull as a book you've already read or a play you've seen. In a volume of poetry published in 1688, Aphra Behn rewrote this dubious genre from a woman's perspective. Given the short attention spans which these poems against fruition acknowledge, she points out that one 'surrender' will turn a woman into a 'short-liv'd nothing' in a man's eyes. And you can't win whether you postpone or decide to have sex right away – they'll soon be chasing the next woman either way.

Behn warns her readers away from men who've learned to move on quickly 'after fruition'.

Enjoyment and *fruition* sound rather innocent to modern ears, but some early English descriptions of orgasm are peculiarly wet and wild. Like today's fashion for 'squirting' in porn, some early medical writers who thought women released 'seed' like men described female climaxes very moistly. A 1655 English translation of a book by a famous French doctor, Lazare Rivière, was hyperactively liquid. When a woman orgasmed, female seed supposedly 'poured forth in that pang of Pleasure', her 'womb skipping as it were for joy', sucking up semen so she can 'sprinkle it with her own Sperm'. There might be something in this (well, not the female sperm, obviously, or the high-kicking uterus): modern science has discovered that it's the swelling, stiffening, contracting and releasing of many muscles that builds our pleasure. But before ovulation was fully understood, female orgasms needed to work a bit like ejaculation. Hence orgasming is described as *melting*, the womb enthusiastically contracting and gulping and gushing. Even so wrong-headed, this imagery is more exciting than modern sexology's four stages: first excitement, then plateau, orgasm and resolution. *Plateau* seems a rather static word for what comes before the big bang. More like chasing a word on the tip of your tongue around your memory, perhaps? There's pleasure when it's found, when the hunting stops, when you know what's *coming*. But one wrong move, one thought out of place, and sometimes it's lost again.

Female orgasms were, as you can see, enthusiastically described in the English of the past when they were linked with fertility and with men's own climaxes. But what about the other routes to the top of the hill? To find the first flutterings of women's sexual pleasure created by and for other means, we need to turn away from the language of medical science or religious doctrine and head in the direction of poets and playwrights. One of the earliest descriptions of a sex aid, for example, is written by an upstart poet called Thomas Nashe. He borrows the earliest English name, that funny word *dildo*, from the nonsense choruses of popular songs. *Sing doe with a dildo!* you might bellow with enthusiasm in Tudor England. These gibberish syllables were often somehow bawdy: *hey nonny nonny*, for example, conveniently rhymed with *cunny*, that slang word for vagina or vulva. A multilingual dictionary lets the cat out of the bag, saying that Italian *fossa* or 'pit' can be a nickname for 'a womans pleasure-pit, nony-nony or pallace of pleasure'.

Nashe turned to writing erotica for his patron, Ferdinando Stanley, Lord Strange, when the theatres were closed in the 1590s thanks to the plague. In Nashe's poem 'The Choice of Valentines', a man called Tomalin finds his country girlfriend, Frances, working in a brothel. Reunited with his love but now taking the role of a sex buyer, he finds things too much for him and ejaculates too soon. Once revived, they try again, she slowing him down so they keep 'crotchet-time/And everie stroake in order lyke a chyme', like a musical striking clock or a bell. Despite this steady clockwork rhythm, he again orgasms before her. He's half asleep, so she uses a dildo to satisfy herself, an object that Tomalin hates, angry at his own short-lived performance. It's suspiciously soggy: the dildo stomps along 'clammie ways' and 'plasheth and sprayeth', splashes and sprays. (The thought that women were given pleasure by male ejaculation perhaps explains why some early sex aids could be filled with fluid.) The poem's full of gender-bending (Frances has a 'mannely thigh'), and thus probably not to be trusted for reliable info about women's self-pleasuring.

Neither were later descriptions of dildos in satirical songs and poems. In the early eighteenth century, dildos gained posher nicknames – *Monsieur Thing* or *Seigneur Dildo* – to make them seem like Continental fashions, but they were still strangely hydraulic. A 1722 poem says that these gadgets could inject 'Warm Milk, or any other Liquid softer,/Slow as they please, or, if they please, much faster'. These lines are more male fantasy than user review, I think. By 1785, Francis Grose's *Classical Dictionary* of slang defined the word *dildo* more solidly, though still dosed with fantasy: an 'implement' made of wax, horn and leather, used by 'nuns, boarding school misses' and anyone else wanting to be celibate or to avoid pregnancy. Grose says that you could buy one at 'many of our great toy shops and nick-nackatories' (a *nick-nackatory* was a shop full of knick-knacks and trinkets). Whether true or not, this spelling-out of women's self-directed pleasure was soon deleted in Grose's second edition only three years later, replaced with some much vaguer phrases in English and a definition in Latin, 'Penis Succedaneus' [i.e. substitute penis]. What had once been an explanation to be read by everyone who dipped into the dictionary was now more hidden, accessible only to those with a classical education.

Thomas Nashe wasn't the only writer who turned to erotic verse in the time of plague. In William Shakespeare's poem *Venus and Adonis*, written for another rich patron, Henry Wriothesley, Earl of Southampton, the goddess Venus tries to seduce an inexperienced boy, the youthful huntsman Adonis. For all that Shakespeare has Venus flaunt her own body, Adonis just isn't interested. Bits of it are very funny: the oversized Venus carries Adonis under her arm and chucks him on his back, but he won't have sex with her. I'll leave you to puzzle out the psychology of two men bonding over how insatiable and yet resistible women supposedly are.

Nonetheless, even in its weird way, Shakespeare's poem gives us a taste of something which hardly registers in early English: cunnilingus. This Latin word first describes the doer – the person who licks or tongues the *cunnus* – before English borrows it in 1864 to name the act itself. In what may be the very first mention of this sex act in English, admittedly a rather oblique and allusive mention, Venus offers Adonis the chance (though he declines) to roam across her body:

> I'll be a park, and thou shalt be my deer;
> Graze on my lips; and if those hills be dry,
> Stray lower, where the pleasant fountains lie.

First he can kiss her lips and then wander down to moister lips below. You'll remember that the labia and clitoris were sometimes called *nymphs* by medical writers: it's not hard to guess where the *pleasant fountains* might be located. Once printed in 1593, the poem was hugely popular, running to many editions. Some commentators fretted that women and girls were secretly reading it and being led astray, though in reality it was young students and courtiers who were fascinated by this sexually demanding, sexually explicit goddess-cougar and the young man who resists her.

Another early murmur of *gamahuching* (a peculiar word of unknown etymology meaning 'cunnilingus' or 'fellatio' which English borrows from French slang in the 1700s) comes in a love poem by Thomas Carew which bossily begins, 'I will enjoy thee now, my Celia, come'. It's more a shared fantasy for writer and reader than anything else: Celia is a name given by many poets to their imagined mistress-muses. Buzzing around a daydreamed body like a bee, Carew says he'll explore where this torso 'doth divide/Into two milkie wayes', which must be two pale legs. Then his 'lips shall slide/Downe those smooth Allies'. Like Shakespeare, Carew gives us an anatomical clue: labia were, as we've seen, called 'wings' by medical writers and wings in French are *ailes*, so Carew's lips will end up somewhere between *alleys* and *ailes*.

Rereading Renaissance poems like these, the love lyrics I studied adoringly when I was an undergraduate, they're not always very convincing. John Donne is a cocktail of two parts misogyny ('Hope not for mind in women' says the speaker of 'Love's Alchemy') and one part objectifying groper ('my roving hands, and let them go,/Before, behind, between, above, below'). Andrew Marvell would famously take all the time in the world to praise the forehead, eyes and breasts of his 'Coy Mistress', but in his own life he doesn't seem to have had a mistress at all, coy or not. Robert Herrick, who wrote delicious lyrics about Julia's fruity breasts and nipples, had a mother called . . . guess what . . . Julia. Perfect training material for baby poets, but not, I see belatedly, a practical guide to making love. Thank heavens that the young man who once read this verse to me late at night and early morning understood that I was mostly real. I'm grateful to him, and to others who were open-minded enough to make sex feel improvised and unscripted, each time a dialogue. With them I began to understand *intercourse*, first a Renaissance term describing trade back and forth between countries, and then a synonym for 'conversation', before – aptly, I think – becoming a euphemism for sex in the early nineteenth century.

These dialogues of young love, shared between university students just as the internet was beginning to burgeon, weren't as shaped by the presumptions of pornography as many first sexual experiences are today, when online porn often pre-sets expectations. In contrast to more free-flowing conversations, pornography puts forward a narrower range of sexual scripts (as sociologists call the cultural norms and assumptions which guide our sexual behaviour), more a monologue of certain kinds of masculine desires than a flexible collaboration by all parties. Even the word itself has a revealing history. The etymology of *pornography* shows this term's origin to be writings about prostituted women, from the Greek *porne*, 'a prostitute', a word linked to a Greek verb meaning 'to sell'. In first French and then English, *pornography* was thus originally a name for writings about prostitution, often in relation to public health concerns about contagious venereal diseases. One Victorian medical dictionary offers this definition: 'Pornography, a description of prostitutes or of prostitution, as a matter of public hygiene'. *Pornography*'s now-more familiar meaning only takes over as this other sense fades into the background.

Though the vocabulary of much early erotic and pornographic writing is lively, often seeming to give voice to women's enjoyment of sex, this narrowness of perspective should make us tread carefully within its narratives. In seventeenth- and eighteenth-century English erotica, many of the speaking voices are, surprisingly, those of women: older, more experienced women brazen-hussily explaining sex to younger ones. But these are conversations for men to eavesdrop and enjoy. The scripts these women rehearse are mostly one-dimensional: heterosexual, goal-oriented, penetrative, starting with sufficient foreplay (a word which always sounds to me too much like some type of golf tournament) and ending with simultaneous climax. Even though they feature happy whores, experimenting nuns and enthusiastic country girls, and though women actively enjoy sex in their pages, these books are written by men for men.

Masturbation and lesbian sex are mere overtures in these texts while the star event is penetration, that imperious acronym *PIV*, penis-in-vagina sex. If penises *penetrate*, persistently, piercingly, what does the vagina do? Just passively receive? Not true: when aroused, the legs and bulbs of the clitoris swell and brace, the cervix and womb retract, the vagina lubricates itself, its walls 'tenting', pulling themselves outwards. What verb could capture that? The French artist Marcel Duchamp nearly had it when he told the art critic Lawrence D. Steefel that he wanted 'to grasp things with the mind the way the penis is grasped by the vagina'. Rewriting Duchamp's grammatical passive, we might say that the vagina-mind grasps – slippery, accommodating, self-expanding, self-protecting.

Perhaps the most explicit of these seventeenth-century erotic texts was Michel Millot's 1655 *L'école des filles*. Samuel Pepys records in a 1668 diary entry that he bought this French book in a cheap binding so he could burn it after he'd read it. Even though he found it 'mighty lewd', and mighty arousing, he did as promised, sending it to the flames. In *The School of Venus*, as the 1680 English translation of this French work is called, the translator invents his own verbs for penetrating and withdrawing, to *encunt* and *discunt*. Though it's men that do the *incunting* in this book, we could turn that on its head, the vagina centre stage, *encunting* what it encounters. And early English's slang for having sex, verbs like *swiving, fucking, sarding* and even *occupying* (which might sound territorial but could also mean 'keeping busy'), are encouragingly gender-neutral. John Florio's 1598 dictionary of foreign words for English speakers defines *fottitrice*, a feminine noun in Italian, as 'a woman fucker, swiver, sarder' and, in a later revised edition, 'a woman occupier'. Not a man occupying a woman, but a woman who occupies a man. Though medicine and religion wanted women to be passive, early erotica describes men and women keeping time together, equal and opposite. But here we need to tread oh-so-carefully: aren't these just stereotypes of women's supposed lustfulness and lack of self-control? Are they fantasies which mostly suit men's priorities? *Phallusies* are inescapable, contaminating almost every description of female desire and pleasure in English's early centuries.

We should thus be grateful for the few words about women's sexual desire which come straight from the horse's mouth in early English. Margery Paston, a Norfolk gentlewoman, dictated a postscript to a letter written on the first day of November 1481 full of gossip for her husband. If John Paston III stays in London on business for a considerable time, she hopes he'll send for her, 'for I thynke longe sen I lay in your armes', it's been a long time since I lay in your arms. And Maria Thynne, writing to her husband Thomas in around 1606, finds eloquence in euphemism. Maria and Thomas married secretly as two sixteen-year-olds in 1594 thanks to family scheming which would take too long to explain. Scholars have wondered whether their story was half in Shakespeare's mind as he was writing *Romeo and Juliet*. They were certainly in love a decade later: Maria thanks Thomas for his 'kind wanton letters' which have made her blush. She reminds him that he's 'threatened sound payment', and she's promised 'sound repayment', and, so she says, 'when we meet, there will be pay, and repay, which will pass and repass'. She turns the Church's language of marital debt, the promise not to withhold sex made by each spouse to the other, into a commitment to back and forth and taking turns. *To pass and repass* is to travel across the sea and return safely – she anticipates their intercourse, their fair trade in pleasure.

In the privacy of her letter, Maria felt able to put her sexual desire into words, albeit lyrically metaphorical ones. But when it came to those sexual activities of which Church and society didn't approve, there was much more incentive to keep quiet so early words are even harder to find. Before more modern categories of *gay*, *bisexual* and *straight* (all first used in relation to sexuality in the twentieth century), classification of sexual activity was based on what was supposedly 'masculine' and what was 'feminine'. The Church put forward the narrowest idea of what was supposedly 'natural': an active penetrating male above, a passively receiving female below. Christian doctrine designated most sexual pleasures as sinful, keeping the terminology of desire and lust versatile, vague and judgemental. Pulpit-thundered, spittle-flecked terms like *lechery* or *fornication* were categories which could include premarital sex, adultery, a priest keeping a mistress or a wife, and even some sexual activities within marriage (given that some doctrinal hardliners thought that anything which wasn't aimed at procreation was sinful, including most non-missionary sexual positions).

Before seventeenth- and eighteenth-century erotica generated more explicit descriptions of women loving women in order to titillate male readers, lesbian sex was often belittled or pushed out of mind in earlier English and so its first language is evasive. This vagueness about what women did with women stretches as far back as the Bible. St Paul, writing to the Christians of Rome in one of the letters preserved in the New Testament, begins his epistle with a summary of types of human sinfulness. On his list are women who've switched from 'natural' practices to ones which are 'against nature', but he's tight-lipped on details, as were those churchmen who made lists of sins and how they should be atoned for. The word *sodomy* (coined to describe those activities popular in Sodom and Gomorrah which made God so cross that He destroyed both cities with a downpour of fire and brimstone) could categorise not only anal sex – as in its more modern usage – but also masturbation and other sex acts, including what women might do with women. It's not that these acts were interchangeable or that anatomy was irrelevant, but that authorities preferred to be circumspect and let the context do the work.

Even in our explicit age, words sometimes seem in short supply to describe how women's bodies move sexily or sexually with each other. At the 2021 GRAMMYs, Cardi B and Megan Thee Stallion's scissoring and thrusting in the dance routine for 'WAP' prompted the conservative commentator Candace

Owens to tweet her anatomically perplexed opinion that 'popping your vagina into another woman's vagina in front of the world' was far from truly empowering. Even if she meant vulvas, it seems a tricky manoeuvre. Similar bafflement can be found in a poem dedicated to Cecily, widowed Countess of Hereford, written by Étienne de Fougères, a royal clerk writing in the 1170s. It's written in French, or Anglo-Norman as the French spoken by England's elite after the Norman Conquest has been called. The poem works its way through each part of society and their characteristic vices. When we get to courtly ladies, we're told they have a new fashion which Étienne thinks very sinful. They bang 'coffin' on 'coffin', 'shield' on 'shield', and they don't have a poker, lance, pointer, handle, rod or pestle to hand – is there nothing to which the penis can't be compared? Two women having sex, in this satirical view, are empty boxes banging together or clashing shields which really ought to be penetrated by an arrow or a spear. But around the edges something more expressive creeps in: Étienne also names this new game 'l'escremie del jambot', combat with the legs or, as we might call it, *thigh-skirmishing*. That sounds more fun. I wonder what the countess, who had outlived three husbands over her eighty-odd years of life, made of this part of the poem?

Almost by accident do these descriptions streak like comets through our language. Two hundred years on from the *thigh-jousters*, John Gower, a South London lawyer and friend of Geoffrey Chaucer, wrote a long poem in which a would-be lover confesses his failings and one of Venus's clerks gives him advice. To illustrate the point that many surprising things can happen in love, the clerk tells his version of one of the stories in Ovid's *Metamorphoses*. A girl is secretly brought up as a boy named Iphis because her father the king has threatened to kill any female child. Aged ten, Iphis is betrothed to another girl, a duke's daughter called Ianthe. They grow up together, often sharing a bed, 'sche and sche', she and she, as Gower's delicate phrase has it. Falling in love, they begin to experiment one night. Gower has an interesting explanation for what is going on: Nature makes everyone marvel at (or perhaps 'study' – the word he uses, *muse*, can mean both things) her laws, our natural instincts, and so Nature compels the girls to 'use/Thing which to hem [i.e. them] was al unknowe'. Something unknown to them until that moment, or perhaps something unthinkable, unsayable. *Thing* (remember Chaucer's Wife of Bath talking about male and female sex organs as 'thynges smale') could be a word for genitals. What is it that Gower is nearly-not-quite describing here? Whatever it is, it vanishes in a trice. The god Cupid, moved by the girls' love for each other, steps in to quickly overwrite their story with a much more limited idea of what is 'natural'. He turns Iphis into a man so that the two of them can live as husband and wife.

Firmer descriptions of what one woman might do with another begin to appear in the Renaissance thanks to old myths made popular once more by sixteenth-century anatomists. When Falloppio described the clitoris, he cited, as supporting evidence for his new 'discovery', medical authorities who'd apparently seen clitorises grow so large that they could be used to penetrate other women. This bit of medical gossip lumped together two separate bits of anecdotal evidence which had been floating around since the classical era, one a kind of person and the other a kind of atypical body. The first ingredient was the figure of the *tribade* (a noun deriving from a Greek verb meaning 'to rub') or *fricatrix* (from an equivalent Latin verb). Since antiquity, *tribade* and *fricatrix* were labels for women who, when it came to sex, weren't passive and merely receptive: women who were highly sexed, who were attracted to other women, and those who took an active, supposedly 'masculine' role in bed or in life.[1] Male writers speculated about what the imaginary *tribade* might do to her partner, sometimes 'rubbing' and sometimes hinting at the use of a dildo. The *tribade* was alive and well in the mid-sixteenth century when al-Ḥasan ibn Muḥammad al-Wazzān al-Zayyātī (known to the West as Leo Africanus) wrote an account of Africa and its peoples. Describing the Moroccan city of Fez where he'd been educated as a boy, he told stories of 'women-witches' (as an English translation of his book published in 1600 calls them) or *fricatrices* who, under various devilish pretexts, enticed married women to sleep with them, having mysterious skills which the wives found to be a 'delight'.

The second ingredient, originally unconnected to the *tribade*, was that of ancient Greek and Latin medical accounts of unusually large clitorises. These enlargements, it was thought, might cause considerable sexual desire, perhaps because they rubbed on clothing giving constant arousal. Once the anatomists had amalgamated these two strands, sexism's confirmation-bias machine bigged up the connection between the oversized clitoris and female desires which were something more than passive or receptive. Doctors theorised that a large clitoris might make one lusty (or, turning that idea on its head, that being lusty, especially enjoying masturbation, might cause your clitoris to grow). The English anatomy writer Helkiah Crooke (for all that he could give a fairly accurate account of the average clitoris) also copied Falloppio in scaremongering about a self-erecting organ which 'strutteth and groweth to a rigiditie' like a penis.

Those 'wicked women' called *tribades*, said Crooke, used this organ for their mutual sexual pleasure. As other authors followed Crooke's lead, the *tribade* got a new English nickname, the *rubster*. What's more, women thought to desire other women, such as the ancient Greek poet Sappho who wrote passionately about other women in her lyrics, were reinvented as *tribades*. An early eighteenth-century English translation of a French book which promised to unveil the mysteries of 'Conjugal Love' gossiped that Sappho wouldn't have 'acquired such indifferent reputation' (a roundabout way of disapproving of her supposed sexuality) 'if this part of hers had been less'. Quite how anyone might reliably know about the clitoral dimensions of a woman who'd died in the sixth century BC isn't made clear. Once the connection between the *rubster* and the poet Sappho had been invented, adjectives like *sapphic* and *lesbian* (from the island of Lesbos, where Sappho lived) appeared in the eighteenth century.

These adjectives are first found in the disapproving tones of moralists and in smears made by satirists, not in self-descriptions by women themselves. Towards the end of the seventeenth century there was a new nickname for lesbian sex, the *game of flats*, *flats* being playing cards or thin counters used in games. The phrase probably also evokes the image of two bodies without appendages rubbing against each other. In the first of a pair of popular ballads published in 1698, women who name themselves in the song as 'whores' complain to Venus, goddess of love, that men are too busy having sex with each other for them to earn a living. Venus replies, in a ballad published a year later, that that's because you women are too busy playing 'flats' with a 'swinging Clitoris'. Here's the tribade's self-erecting mini-dick in a new, mobile guise, muddled up with whatever *flats* might be. Those outraged (whether for real or for amusement) at the popularity of gay and lesbian *amours* aren't really concerned by the accurate subtleties of hips, lips, fingers, movement, angles and pressures.

A century later, however, one woman did set about finding her own vocabulary for her same-sex desires. Anne Lister was a Yorkshire woman given the nickname 'Gentleman Jack' for her gender-nonconforming choices of clothes and behaviour. In York in 1804 her first sexual experiences as a teenaged schoolgirl were with Eliza Raine, an Anglo-Indian girl sent from Chennai to Britain for her education. Eliza and Anne imagined themselves married, Eliza the wife and Anne the husband. Throughout her life, Anne kept diaries detailing her business dealings, her travels, her reading, and, in a cypher she'd invented, her sexual relationships with other women. In doing so, she found words for Gower's *thing unknown*, the things left largely unsaid. As she began her first serious relationship as an adult, she made herself a glossary of Latin sexual words with the help of etymological dictionaries from her reading in the Classics. But she also created her own slang, a code within a code, calling orgasms *kisses* and her vulva her *queer*. No one is quite sure how Anne arrived at *queer* well before it first became a derogatory term for homosexual men around 1900 and then was gradually reclaimed mid-century by some of those it initially stigmatised (though for others it remains an irredeemable slur). Anne was the first queer practitioner long before academics popularised queer theory in the 1990s. Perhaps it reflected how she felt off-kilter or unusual, calling her preference for women her *oddity*.

The gaps which Anne Lister sought to fill in may have come about because the authorities were unwilling to officially admit to the existence of lesbian loving. It's a myth that woman-with-woman action was completely ignored by the law: lesbian sex was criminalised in parts of medieval and Renaissance Europe though before 1800 only a handful of women were prosecuted. New England Puritans, setting up their communities on America's Eastern Seaboard, experimented briefly with criminalising lesbianism in the 1600s, though prosecutions were likewise sparse or non-existent. The story that Queen Victoria found lesbianism impossible to believe and refused to allow a law against it is also complete fantasy, but it's true that the English legal system didn't in its history specifically outlaw women having sex with women. The 1533 Buggery Act, the first English civil legislation in this area, hadn't defined specific sexual acts but prosecutions targeted anal sex, bestiality and the sexual abuse of children.

In 1921, it was proposed to add an offence of 'acts of gross indecency between female persons' to the statute book. The House of Lords thought this was a terrible idea. Their Lordships feared that sociable women who like to bedroom-share, girls who had passionate teenage friendships and those women squashed three-in-a-bed in small houses would all be at risk of blackmail and malicious accusations. And they were gloriously confident that most women didn't know any details about how lesbians might have sex. Apart from sophisticated people in big cities, the Lord Chancellor thought that 'of every thousand women ... 999 have never even heard a whisper of these practices'. If Parliament passed a law against such activities, the court cases that might follow would publicise them much more broadly. Like the medieval Church, the Lords thought that keeping mum about lesbian sex would ensure it remained suppressed and so the amendment was rejected.

The Lords' assumption that hardly any woman would know a thing about lesbianism shows how terms for certain subjects can be lost, or wilfully forgotten, or ignored. Whatever nicknames this subject once had were hushed up as Victorian decorum descended. Yet, while enjoying the rediscovery of thigh-skirmishings and swinging clitorises, we should, I'm afraid, be pretty pessimistic about how far the past could really put female sexuality into words without considerable distortion. Any delight we might find in these first descriptions must take due account of *phallusies* about women's bodies whose roots go very deep. Some of these myths still underpin insults like *nympho* or *frigid* which claim that a woman's sexuality is too much or not lusty enough.

Never just right, we're always being accused of either running too hot or blowing too cold. In ancient and medieval medicine, female bodies were supposedly 'cold' in physiological terms, yet women were said to burn with lust. Perhaps we were like damp wood, experts theorised, slow to ignite but burning hotter and for longer once the fire got going. Or perhaps the 'cold', 'moist' womb was hungry for 'hot', 'dry' semen, hence women's greater lustfulness. Or, if you preferred a scriptural rather than medical reason to stigmatise women's sexuality, Eve being made from Adam's flesh and not dust and mud meant that she was more in thrall to her body than him. Hildegard of Bingen, a twelfth-century polymath who juggled her studies and books with her day job running a German monastery, has some fun with that, saying that Eve's mind was therefore 'sharper and loftier' than Adam's because it wasn't weighed down with all that earthiness.

The clever girl at the back of the class might now stretch up her hand to ask how women could be both excessively lustful and yet perfectly passively receptive. Something about their lesser reason, their hungry wombs, the chap in the cassock would reply, not making much sense. Before our modern version of the sexual double standard, in which women are called sluts for behaviour which might be admired, or at least overlooked, in men, a different asymmetry operated. Women were enslaved by their bodies while men (so the sexist logic went) could function with more self-control. English has always had a plentiful vocabulary of nouns like *slut* to label women on the basis of their sexual appetites. Would you rather be a *tickle-tail*, a *trull*, a *stewed strumpet*, a *harlot* or a *lightskirts*? There are far fewer words for men who pursue and desire sex with enthusiasm.

To my dismay, the first recorded use of *slut* happens to come in the verse of Thomas Hoccleve, the medieval poet whom I've spent much of my academic career studying and translating. The origin of *slut* is unclear, perhaps coming from older words for wet or dirty snow (a bit like Modern English *slush*). *Slut*, like *slattern*, another insulting word, tarnishes women's sexuality with associations of dirtiness or messiness. It was also used as a name for a lowly female servant (often in the now odd-looking combination *cook, slut and butler* which once described the minimum number of servants which a household needed) or a woman who doesn't conform to society's standards. The connotations of words like this reverse the much more likely state of affairs. *Slut* excuses men's blushes by redesignating poorer women who are vulnerable to sexual exploitation as women who are notoriously promiscuous.

Terms like *slut* continued to flourish even when the myth of greater masculine self-control got switched out in favour of the myth of men's almost-uncontrollable sexual appetite. And nineteenth-century doctors and scientists were still energetically inventing and updating *phallusies* about female sexuality behind the scenes. Experts pathologised women's desires, whether too little or too great, as abnormal. On the one hand, the new field of sexology freshened up sexism with novel syndromes such as *nymphomania*, a diagnosis for excessive sexual desire in women. The origin of this name *nymphomania* is a bit of a mystery. Perhaps, like hysteria, it sought to emphasise how part of the female body could easily malfunction (either the labia or the clitoris, both of which, as we have seen, were called *nymphs* in ancient medicine). Or, given the pairing of nymphs and satyrs, perhaps it was the female equivalent of *satyriasis*, a name for hypersexuality in men.

On the other hand, those who didn't enjoy or desire sex were now called *frigid*. When used to describe human physiology, this word for most of its life in English described the cold, sluggish constitutions of older men who often suffered from erectile dysfunction. A 1699 dictionary defines *frigid* as 'a weak disabled Husband, cold, impotent'. It was the keenness of Victorian gynaecologists (and a little later that of sexologists and psychoanalysts) to present themselves as experts about women's many supposed malfunctions which one-eightied this term. By the first decade of the twentieth century *frigid* had flipped to become a label for psychosexual problems supposedly characteristic of women. Since then it has become an insult to be slung at those who reject sexual advances.[2] Women have found themselves up against new 'scientific' versions of older myths, sometimes expressed in scientific coinages but sometimes described with older words given fresh meanings.

Early feminists who wanted to improve the lot of women in society thus knew that language should play an important part in their campaigns. Sex educators, from Victorian pioneers onwards to the present day, had to fill silences with words and change the terms of the discussion. This was particularly difficult at a time when society prioritised decorum and modesty, and obscenity laws made taboo subjects difficult to explore. One campaigner who knew the significance of words was a New Hampshire farm girl with the tongue-tripping name of Angela Fiducia Tilton Heywood. Heywood moved to Massachusetts in 1871, becoming one of the Free Lovers, social radicals who campaigned for the abolition of slavery and reform of tax and labour laws, as well as rights for women. Alongside her husband, Heywood published magazines and pamphlets aimed at overturning the idea that silence about particular topics, not least about anatomy, could somehow guarantee 'social purity', as some of society's moralists argued.

Heywood wrote what were, for the late nineteenth century, shockingly frank articles about sex education and marriage guidance. Growing up with a plain-speaking mother, she said that 'it never occurred to me that it could be considered indelicate or "vulgar"' to call things 'by their proper names' rather than hiding them behind euphemism or formality. 'Latin names and devious phrases', she wrote, could never be as useful as more open-minded, open-access language for discussing what she

called 'the Human Crotch Fact', the everyday realities of sexual
activity and human reproduction. She urged society to stop
being prudish and to use 'plain English words' (including what
we would call slang or obscenity) to rationally evaluate relationships between men and women. She demanded this 'sex realism'
as one step towards greater equality in marriage.

Moving closer to the present day, the power of collective and
individual voices was vital for the development of Heywood's
sex realism. Fifty years ago, a group of Boston women formed a
Women's Health Book Collective and sold a stapled pamphlet
titled *Women and their Bodies: A Course* for 75 cents a copy.
Rather than either relying on the limited information provided
by medical experts or remaining in ignorance, they researched
and wrote their own textbook. At the heart of it was information about sexuality, relationships and the female body: 'For us,
body education is core education. Our bodies are the physical
bases from which we move out into the world'. This pamphlet
became *Our Bodies, Ourselves*, one of the most influential books
of the twentieth century, selling many millions of copies and
inspiring versions in thirty-odd languages.

In their chapter on sex, the Collective noted the power of
the first-person singular and plural, *I* and *we*: 'we felt that our
own voices, our own histories rang the clearest and truest and
helped us to reclaim the mysterious topic of sexuality as familiar
and ours'. More important than even the words themselves is
the right to speak on our own behalf. Thanks to *Our Bodies,
Ourselves* and many others, and to the unflagging work of campaigners and educators, we now speak much more openly about
sex and sexuality. We may be stuck with the terminology of
Renaissance anatomists and Victorian sexologists, but we can
use those same words much more freely, pulling hard against
the deadweight drag of history's myths and scripts which might
circumscribe what we want to say.

Four

MATRIX

The Womb's Words

—

These days sperm can meet egg on a microscope slide while semen might be launched inwards by a syringe. The real business of coming alive, however, still occurs *in utero*. Our first unremembered thoughts and feelings start in what was once in medieval English called the *matris*, *matrice* or *matrix*, not a computer simulation but the womb's crimson nightclub, dimly lit, its heartbeat-bass thumping. *Matrix* seems a fitting name for the place in which our existence is generated. First in Latin and then in English, *matrix* describes a thing which produces something else, especially a means to reproduce an item more than once. Across the course of its history in English, *matrix* has named not only the womb but also the metal blocks in which letters are engraved for the casting of type, or the die or stamp on which coins are struck, or the engraved tool which you press into wax to seal a document. From these practical usages, *matrix* becomes a technical term in maths, logic, computing and electronics for a framework that supports or produces an entire system. Just so, one human can give birth to several new humans.

Compared to the powers of the *matrix*, our contemporary

set of maternity words is underwhelming. Everyday words for childbearing seem rather humble and modest, like the maternity dresses of yesteryear which muffled baby bumps with drapes and frills. They downplay so much of the substance of it. The verb phrases are more states than actions – *being pregnant*, *having* or *expecting a baby* – which present maternity as a passive time of waiting, being or receiving. *Gestation* sounds like a more active process, comparable to cogitation or digestion, yet it derives from the Latin verb *gestare* which simply means 'to carry'. *Gestation*'s first appearances in English come as a fancy name for ways to give fresh air and exercise to those too weak to move themselves, carried in a sedan chair, for instance, or taken out in a boat.

Etymologically at least, *gestation* thus implies that the womb is a mere carry-case in which the foetus mostly grows itself. Images of babies *in utero* often appear in close-up, as if the foetus floats in a bubble or a jar, the body which sustains it being cropped out. But maybe we don't want to be cheerleaders for maternity? Nowadays we might keep quiet so that the old equation – woman equals mother – isn't reinforced. Perhaps it's immodest to over-egg our part? If all goes well, we might feel like the pilot of a self-driving car, the body doing its own thing without conscious inputs. But this important journey, the route to everyone's beginning, has considerable physical and mental risks, so it deserves more than lip service. If we do speak up boldly about increase and loss, fertility and infertility, what words are there to use and where did they come from?

The question of whether gestation is a passive or active process runs far back into the early science of human reproduction and shows up frequently in its choices of vocabulary, even in descriptions of conception itself. Among experts and authorities, there was much uncertainty about the exact details before science fully understood how egg and sperm matched up their chromosomes. Did women contribute 'seed' to make an embryo or was it just the men? If there was only one seed in play, was the womb not much more than an incubator? One might suspect experts in the past of downrating the female contribution wherever possible. As the origin of such minimising, we could (and many would) heap much blame upon the head of one of the founding fathers of philosophy. Once Aristotle's works were available to be studied in Latin in medieval universities, his bio-logical–philosophical reasoning set the terms of knowledge in Western Europe for centuries. But, just as the findings of a dense academic study might be first condensed by a press officer, then written up by a journalist, then sexed up by a headline writer, there's often quite some distance between Aristotle's perplexing prose and what a potted summary says.

On human reproduction, for example, a handy Aristotle explainer might read as follows: females merely provide the 'matter' to which, via semen, males give both the 'form' and the important bits of the soul. The male is active and independent, informing (in the sense of organising and giving meaning to) female stuff which waits passively, dependently. That version is the bedrock on which so many *phallusies* have been built: as active is to passive, as form is to matter, as soul is to body, so male supposedly is to female. *Matter* can sound inert and claggy, though it can also feel significant, *what matters*, *the heart of the matter*, something of substance and importance. *Matter* in our modern English comes from Latin's *materia*, the word which the Roman over-achiever Cicero, lawyer, politician and author of many works, chooses to represent the Greek word which Aristotle uses. Aristotle's term for 'matter' is *hyle*, in everyday usage meaning 'lumber' or 'timber', a particular kind of stuff needed to make particular kinds of things. Cicero translates *hyle* with *materia* in part because of its relation to the Latin word for 'mother', *mater*, tying the closest of knots between the maternal and the material.

Yet two millennia and more on from Aristotle's putting stylus to wax tablet, philosophers are still debating whether we've been reading him entirely right. Several recent academic books argue that Aristotle gives the female a bigger role in reproduction than merely being some lumpen block of multipurpose stuff. The female body supplies the specialised materials containing the potential ready and waiting to make a human body which can be animated by a human soul. Before we make him too much of an ally, however, Aristotle does say that the female body has 'an inability of a sort' (though as the philosopher Sophia Connell notes, he *is* trying to be tactful, it's just *of a sort*, not *really*).[1] The female can't complete the task of reproduction single-handedly, because her 'colder' body can't fully convert nutrients into the semen. The male's physiologically 'hotter' body, which does have the necessary 'heat', is the final piece of the puzzle, providing the initiation which completes what's needed for reproduction. Via his seed, the male is the trigger, setting in motion the chain of events which lead to a baby. But though the male is needed to complete reproduction, this means little without the right material already primed to respond to it. Much of what Aristotle describes is a system of mutual reliance and dependence. (Though doesn't it sound more exciting to be the initiator and completer than the great DIY shop of the flesh?)

The trouble is that mutually reliant contraries can so easily be tipped over into plain old hierarchies with male up top and female down below. When first Arabic and then Judaeo-Christian thinkers got their hands on Aristotle's writing, they swung his ideas violently towards the vertical. Clerics and academics proposed analogies between the male role in reproduction and God's setting of creation in motion. Other extrapolations from Aristotle were yet more sexist. If the male seed supplied the intellect, said certain medieval philosophers, the part of the mind that thinks and understands, men therefore had much reason and women very little. In the wrong hands, Aristotle's balance was easily upended into mutually reinforcing subordinations: heaven governs earth, humans govern animals, mind governs body, form rules matter and men have power over women.

While the men of the medieval church and universities capitalised on the latent sexism in Aristotle's thinking, medical experts often took the different route set down by Galen and the writings attributed to 'Hippocrates'. In this way of thinking, men and women each supplied a seed, their contrary natures, 'hotter' and 'colder', balancing each other out. By the Renaissance, English medical descriptions of conception were mix-and-match, combining elements of both theories. Though Thomas Raynalde had already included some of the new Vesalian anatomy in his 1545 *Womans Booke*, the first anatomical textbook in English is often credited to a London barber-surgeon named Thomas Vicary, published in 1577, sixteen years after his death. Vicary's *Profitable Treatise of the Anatomie of Man's Body* was a cheap-and-cheerful crammer drawn from medieval sources, intended for apprentice barber-surgeons whose Latin wasn't up to scratch. The womb, writes Vicary, is the 'felde of mans generation', the place where 'by the tillage of man', the 'kindly heate' (that hot-hot-hot essence which initiates and completes conception) is sown. So far, so very traditional: the womb like mother earth awaiting men's cultivation. And thus at first in Vicary's explanation, man's seed actively *works* while the woman's seed passively *suffers* (that is, it allows the male seed to work on it). But soon they tumble together indistinguishably, both passive and active, making an embryo: 'each of them worketh in other, and suffereth in other – there is engendred Embreon'. Both seeds actively work and passively permit.

Thomas Raynalde, writing for his readership of mothers and midwives, had gone even further in his *Womans Booke* published twenty years earlier. The womb, he wrote, was the place where 'the seed of man is conceived, foetified, conserved [i.e. kept safe], nourished, and augmented, unto the time of deliverance'. *Foetified* seems to be a word Raynalde invented himself, meaning 'made into a foetus'. What's more, he says the uterus isn't just some manured and passively fertile field but more like a workshop, the perfect place where Nature (a personification whose pronouns are she/her) can 'at leisure work her divine feats'. Helkiah Crooke, in the section of his *Mikrokosmographia* which escaped the College of Physicians' censorship, followed Raynalde's lead. Both sexes, says Crooke, provide 'fruitfull and pure seedes which are poured out into the wombe as it were into a fertil field'. Then the matrix takes over: 'the wombe rouseth and raiseth up the sleepy and lurking power of the seeds, and that which was before but potentiall, it bringeth into act'. Here Aristotle's hierarchy is inverted like an hourglass: the womb is now the active partner, energetically shaking the seeds awake like drowsy teenagers and initiating the life-building possibilities hidden within them.

There was similar uncertainty about whether a pregnant woman was a passive carrier or an active creator as an embryo grew to a full-term baby. Is this real bodily work or not? These tensions play themselves out in the vocabulary we've inherited for the processes of gestation as well as conception. By the middle of the sixteenth century, the medieval misogynist version of Aristotle's theory of human reproduction, in which women contributed not much at all, seemed distastefully old hat. In 1559, a Dutch doctor called Levinus Lemnius wrote a book called *Occulta naturae miracula* (the 'secret miracles of nature'). Books of secrets such as

Lemnius's *Occulta* were the non-fiction publishing craze of their day, a mix of self-help, how-to and amazing facts. The *Occulta* wasn't translated into English until 1658, but it was read in Latin and in French versions – Shakespeare alludes to it in *Hamlet*.

In his chapter on human reproduction, Lemnius says he'll answer very accurately the 'great question' of which sex does what in reproduction, because some jokers like to 'persuade women that Mothers afford very little to the generation of the child, but only are at the trouble to carry it'. They tease women that pregnancy is just a 'tedious time of nine Moneths, as if the womb were hired by men, as Merchants ships are to be fraited [i.e. filled with cargo] by them'. Lemnius worries that such cheapening makes women love their children less (a mother's place is always in the wrong, it seems, even when misled by pseudo-Aristotelian biology). As an uncoverer of nature's mysteries, Lemnius could hardly have imagined the science which permits today's commercial surrogacy, in which wombs are indeed hired and eggs are bought. A woman paid for the work of her womb is now sometimes called, tautologously enough, a *gestational carrier* rather than a *surrogate*.

While the modern language of commercial surrogacy tends to downplay its commodification of human reproduction, earlier descriptions of pregnancy reflected the flourishing of Britain's economy. The historian Mary E. Fissell has discovered that, in the years either side of 1700, books written by doctors about women's reproductive health often compared pregnant women to laden ships on a dangerous journey, 'a Voyage so long and perilous through such rough and rocky seas'.[2] They chose this imagery to make women feel yet more anxious about pregnancy and labour, offering their own advice as the means to return safely to harbour. They promised to explain how a pregnant woman can achieve 'her right Unloading and Delivery', as if giving birth to a baby is just like having a shipping container craned out of your innards. To *deliver* has been used to mean 'give birth' since the Middle Ages, the baby imagined as a burden or a load of which you are eventually relieved. It's just a figure of speech, these doctors would say.

Yet these metaphors sprang up just as Britain consolidated its status as a trading and financial super-power thanks to its colonies and merchants. Britain traded not just in goods but played its part in the buying and selling of enslaved Africans, a trade in which its companies dominated from the 1640s onwards. New York University's Professor Jennifer L. Morgan has tracked the dehumanising language of slave-owners as they profited not just from the manual labour of enslaved women but also from their reproductive labour.[3] Children which these women might have were described in wills as their *future increase*, bequeathed as property from one slave-owner to another. Relationships of kin and family were redacted by the 'logic' of property law. In the English colony of Virginia, a 1662 law code said the legal status of a child was matrilineal, inherited from the mother. If your mother were enslaved, you were enslaved. In the words of a Latin tag added in when a nineteenth-century historian wrote up the history of Virginia's laws, 'partus sequitur ventrem', the offspring follows the belly.

Increase as a noun could mean not only what we would call procreation or reproduction but also profit and growing wealth. In the 1760s, a philanthropist and governor of London's Foundling Hospital, Jonas Hanway, raised funds to look after abandoned and orphaned babies. He argued that Britain's economic and political success required many new humans and so it was important to nurture and educate every foundling child: 'Increase alone can make our natural Strength in Men correspond with our artificial Power in Riches, and both with the Grandeur and Extent of the British Empire'.[4] He's unafraid to say imperialism's quiet bit out loud. Britain needed a plentiful supply of human beings, 'some millions', Hanway thought, 'to people the countries subject to the crown of these realms'. This *increase* would fight on Britain's behalf and sustain the economic exploitation of its growing empire.

Reproduction has the same pair of meanings, one biological and one economic, which also cosy up inside *increase*. This word for making fresh humans can seem, at least from our modern perspective, rather mechanical or technological. Our suspicions about *reproduction*'s connotations might be heightened because this new usage of an older word emerged during the decades of the Industrial Revolution. Some historians have thus been tempted towards greatly simplified stories about the replacement of older words like *generation* and *procreation* by this new sense of *reproduction*. Some have claimed it represents a shift in thinking from *generation*'s more natural fruitfulness to *reproduction*'s more dehumanised abstraction. Others have seen it as a move away from a more religious view of procreation to something more economic or industrial. Most damningly, some claim it as evidence of a turn from a more woman-centred view of gestation to seeing female bodies as mere baby-making machines. Yet however appealing these super-scale narratives are, they're just not sufficiently true. Professor Allison Muri has uncovered how little historical evidence there is for any of these broad-brush theories.[5]

It *is* true that, over two centuries and more, formal English has tended to increasingly use *reproduction* in place of *procreation* or *generation*. And it's also right that two new senses of the word *reproduction* appeared at roughly the same time in the second half of the 1700s. One came from natural history, a term to describe the general process by which plants and animals continued their species. The other emerged from the new science of political economy, first of all specifying the regeneration of natural resources (such as nature's annual harvest). Soon *reproduction* also described those conditions which allowed economic activity to be *productive*, creating profit and increasing wealth. Only from the mid-nineteenth century did *reproduction* really start to shove *generation* aside as a word for species propagation. At the same time, as new technologies made precise replication ever more possible, *reproduction* acquired its associations with mechanical duplication.

The theories of eighteenth-century economists divided up human activity into *unproductive* and *productive labour*. *Productive labour* turns raw materials into a product, something that can be sold for a profit, generating capital which can be reinvested to create yet more economic growth. But despite *reproduction's* simultaneous use as a word for procreation, political economists from Adam Smith to Karl Marx and beyond generally ignored gestation and child-rearing. The value to society of childbearing and other kinds of care work needed to supply an economy with workers and consumers was labelled *unproductive* in their economic models. Perhaps what really matters in the history of the word *reproduction*, then, is not some grand epochal shift, but rather the fact that these economists, and the societies in which they wrote, took human-making for granted as natural, inevitable regeneration, as its older meaning implies. Feminists have had to reclaim *reproduction* in its adjectival form to develop the category of *reproductive labour*, the work done to create and sustain human life, often unpaid and undervalued, done predominantly by women out of public sight in the privacy of the home.

The language of economic reproduction doesn't always fully acknowledge the value to society of *reproductive labour*. Likewise descriptions of the process of gestation don't always do justice to the work of making a baby. We even lack a plain verb to name what the female body does from conception to delivery. We can explain our state by adjectives – *pregnant, expecting* – but how do we say what we're actually doing, something more than *carrying* or *increasing*? Some enthusiastic celebrations of the workings of the uterus pinned women like butterflies in the glass case of motherhood, our bodies seemingly perfectly designed and destined for maternity. Others had reason to make pregnancy seem terrifying.

In the British Library, a notebook-sized manuscript preserves a group of texts written around the year 1200 for young women contemplating the choice between marrying or pledging their life to the church as a nun or anchorite. One work in this early medieval West Midlands collection, *Hali Meithhad* (a title which means 'holy maidenhood'), lays it on thick: better to be a virgin married to Christ than endure sex and maternity. Pregnancy is called the 'burtherne of bearne', the burden of the child, when the baby will 'fehteth o thi seolve flesch ant weorrith with feole weanen o thin ahne cunde'. It will fight against your own flesh and make war against your own nature with many miseries. That metaphor anticipates the insights of recent research: it's not so much that the mother's body generously provides but that the foetus unstoppably demands what it needs. In a rather tongue-in-cheek pamphlet defending women which he dashed off after graduating from Oxford in 1620, Christopher Newstead pointed out that we should all be natal-grateful for such accommodation. A mother-to-be is 'a good Land-Lord to her childe, giving it both house-roome and nutriment, when it, like an unruly Tenant, doth grieve and vexe her'. Busybodies tease the pregnant about *eating for two* but they miss the mark: when pregnant, we're living, breathing, existing in tandem.

Medieval English does at least try out a few verbs. In one medieval romance, a duchess who's had sex with a devil disguised as her husband grows bigger by the day as her pregnant belly swells. As its author writes, she 'gretid' – in modern spelling we might say she *greated*. Another Middle English verb, *to child*, could describe the process of giving birth and also pregnancy itself. *I'm childing*, you could say, a more direct statement than the round-the-houses formality of *being with child*. My favourite medieval English pregnancy verb is, admittedly, quite a rare one. Dictionaries record it in this sense only in a book written by a London citizen called Henry Lovelich, a merchant who traded in skins, hides and furs. At the request of a fellow skinner, Lovelich translated two French romances about Arthur and his knights of the Round Table. Describing King Arthur's mother Igraine, another victim of sex by deception (this time not a demon but her future husband – medieval romance can't resist a conception with consent issues), Lovelich says she 'barnesched wondir faste', she grew with child amazingly quickly. *Barn* means 'child', so Igraine is not just *blooming* but literally *barnishing*, child-making.

Barn, from the Old English word for child, *bearn*, survives in English today in the Scottish and Northern English dialect term *bairn*. The *bearn* is the thing which is born, carried and brought forth. Such words have deep linguistic roots forged far upstream in the early history of our language. In proto-Germanic, one of the dialects spoken around 500 BC by the tribes living on the western shores of the Baltic (and the dialect that happened to become the common foremother of English, Dutch, German and the Scandinavian languages), linguists have reconstructed the verb *beran*, meaning both 'to carry' and 'to give birth'. In many of the daughter and granddaughter languages which descend from proto-Germanic, you find the same combinations of meanings: carrying, giving birth, producing, yielding up. In English *beran* proves very productive, giving us words like *born*, *bearing*, *birth*, *birthing*. Spelling convention sometimes separates *born* from *borne*, but both of those adjectives are past-tense forms of the verb *to bear*. When we say so-and-so *was born* or is a *bairn*, we mean (whether we remember it or not) that a body bore them and brought them forth. Our modern word *burden*, meaning 'something carried, a load', was originally spelled *burthen* or *birthen*, because it too derives ultimately from *beran*.

To bear is used in early English for agriculture and farming as well as for human reproduction: we bear children as a tree bears fruit or an animal bears offspring. Those sorts of usages feel dehumanising today, though earlier English speakers often used *breeding* as a synonym for pregnancy and childbirth. 'She may be breeding', one husband writes to his brother in 1658, worrying about his wife's ill health. 'She breeds them very painfully', a mother says of her daughter, praying that God will keep her safe in labour. (This daughter, Aletheia Howard, Countess of Arundel, survived at least six pregnancies, and was one of the first women to author a published English work of experimental science and 'practical observations', not only medical recipes but instructions for 'Chemical Extractions' and technical knowledge). Around the same time, Alice Thornton, a Yorkshire gentlewoman, decided to write her autobiography, what she called 'my own book of my life'. She records that she was 'exceeding sickly in breeding' at the start of one of her pregnancies, probably suffering from what we'd call, if we could get its many syllables in the right places, *hyperemesis gravidum*.

Breeding and carrying aren't, however, the only ways in which the earliest English puts pregnancy into words. In Old English, *eacnian* not only meant 'to conceive', 'to be pregnant' and 'to give birth', but also 'to increase', 'to flourish' or 'to bring forth wisdom'. It's a verb which has left hardly a trace in later English apart from our vague sense that you can make something last a little longer, that is make it a little bigger, by *eking* it out. But *eking*'s earlier spread of meanings makes sense: reproduction is, at base, an increase, two people becoming three (or more). *Eacnian* had a related adjective, *eacen*, whose usage was split down gendered lines. On the one hand, those who are *eacen* are full of excellence. When Beowulf, that Swedish superhero who stars in English's famous early epic – the Anglo-Saxons weren't averse to a spot of cultural appropriation – first appears in the story he's called both *æþele*, 'noble', and *eacen*, usually glossed as 'mighty'. On the other hand, the same word describes women who are pregnant or who are giving birth. Both heroes and those of us who are pregnant are endowed and augmented. Pregnant women are *bearn-eacen*, a compound defined in the *Dictionary of Old English* as 'big with child', but one we might reconceive as *child-flourished* or *child-mighty*.

Beowulf's virtues are mental as well as physical; he has not only superhuman strength but wisdom and bravery. So too the language of generation in previous centuries didn't neatly divide the processes of the mind from the workings of the body, even though we think of pregnancy as a mostly corporeal business. Old English verbs like *cennan* and *acennan* mean 'to be pregnant' and 'to give birth' but also 'to make known' and 'to reveal'. An inkling, the beginning of a thought is, like an embryo, small, hidden, internal. Only gradually, by writing or speaking, is thinking brought out into the open. Just so, if all goes well, the belly swells over nine months, gradually testifying to what's within until a baby is brought forth. The same doubled meanings entwine in words which English borrows from Latin: a *conception* is both the meeting of sperm and egg and also an idea, something that the mind produces like the womb. *Conceiving* can be intellectual or embryological. Rather than strictly separating the fleshly feminine and the rational masculine, the vocabulary of the past often entertains the notion that thinking and baby-making are comparable.

Pregnant too has this mix of meanings in early English. When the word first arrived, borrowed via French from a Latin root, it ran on several tracks at once, not only the familiar reproductive sense but also, more metaphorically, describing both imaginative or lively thinking and something full of significance and deep meaning. This explains why a *pregnant pause* is a silence full of consequence or import. The first dictionaries of English jostle these different senses together. Robert Cawdrey's 1604 dictionary defines *pregnant* as 'wittie, substantiall, with child'; John Kersey's *New English Dictionary*, published a century later, has 'great with child; also subtil, refined, substantial'. Childbearing is literally and metaphorically an act of substance and weight.

In today's super-formal medical terminology, pregnancy is called *gravidity*: you're a *primigravida* when having your first baby, and then, if pregnant again, a *multigravida*. *Gravid* (an old word for 'pregnant') and the adjective *grave* both come from Latin's *gravis*, a word which can describe things which are heavy or burdensome or, more positively, things which are serious or important. Being pregnant involves all of *grave*'s aspects. The physical burden isn't to be underestimated: with joints loosened temporarily by pregnancy hormones, feet can get permanently bigger while ribcages are shoved upwards. The downward pressures of several kilograms of baby can cause pelvic girdle pain, both during pregnancy and afterwards. Our bodies take the strain, becoming ever more weighty and substantial. The heart beats faster, grows bigger, pumps greater volumes, while our veins hold more blood and our tissues more water.

Given pregnancy's unavoidable gravity, it's peculiar that *pregnant* can also mean 'refined' or 'witty'. An early dictionary explaining hard and unusual words, Bulloker's 1616 *English Expositor* defines *pregnant* as 'Quickewitted, that will soone conceive' and *pregnancy* as 'Quickewittednesse'. It's not that he has biology back to front, pregnancy followed by conception. Rather, he says in the introduction, that if a word has an everyday usage and a more difficult one, he'll only give the trickier one. This metaphorical sense of *pregnant* comes from *quick*'s older

meaning, not 'fast' but 'living' (as we'll see later in this chapter
when we get to that mysterious old word *quickening*). Wits which
are *quick* are as much lively as speedy. A brain full of animated
thoughts is like a belly propagating new life. If a mind *teems* with
thoughts, it's literally breeding them, for *to teem* originally meant
'to bear children'. Your *teeming-time* was your fertile years; a *teem*
(or, as we would spell it, a *team*) referred to a family's offspring
before it became a word for a group of people working together.

It feels right that the language of pregnancy is sometimes a
Möbius strip of body and mind, not easy to peel the two apart.
For those of us who don't fall pregnant when we want to, the
mind teems with doubts, disappointments and what-ifs. For
those of us who know we're pregnant and are happy to be so,
the earliest weeks breed worries and fears aplenty. Conceptions
about conception have time and space to multiply because
we often keep these hopes, fears and torments quiet. When I
could think of nothing but wanting to be pregnant, I pasted,
for the benefit of family and friends, the same bland expression
on my face across two weeks of hoping, one week of despairing
and one week of trying out every gobbet and google of advice
I could gather up as the months ticked by. Those who endure
unexplained infertility and recurrent miscarriages face the fear
that there's no interface at all between what the mind wants and
what the body does.

Such heartache can be found in the writings of privileged
women whose anything-you-want wealth couldn't buy them
a child. Niece, daughter and sister to kings and queens of
England before becoming monarch herself in 1703, Queen
Anne was pregnant at least seventeen times following her
marriage in 1683. There are records of a dozen miscarriages
and stillbirths, two babies who died as neonates, and two girls

who died of smallpox as toddlers. Heartbreakingly, Anne's one surviving son, Prince William, also died of smallpox aged eleven. After a decade of this, she wrote to her closest confidante (imagine a younger Olivia Colman to Rachel Weisz, if you've seen *The Favourite*) that she had ordered a medicine 'not proposed to me by anybody', not prescribed by any doctor. It was one that had just occurred to her as something she'd not yet tried. She was, she confessed, 'so desirous of children I would do anything to go on'. *Going on* or *going through* were informal ways to describe carrying a pregnancy to term. I don't know how she kept going, kept trying to *go on*, the eyes of the royal court always upon her.

It's easy to imagine everyone in the centuries before reliable contraception living in football-team-sized families, rather than, like Queen Anne, haunted by a posse of infant ghosts. Many women did have many children, but plenty didn't. Whether by choice or circumstance, a good number of women remained unmarried. Caroline Fenwick's calculations, based on the English poll tax records of 1377, show that in that year just under 30 per cent of adult women were single, and this figure, which doesn't include widows, is probably an undercount.[6] Amy M. Froide's sample of a hundred English communities between 1574 and 1821 confirms that figure for later centuries: on average about 30 per cent of adult women in both urban and rural localities were unmarried. Demographers have calculated that from the fifteenth to the nineteenth centuries on average around one-fifth of women and men didn't marry.[7] Some of them, no doubt, cohabited without marriage and had children out of wedlock, but, given the pressures of community and Church, most of them didn't. Many of them lived and worked in someone else's household.

Furthermore, those who did marry were by no means certain to procreate. In the families of medieval English dukes and

duchesses whose grand titles make it possible to track descendants accurately, 17 per cent of women whose marriages lasted
through their fertile years had no living progeny. We can't tell
whether their childlessness was due to infertility, miscarriage,
stillbirth or neonatal death. Later in time and lower down the
social scale, researchers working with English parish records
have calculated that 7 to 10 per cent of first marriages between
1540 and 1750 in which a woman lived to the age of fifty didn't
produce a surviving child.

Women-blaming, though a popular pastime for almost
every kind of pre-modern Englishman, wasn't necessarily the
automatic response to infertility, though medical books did
enthusiastically catalogue what could go wrong with wombs.
Historical research on infertility in the Middle Ages and
Renaissance makes clear that sterility was seen as a potential
problem for men and women, with treatments offered not just
for erectile dysfunction but for men who could have penetrative
sex but didn't become fathers. The overlap of animal and human
in words like *breeding* and *teeming* also gives us infertility's cruel
vocabulary of words like *sterile* and *barren*, used of fields, creatures, plants and would-be parents. Words like *barrenness* and
impotency were first used for both sexes; it was only towards
the end of the 1600s that *barren* became mostly, though never
exclusively, a word targeted at women.[8]

There was often more sympathy than finger-pointing. The
historian Daphna Oren-Magidor has studied a memoir written in the 1660s by Mary Whitelocke, whose sixteen-year first
marriage was childless. Mary wrote of the kindness of her first
husband who, knowing her hopes and sorrows, never mentioned
wanting to have children in her presence or blamed her for their
childlessness. After his death, Mary became the third wife of
the lawyer-politician Bulstrode Whitelocke. She took on his ten
children and together they navigated the political aftermath of

the Civil War. Yet though, as she wrote in her biography, she knew she had 'as much outward comforts as this world could afford', she admitted asking God, 'what is all this to me seeing I goe childless?' In fact, it's much more likely that it was Mary's first husband rather than her who was infertile, for she wrote her memoir for her son, born nine months and twenty-five days after her second wedding and followed by six more children. Her husband Bulstrode called this first baby a 'childe of prayers', a boy conceived as much from devotions and longings as he was from flesh and blood.[9]

It wasn't just women who thought long and hard about infertility and sometimes put their troubles into words. For all his #metoo-worthy assaults, seductions and affairs, as well as many years of marriage, the Navy bean-counter and undoubted sexpest Samuel Pepys hadn't fathered a child. (*Long-suffering* would be precisely the wrong epithet for his wife Elizabeth, who, on finding him embracing Deborah Willet, her maid, grumbled and raged at length, eventually threatening to leave him.) In his diary, Pepys records attending a 1664 dinner to celebrate the birth of a friend's baby. When the female guests retired after the meal, he went upstairs with them and, seizing his moment, 'began discourse of my not getting of children and prayed them to give me their opinions and advice'. The thirty-one-year-old Pepys didn't put the blame on his wife: his chit-chat is about his own *not getting of children*. (I hope he was in earnest – perhaps this was just a creepy way to talk to boozed-up women about sex?) The ladies obliged, giving him their top tips, some of them familiar (healthy diet, loose underwear) and some less so (do the deed with your feet higher than your head). Nothing worked, for the Pepyses were still childless when Elizabeth died four years later.

*

Several years earlier, in the very first entry of his famous diary, Pepys recorded that Elizabeth, having not had a period for seven weeks, 'gave me hopes of her being with child'. On New Year's Eve her 'terms', as Pepys calls menstruation, returned. It may be that Elizabeth had had an early miscarriage. The dashed hopes and fears of miscarriage and stillbirth make some of our pregnancy words tentative, contingent and sometimes helpless. Saying *I'm having a baby* in these early months of a pregnancy might feel like tempting fate. These days we're cautioned not to make announcements until safely scanned at twelve weeks. For these early stages, the historian Lara Freidenfelds has suggested that we could revive earlier metaphors, used from the ancient Greeks onwards, which imagine early pregnancy botanically as blossom or fruit. If wombs are fields and menstrual blood is flowers, embryo and foetus are buds or seedlings. Freidenfelds suggests we could call the early stages of pregnancy a *sprout*, a word which accepts 'that not all seeds sprout, and not all sprouts grow and bear fruit'.[10]

We do need words for something so very common: at least one in four recognised pregnancies ends in miscarriage. The etymology of *miscarriage* might give the impression that something which should have been safely carried has been let slip, unhelpful connotations when we're so willing to blame ourselves. In fact the word *miscarriage* is used in English for many kinds of mishap – hence that phrase *miscarriage of justice* – before it's recorded for the first time as a word for pregnancy loss (thanks to our friend Helkiah Crooke in 1615). More euphemistically, miscarriages in our modern medical sense were called *mischances* or *misfortunes*, something like the uncontrollable weather or, in a devout age, the mysteries of God's will. Such mysteries preoccupied Mary Jackson, a Northumbrian girl who, on her first marriage, became the grander-sounding Lady Carey. Thanks to her second marriage and the English Civil War, she spent a decade as a military officer's wife moving between garrisons. In her late thirties and her forties, she wrote prayers and poems, writings which recorded a life lived according to Puritan devotion.

Having lost five of her seven children in infancy, Mary was consoled by her faith. On New Year's Eve in 1657, aged forty-eight, she composed a final poem, lines written 'Upon the Sight of my Abortive Birth'. Her poem begins with questions: 'What Birth is this? A poor despised Creature? A little Embryo void of Life?' Can words, even paradoxes, make sense of what she and we see in the poem, 'my dead, formless Babe'? Language lurches between life and death. Parents' grief can be compounded when their babies-to-be are redefined tactlessly by health profession-als as a *blighted ovum* (an early miscarriage when the embryo is reabsorbed leaving behind an empty gestational sac) or as the *retained products of conception* (the tissue which remains in the uterus after a miscarriage). Mary, like many of us, wants to know what's gone wrong. 'What is the thing amisse?' she asks God. The answer she imagines the Lord giving is spiritual rather than physical, one which is witness to her deep faith as well as women's tendency to blame themselves: this has suppos-edly happened because of lack of liveliness in her own religious devotions.

As you can see from the title Mary chose for her poem, what we would call a miscarriage was also in the past called an *abor-tive birth*, an *abortment* or *aborsement*. The first vocabularies of miscarriage and abortion were interconnected rather than separate. A 1672 English translation of a French textbook on midwifery divides up pregnancy loss into three categories. An early miscarriage is termed 'an Effluxion or a sliding away of the Seeds', *effluxion* being the flowing out of a liquid. When a 'false Conception' miscarries, what we would call a molar pregnancy (that is, a fertilised egg with abnormalities which mean a baby and placenta will not develop normally), it's called 'an Expulsion'. Only a miscarriage in late pregnancy, 'when the Infant is already formed, and begins to live', is called 'an Abortion'. What we would think of as an *abortion* today, the intentional ending of a pregnancy, is by the 1600s specified by the addition of an adjective like *procured* or *induced*.

Before such specificity, the early language of what we now call abortion was hard to pin down.[11] Some historians have imagined, with more enthusiasm than evidence, that women had secretive expertise in this area which the authorities sought to suppress. Others think it likely that any such knowledge was very sketchy and scattered. Some scholars have argued that descriptions of emmenagogues (substances which might regulate or bring on menstruation) in medical books are really coded references to methods for ending a pregnancy. But in an age when regular menstruation was thought beneficial for physical health, perhaps we shouldn't be second-guessing this subject. Emmenagogues, herbs which might *bring down the flowers* as some authors described their workings, may well have been taken to promote fertility rather than suppress it. The medical historian Monica H. Green points out that emmenagogues attract no particular concern or warnings about their use.

The backstory of abortion's treatment by the law is likewise not straightforward. This hazy history might have once felt dustily academic, but it now seems a very pressing matter. The early language and law surrounding abortion was recently discussed in detail in the US Supreme Court decision overturning *Roe v. Wade*, the 1973 case which regulated the ability of individual states to restrict access to abortion. Some of the 2022 Supreme Court ruling hangs on the meaning of old words like *quickening* and *misprision*, as well as the question of whether abortion was criminalised in the common law of medieval and Early Modern England. Whether seen as a sin or a crime, abortion has never been a simple topic.[12] Early medieval penitentials listed the years of atonement due if a woman confessed to the destruction of a foetus. But even by the eighth and ninth centuries, churchmen knew that there were complexities to be argued out. Abortion was not the same as the murder of a living person. Its degree of sinfulness depended on the stage of pregnancy, or whether the woman in question acted out of poverty or a desire to cover up fornication.

In the thirteenth century, one kind of abortion did come to the secular courts as a common-law offence. As Professor Wolfgang Müller has explained, these cases were not abortion in our sense of the term, but rather *assault and battery*, in which another person injured or poisoned a pregnant woman leading her to miscarry.[13] These felony charges were usually brought by the woman whose baby had been lost. Yet between the mid-fourteenth and the mid-sixteenth centuries, cases of culpable miscarriage like this ceased to be prosecuted. Law books, giving their legal theories and examples of precedent cases, offer some explanation of this change. These crimes could not be prosecuted because the foetuses in question were nameless and weren't present *in rerum natura*, one of those quaint legal phrasings which means 'in the nature of things', as fully part of our world. They didn't yet have *legal personhood*, as we would call it today. Even in the case of miscarriage caused by assault, no crime had thus been committed.

In later centuries, as the legal scholar Carla Spivack explains, guides to the common law show that some abortions were considered crimes.[14] The seventeenth-century legal expert Sir Edward Coke wrote that if a woman 'be quick with childe' and 'killeth it in her womb' by some means (or if someone else kills it), 'this is a great misprision, and no murder'. A *misprision* was an offence less serious than a felony. Coke follows the same logic that this cannot be murder because the victim does not yet exist *in rerum natura*. *Quick* on its own can mean simply 'alive', as in that strange pairing *the quick and the dead*. But *the quickening* was the point in pregnancy when a woman could feel the foetus's movements within her. To be *quick with child* was to be in later pregnancy. Before quickening, abortion wasn't criminalised, though the Church considered it sinful. After quickening, it wasn't a felony offence. Spivack notes that such prosecutions as there were generally targeted assaults on pregnant women and cases relating to illicit out-of-wedlock sex. At a time when knowledge of menstrual cycles and due dates was much less exact and purges and emmenagogues much more common, with the woman herself the main witness to *quickening*, the law couldn't easily penetrate the bounds of marriage and the private home.

Today's arguments about abortion often take place at the extremes of *pro-life* or *pro-choice*. But earlier debate wasn't quite so certain about the starting-point of *life* and where a foetus fitted *in the nature of things*. Most medieval and Renaissance experts believed that the foetus did not come fully alive until it had been given a soul. Authorities gave various timespans for this *animation* (a word which derives from Latin *anima*, 'the soul') or *ensoulment*. Some said forty days, some longer. By the eighteenth century, religious opinion had changed its mind and now believed that the foetus was alive from the very beginning (even if it wasn't certain when it was ensouled) and hence should be protected. Soon the law followed suit. In Britain, post-quickening abortion was criminalised by Act of Parliament in 1803, with a second 1837 Act criminalising abortion at any stage of pregnancy. What had once been somewhat out of reach of the law was now definitively illegal.

*

It's only very recently that doctors have been persuaded to let go of one hangover from this older English and stop calling miscarriages *spontaneous abortions*. Nowadays there should be no linguistic overlap at all between the intentional decision to end a pregnancy and an early pregnancy which is lost. In the language of the past, miscarriages were once imagined as blossoms or fruit swept away by strong winds or rain. One such metaphor turns up in an English translation of a gardening guide written by the French lawyer-turned-designer who planned the kitchen garden at Louis XIV's palace of Versailles (quite the celebrity endorsement . . .). Blossoms which 'shed without knitting for Fruit', whose petals fall without their fruit setting, are in French described with the verb *couler* which means, so the English version explains, 'to slip, or slink like an Abortive Birth'. These verbs suggest that the womb's job is to hold on tight, just as today we pray that pregnancies will *stick*.

Other euphemisms, those wordings that carefully step around a difficult thing for kindness's sake, described pregnancy loss as an early arrival, a child *born before time* or *untimely born*. Perhaps the old ideas about the stages of gestation were some consolation. Once you felt the baby quicken, you could be more certain that you had a human-to-be inside. It's hard even in the age of ultrasounds and scan pictures to find a single word to describe what grows within us from the first nauseous gags and strange twinges to those final days with a giant bump that transfixes onlookers as bony baby shoulders and heels poke into view. The whole point is that the thing co-inhering with us changes: first a *zygote* and *blastocyst*, before becoming an *embryo* and then, after eight weeks, a *foetus*.

Even harder to find the right words to use when pregnancy ends in tragedy at a later stage. For the mothers of the one in every two hundred and fifty British babies who died *in utero* in 2019, it is, unavoidably, *still birth*, still labour and delivery with all their efforts and risks. The sixteenth-century phrase *born still*, describing a newborn without breath or movement, became first an adjective, *still-born* and then, a century afterwards, the noun, *stillbirth*. A more tactful word, perhaps, than the equivalents *misborn* and *dead-born* used in medieval and Renaissance English. Even further back there's an Old English charm preserved in a manuscript copied around the year 1000. It gives a spell which a woman could be taught in order to pray she has a living child. She should wish that her pregnancy ends 'mid fulborenum', with a baby that is *full-born*, fully formed and living, rather than with one who is 'fægan', a baby who was (in the fatalistic Anglo-Saxon imagination) doomed to die. *Fæge* is, curiously, the early ancestor of our word *fey*, which now means something like 'unworldly, magical'. It reminds me of *angel babies*, that gentle phrasing which helps some grieving parents preserve the memories of their lost children.

When it comes to childbirth itself, the words you choose to describe it matter a great deal. Words like *labour* and, in medieval English, *travail* (from the French word for 'work') see birth as, in essence, hard trouble, difficulty, arduous effort. It's certainly not an easy process, whichever kind of birth the universe plans for you. These days, if you can have a perfectly free choice (not likely given the politics and practicalities of it all), you choose between major surgery or something comparable to the demands of an endurance event, the ultimate *ironwoman*. Most Caesareans are unplanned, so women who deliver their babies this way face first the ultra-marathon of labour and then an invasive operation.

There's quite the backstory to naming birth as hard work, *labour* or *travail*. In the Book of Genesis, when Adam and Eve screwed up in Eden, God appeared with a list of sanctions.

Kicking them out, he tells Adam that, rather than the easy life in Paradise, he'll now have to work for his living. Eve, among other things, is told that she'll bring forth children 'in sorrow'. Putting subsistence farming and childbirth in parallel, this reason-giving myth starts with the question and works backward to invent the answer. Why do women have so much pain giving birth compared to other mammals? Because it's God's punishment for Original Sin. Such a dick-move, isn't it, to blame a woman for the pain of childbirth. A demoralising thought for women in the past already rightly scared of pain, injury, the loss of their baby or their own death. Before the invention of instruments to help mothers deliver babies, before antiseptic and antibiotics, childbirth was dangerous, much more dangerous than today. Accurate calculations are tricky, but in early modern England, historians estimate that around 2,500 women died per 100,000 births.[15] Compare the World Health Organization's figures for 2017: an average of 462 per 100,000 in low-income countries and 11 per 100,000 in high-income countries.

Though much safer nowadays, *Eve's curse*, as the perils and pains of childbirth came to be called, remains exacerbated by inequality and embedded prejudices. Maternal mortality rates are four times higher for black women in the United States and in Britain. Some of these prejudices are tap-rooted deep in history, as Jennifer L. Morgan explains in her book *Laboring Women*. Explorers' accounts of the New World entertained readers with strange and unfamiliar details of the indigenous societies they encountered. In the account of the merchant-explorer Amerigo Vespucci's voyage of 1501–2, for example, translated for English readers by Richard Eden in 1553, South American women were said to 'travayle in maner without payne', to give birth painlessly. In the seventeenth century, colonists in North America likewise reported that Native American women gave birth with comparative ease, perhaps, so these colonists reasoned, because their manual work gave them stronger bodies.[16] (Such logic conveniently allowed a side dish of woman-blaming, the more sedentary lives of European ladies supposedly contributing to their more difficult labours.) In a travelogue published in 1744, William Smith, remembering his journey along the Gold Coast to survey the Royal African Company's forts twenty years earlier, said he too had heard of African women giving birth in under fifteen minutes with 'no Shrieks or Cries'.

Soon 'race science' swept up these dust balls of hearsay about painless births into its racism. If women across the globe shared Eve's curse, their labour pains testified to a shared origin for humanity. But if they didn't, this could be taken as 'proof' that different races were different species. In his *History of Jamaica* (1774), three comprehensive volumes that were comprehensively racist, the plantation-owner Edward Long repeated Smith's hearsay that African women delivered babies with 'little or no labour . . . in a quarter of an hour'. He doubled down on Smith's account, saying that African women 'bring forth twins, without a shriek, or a scream'. Comparing their labours to births of animals because he saw them as less than human, these mothers, Long wrote, were 'exempted from the curse inflicted upon Eve and her daughters'. From such origins descended the prejudiced idea that black people felt less pain and the racist notion that black people weren't fully human.

Silent births, whether the medieval myth of the Virgin Mary's painless labour or the bigotry invented by racists, must have seemed unlikely to English readers in the past. In early English, childbirth was sometimes called *groaning* or a woman's *crying out*. The author of the early medieval book written to scare Midlands maidens into choosing holy virginity over marriage imagines labour in his peculiar twelfth-century English as 'pine over pine, thet wondrinde yeomerunge', pain after pain, that restless yammering, yelling or lamenting. With little or no effective pain relief, many women cried out. Support during childbirth came from family, friends, servants and midwives. Their name meaning 'with women', midwives knew the 'craft' (according to a popular medieval encyclopaedia) to make births easier and less painful. Because it involved tabooed body parts, birth was predominantly women's business, though surgeons might be called to extract a dead baby or attend a dying mother. Guy de Chauliac, author of the most famous medieval guide for surgeons, concedes that dealing with multiple births and difficult births, what we would call malpresentations, was not his concern. This medical work is *haunted* (as the medieval English translation of Chauliac's book has it, meaning 'usually performed') by women, so he won't waste sentences dwelling on it. The author of a medieval English handbook of gynaecology says that a baby can be repositioned and then safely delivered 'by the grace of God and the mydwifes connyng [*cunning*]'.

Craft and *cunning* sound excitingly witchy, a treasure chest of women's secrets, but they could equally be translated as 'art' and 'knowledge'. Once upon a time, feminist historians imagined the past as a golden age when women managed their reproductive health on their own terms guided by the knowledge of midwives. Midwives' expertise and authority, so this tempting tale went, were then targeted by seventeenth-century witch-finders and, from the eighteenth century onward, swept aside by an invasion of man-midwives (the English name for the first male obstetricians), by maternity hospitals and eventually by Victorian doctors who began the modern medical specialties of obstetrics and gynaecology. That fairy story of good and evil is far too simplistic, I'm afraid.[17] Childbirth was never entirely free from the involvement of husbands, the clergy and medics. Midwives in Britain were, happily, no more targeted by Puritan witch-hunters than any other group of women. Because they had no guild or professional body, women working as midwives did face regulation from the Church (from the early 1600s they needed a licence from their local bishop) and a good deal of mansplaining. It's true that from the 1730s childbirth was increasingly a medical procedure. This was as much because wealthier women thought these fashionable new developments were safer as it was because of masculine muscling-in. Whether they were safer or not is also complicated: while forceps and surgical techniques saved many, hospital-acquired infections killed plenty of others.

There's long been a tug-of-war between book-learning and practical experience when it comes to childbirth. Once the two professions were properly in competition, midwives accused obstetricians of being too keen to use instruments, causing injuries to mother and baby, while man-midwives belittled women for their lack of formal training and education. Even today, the language of labour bifurcates along these lines. It's part medical and mechanical (*contraction, dilation, the latent phase*), part vernacular and mysterious (*the show, waters breaking, bearing down, crowning, the afterbirth*). And arguments about how best to deliver babies are still conducted through proxy wars of terminology.

On the one hand are those who idolise vaginal deliveries as 'natural births' and label pain relief and medical assistance as 'interventions' which might unstoppably 'cascade'. On the other hand, obstetricians might be overly keen to medicalise a process which, if all's well, can be 'physiological', something a body can achieve by itself. Elizabeth Nihell, a London midwife who had trained at the leading Paris maternity hospital in the 1740s, published a bolshy treatise in 1760 defending what we would now call midwife-led home births against the popularity of male midwives and hospital deliveries. She reminds her readers that, in order to encourage more women to pay for their services, obstetricians had incentives 'to forge the phantom of incapacity' for pregnant women, to invent dangers or at least to scaremonger that our bodies won't be sufficiently capable. Making our choices (so far as we are able to choose) about where to give birth and who to have in attendance, we still puzzle over what's evidence and what's mere phantom.

Given the push–pull of theory and practice, the first English books discussing childbirth weren't overly prescriptive. Some births are easier, some harder. Each woman labours in different positions, 'as she is accustomed' says one book, *as suits her* or *as she's used to*. Authorities generally agreed that dim lights and privacy were best. For the early stages of labour, most advised a mix of rest and walking around, with nourishment and encouragement from attendants (several note that the midwife should be good at finding 'sweet words' to keep spirits up). Even if churchmen thought that women should suffer Eve's curse of painful labour, Renaissance physicians suggested, for those who could afford them, the taking of pills and drinks which 'alleviateth and unpaineth the birth'. (The verb *unpain* might be optimistic, but, like TENS machines and aromatherapy, one can only hope . . .). Beyond this, much remained an enigma. Even books which publicised the Renaissance's new anatomical knowledge couldn't give detailed descriptions of what our body does in childbirth. They marvel at how the cervix, which, if all is well, stays clamped for nine months, then becomes 'a gate wide open' in labour. Helkiah Crooke, comparing the mechanics of labour to the mysteries of conception and pregnancy, says that Nature's baby-extraction plan is 'the crowne of all the rest, as that which exceedeth all admiration'. One English translation of a French guide says that childbirth 'cannot be comprehended . . . but only wondered at, and admired'.

This admiration is well and good but it makes it sound easy, as if the cervix pops open like a camera aperture. *Contractions,* describing how the muscles of the uterus squeeze to pull open the cervix, was first used in this specific sense in the early 1800s. It's a word that sends your brain off down the wrong track, for rather than narrowing or contracting anything their purpose is to crank the cervix slowly open (half a centimetre per hour is considered good progress), the very definition of *laboriously*. Before they were called *contractions*, they were known as *pangs*, *throngs* or *throws*, plain syllables naming the pain of these spasms. While hazy about the realities of contractions in the first stage of labour, experts did describe the second. Though authorities repeated the older myths that the child simply forces its own way out, they also admired what Helkiah Crooke calls 'the voluntary endevor of the woman', the woman's own efforts. Guillemeau's *Happy Deliverie* encouraged the labouring woman not to 'lie crying and lamenting' but to 'take a good heart, and straine her selfe as much as she can, when her throws come upon her, making them double and increase, by holding in her breath and stopping her mouth, and forming herselfe as though she would go to the stoole'. *Going to the stool* is going to the toilet. Even Renaissance doctors understood what the strange instruction to *bear down* might feel like.

Despite my logophilia, words did not play much of a part in the birth of my daughter. The books I'd read, the talks I'd listened to, the birth plan I'd written and rewritten were gradually rubbed out. My glasses on a high ledge, my clothes on the floor, my speech simplified to groaning, breathing, keening. First managing and then what felt like mostly panic. Its parameters were so uncertain – how much longer, how much further, how much more painful, what forces could I withstand? Obstetricians, when speaking formally, rename the vagina as the *birth canal* during labour. If only the baby did glide like a barge from a tunnel, not bumping the sides. In fact it spelunks inch by inch through the birth pothole, and the body has to stretch, accommodate, be cut or give way. The author of one medieval gynaecology guide says that many births cause 'mischevous grevaunce', distressing injury and pain, because some women lack 'good mydwifes'. Women keep such injuries secret out of shame, yet they 'nedith to be holpen', they need to be helped, he writes, giving advice for their treatment. Birth injuries, especially issues with incontinence, remain taboo subjects, and women still suffer in silence with substandard treatment, though campaigners are doing their best to improve matters.

The philosopher Fiona Woollard argues that physiological birth is often either 'celebrated the wrong way', idolised as 'better' or 'more natural' than other births, or, at the other extreme, unduly minimised and taken for granted.[18] Perhaps, she suggests, we could talk about physiological birth as no more or less than a physical achievement, in the same way that we think of running a marathon. Like a marathon, physiological birth takes physical and mental endurance, yet also needs the good fortune of a body which is able to meet the demands put upon it. Neither feat makes us 'better' than those who didn't attempt them or didn't complete them. But such neutrality is not easy when plenty of us have our birth plans revised and rewritten by Fate, the great editor. Our stories inevitably diverge and conversation without comparison is a hard dance to master. For these reasons, as well as the hesitation which surrounds bodily taboos, labour has its code of silence.

Though there's no sense in idolising historical childbirth before modern science made it substantially safer, women in English's past did have more chance to witness many labours and to talk them over. Before hospital births were the norm, those who'd been chosen or who had volunteered to help, plus a local midwife, were gathered up, house by house, when a woman went into labour. This doorstep-dash even had its own word in East Anglian slang, *nidgeting* or *nigiting*. Before medicine had anything much to offer, these gatherings gave what support they could to birthing women. The midwife Elizabeth Nihell paid tribute to 'that supremely tender sensibility with which women in general are so strongly impressed towards one another in the case of lying-in'. Though the poor and enslaved had no such cossetting, in wealthier medieval and early modern families these gathered-up women would keep the new mother company during her *lying-in* or *confinement*, that is during the birth itself and the first three or four weeks after labour, what we would call the *fourth trimester*. After *lying-in* came *upsitting* or *footing-time*, when the post-partum woman got out of bed and rejoined everyday life. Her lying-in companions would accompany her to her *churching*, once a ceremony of purification which, by the mid-sixteenth century, the Church of England had cleverly rebranded as a service of thanksgiving.

As well as celebrating her churching, a woman's closest friends would be asked to become the baby's godmothers. *God-sib*, literally 'God relations', an early English word for godparents and close friends, gradually becomes our word *gossip*. In the sixteenth century, the word was, by extension, a name for the group of friends who attended a woman's lying-in. Thanks to the stereotypical idea that women gathered together would do nothing but talk, we get our modern meaning of *gossip* with its gendered connotations. Eighteenth-century dictionaries defined a *gossiping* as 'a merry meeting of gossips at a womans lying-in' and a *gossip* as 'one who runs about tattling like women at a lying in'. I hope that the days post-partum were once as brimful of talk as these sexist definitions imply. Lying-in might have offered a chance to debrief and process memories of labour, a time for older gossips to tell their anecdotes and for younger ones to learn what might be in store later in life.

The informal words such gossiping might have used have largely vanished without trace – I can't find you much in the written records. Midwives like Jane Sharp and Elizabeth Nihell who published books mostly adopted the formal tone of the men whose public sphere they joined. This tone endures in the long-lasting words of medical tradition: the ubiquitous use of *delivery* (as if the baby's just handed to us out of the tinfoiled crib of a takeaway food courier) and needlessly cruel phrasings such as *poor maternal effort* or *failure to progress*. So to do justice to pregnancy and labour in everyday language, we need to find words afresh, as women are starting to do in the online spaces where they share *positive birth stories* of every type of birth, as well as valiant testimonies of birth trauma and its physical and mental after-effects. *Positive* is a carefully chosen adjective, making no assumptions about what is a *normal* or *natural birth*. Tucked at the bottom of a drawer I have a baby book, a present when my daughter was born, a cutesy volume in which to record her developmental milestones. Its dotted lines are still awaiting completion – life with a newborn was busier than I'd imagined. Instead I wish I'd been given a blank notebook and the time and space to write down an account of her arrival while it was vivid in my mind. Let's all be gossips about infertility, baby loss, pregnancy and birth, telling our stories whatever path they follow.

Five

Nurse

The Language of Care

—

The word *nurse*, as both verb and noun, holds in its lap a bundle of meanings which dominated many women's lives in past centuries. I'd assumed that *nursing*, in the sense of breastfeeding, was a recent euphemism, a way to avoid saying the tabooed body-part *breast* out loud. In fact, the lactating breast is the source from which many other words flow. *To nurse* or *nourish* – two meanings and spellings which cohabit in one entry in the dictionary of medieval English – come to us across French stepping-stones from the Latin verb *nutrire*, meaning 'to suckle, to feed, to rear, to bring up'. The roots of *nutrire*, and the related Latin noun *nutrix*, 'the one who nurses', run far back into prehistory. Like theoretical physicists whose complex calculations deduce what there might be in the outer reaches of space, historical linguists work backwards through time to reconstruct items of ancient vocabulary. What these experts recreate are more like formulae than words thanks to the conventions which notate their strange syllables. In Proto-Indo-European, the language that migrated with its speakers out from now-Ukrainian river valleys in the fifth millennium BC, seeding its words far and wide as the common ancestor of the Indo-European languages, they've followed the thread all the way back to *sneu-tr-ih2, meaning 'a female who nurses'.

This chapter explores some of English's oldest descriptions of caretaking labour. From *nurse*, this fossil word for a physical capacity, one body providing food for another, comes a much broader range of meanings, words like *nurture* and *nourishment*, with their connotations of comfort, nutrition, support and education. Language often stretches or repurposes words rather than making the effort to invent new ones. So *nurse* first of all named the person, usually a woman, who took care of babies and toddlers, often breastfeeding them herself as a *wet nurse*. From this came *nursery*, the room in a house where young children slept and played or, in its modern meaning, the place where infants are looked after while their parents are at work. By the seventeenth century, a *nurse* not only looked after children, but might also be someone who took care of other groups of vulnerable people such as the ill and the elderly. Now we think of it as a professional title, though one whose gender balance is still sharply shaped by its origins. Whether looking after the sick, the young or the old, *nursing* has predominantly been women's work and remains so today.

Keeping pace with *nurse* during the history of English is *care*, another word whose bundled meanings have commandeered many women's lives. A *carer* can be someone paid to care or someone who cares unpaid within a family. When the state steps in to look after children, the support and protection needed and hopefully given is simplified to the common denominator of *care*. If *nursing*'s linguistic roots are bodily, *caring*'s origins are more in the mind. Old English has a verb, *carian*, meaning 'to have sorrow, feel concern, be anxious'. Even at this early stage, such preoccupations could be both sorrowful yet also useful. To *care* in early English meant not only to lament or to grieve but also to be watchful, attentive, concerned, what dictionary-makers in their formality define as 'being solicitous', paying close attention to someone else's well-being. *Caring* is as much thinking as doing, the voluntary taking on of trouble, turning over your brain to keep track of someone else's needs.

We might be glad that *caring* rather than *nursing* has become the standard term for looking after children. The etymology of *nurse*, rooting care in the breast, invites essentialist thinking: that because female bodies have the equipment for feeding infants, women are inherently 'caring' and so such tasks should inevitably fall to them. Anatomical explanation slip-slopes easily into spurious justification, stitching women into domesticity's small pocket. Yet while women have certainly done most of the caring in English's past, there wasn't always a seamless linguistic fit between womanhood and childcare. Mothering didn't necessarily have the starring role in femininity. Medieval guides setting out how to be a good wife or daughter are mostly uninterested in how to be a good mum. They reflect the real-ity that it was by no means always a child's own mother who nursed and cared for them during their first months and years. The earliest vocabulary of caring in English tends to describe what's done, not who does it: *nursing, caring, fostering*. As verbs, *to mother* or *to father* referred to reproduction rather than to parenting for most of their history. Not till the mid-nineteenth century did *to mother* mean to raise children in some particularly motherlike way.

With maternal mortality high, many babies and toddlers in the past had to be cared for by relatives or by women paid from a parish's charitable funds. More privileged families often employed a wet nurse, either sending the baby to her home or having the nurse live with them. While a *dry nurse* cared for an

infant without breastfeeding them, a *wet nurse* fed them herself.
Wet-nursing was a more parochial version of the chains of care
which now stretch around the globe, care work relayed down
marble runs of inequality from one family to another. Before safe
and healthy formula milk was available, breastfeeding enforced
the anatomical *fiat* that infant care was women's work. Yet wet-
nursing also made it very clear that babies and toddlers needn't
be looked after primarily by their mother. Care could be handed
over, outsourced, extracted under duress and displaced. In
colonial-era America and in the centuries afterward, wet-nursing
could be forced labour, another means of exploiting enslaved
women. Enslaved mothers' own children might thus have to be
nursed by others, weaned early or bottle-fed on whatever 'dry'
substitute nourishment could be provided. How enslaved women
might care for their own children mattered little to slave-owners,
yet these same women nurtured slave-owners' infants.

From the sixteenth century to the nineteenth, experts urged
women to breastfeed their own babies. Even the word chosen
to name our particular class of animals, *Mammalia*, from which
we get our English word *mammal*, may be part of this heavy-
handed encouragement. As the historian Londa Schiebinger
has explained, the Swedish scientist Carl Linnaeus invented this
word, meaning 'of the breast', in his 1758 *Systema naturae*, a book
which classified the natural world into an ordered taxonomy.[1]
Mammalia put in one category those creatures who feed their
young by milk from mammary glands. Linnaeus had, six years
earlier, written a pamphlet arguing that mothers should suckle
their infants rather than make use of wet nurses. By selecting
this shared feature rather than any of the others (their four-
chambered hearts, their configuration of teeth and ear bones,
or their warm-blooded hairy bodies), Linnaeus's new name put
breastfeeding offspring right at the centre of this category of
beings, as natural for humans as other mammals.

Other experts sought to shame women into breastfeeding by suggesting that motherhood itself was transferrable to who-ever did the job of caring. In the early 1520s, Juan Luis Vives, a Spanish academic with a visiting-lecturer gig at Oxford, was encouraged by Katherine of Aragon, Henry VIII's first queen, to write a book about how to bring up girls. With young Princess Mary to educate, this was a topical matter – a good job Katherine had no problem reading Vives's original Latin. From our perspec-tive, his *Education of a Christian Woman* is infuriating: Vives widened women's intellectual horizons but nevertheless kept them boxed in as wives and mothers. Encouraging women to nurse their babies themselves (and hence to be on hand as their earliest teachers), Vives, in the English translation of his work which soon followed, warned guilt-trippingly that 'nurces be wonte also to be called mothers', *nurses are often called mothers*. If a mother nurses her own child, 'none of the mothers name shall be taken from her and put unto any other'.

Such emotional blackmail didn't work on everyone. Another sixteenth-century education expert, the Dutch academic Erasmus, published invented conversations for language learners which showed you how to make your Latin sound fluent and lively. As subject matter for these model chats or *colloquies*, he chose hot topics and juicy debates. In one, a new mother spars with a male visitor who notes that her baby has a nurse. He asks (in the English translation published in 1606) why she would 'willingly resigne more then halfe your title of Mother unto another woman', a question not so much loaded as swamped by disapproval. The young mum Fabulla (whose name means 'talker', though he's chattier than she is) is having none of it and does the maths differently: 'I divide not my sonne', she tells him, 'I am the whole and sole mother'. For her, nursing doesn't equal motherhood.

Just as progressive thinking today sometimes accelerates

into relentless purity spirals, some parts of the Renaissance's zeal for reform of religion and education spun themselves into Puritanism, the drive to live an exemplary life according to Christian teaching. We might find the popularity of bestselling conduct books mystifying – why would anyone pay to be told how to be holier-than-thou? But perhaps it's not so unfamiliar. Our vices and virtues may be different but we still like domineering books that tell us what to do or how to think. Puritan rhetoric about breastfeeding could be extreme: Cotton Mather, preacher and Salem witch-trial expert witness, compared non-nursing mothers to the Bible's description of the bone idle, 'dead while they live'. Yikes.

Yet other voices were more thoughtful, or at least more conflicted. Having survived eighteen pregnancies, Elizabeth Clinton, Countess of Lincoln, published her first and only book in her late forties. This 1622 work, called appropriately enough her *Nurserie*, sang the praises of breastfeeding as enthusiastically as any zealous La Leche League peer-supporter. But in Clinton's case, it wasn't that years of nursing made her (as she thought some readers might assume) 'more busie to meddle', keen to write a book to 'make them to be blamed that have not done it', shaming women who did not nurse. She writes from regret, having been dissuaded from nursing by 'anothers authority' (perhaps her husband, as men often encouraged wet-nursing so that their wives' fertility would not be impacted by lengthy periods of breastfeeding) and by 'ill counsell', by bad advice.

She recognises too that breastfeeding your own child is idolised as somehow better, more motherly. A nursing mother, she gushes, is 'a mother deserving good report . . . a mother winning praise for it'. Then as now, it's hard to recognise breastfeeding's own value and effort without setting up a motherhood scoreboard. But those who do nurse their own babies should steer clear of smuggery, says Clinton, and instead give thanks for the 'ability and freedome' to do what 'many a mother would have done and could not; who have tried and ventured their health, and taken much paines, and yet have not obtained their desire'. She knew first-hand that it takes more than pure willpower or virtue: you need sufficient support and knowledge, plus a body and a baby that cooperated. *Taking much pains* is a good description of the physical and mental fortitude breastfeeding often demands of you, whether you continue to nurse for many months or stop after a few days.

As Elizabeth Clinton's experience shows, many families chose or were compelled to ignore experts' campaigns against wet-nursing. The early language of infant care had to accommodate these unpredictabilities. Some organised wet-nursing well in advance while others rushed to find a nurse when plans went awry. Frances, second wife of the governor of Guernsey, had set her heart upon nursing her child but pain made it impossible and so a wet nurse was found. She was so disconsolate that, as she wrote to her husband in 1678, she thought she would 'never be cheerful again'. Authors recognised that, in practical terms, nurses and mothers did pretty much the same thing. A popular medieval reference book first says that the *mother* is the one 'to norische [nourish] and keep the childe' but, turning over a few more pages, almost the same words define the job of the nurse, 'to norische and to fede the childe'.

Even with encouragement and information on your side, the job of a nurser demands stamina. To fill and refill a stomach the size of a cherry (then a walnut, then a plum – after a month only an egg!) takes so many minutes of the day and night. It's not the easiest skill for a first-timer and a newborn to grasp. The learning curve is near-perpendicular, made more stressful these days, as it has to be, by scales and charts. The baby must *thrive*, that strange old verb, it must put on weight and get strong enough to feed and grow. Thank heavens for the safety net of formula.

Once up and running, breastfeeding is often low maintenance and sometimes perfectly symmetrical, we *suckle*, the baby *suckles*, the same verb does for both. But at the start, the system's often laggy. A growing baby who needs more calories can be nothing but insistent – *more, more, more* – and send its signals by feeding endlessly for a day or two.

Then, hopefully, the nursing body catches up. Nurser and baby are interdependent, their two-to-tango not easily paused without planning and pumping. The *whusssh-hmpf* of a breast-pump shows how *suckling*, for all its luscious gentle consonants, doesn't really convey the forceful siphon which baby bellow-cheeks generate. Another medieval verb for breastfeeding, *to give suck*, gets nearer to reality. Likewise, the *latch* of a baby's mouth isn't some mere nibble but a veritable clamp, something powerful enough to lock very tight, as the word itself suggests. Mispositioning can cause much pain and damage. Jane Sharp in her 1671 midwives' guide notes that 'Clefts [cracks] and Chaps of the breasts are troublesome, and usual to Nurses'. My first days of feeding were a tutorial in suction and friction.

What anthropologists call *matrescence*, the changes in body, personality and identity brought about by motherhood, is often a sharp lesson that, whatever your own needs, your hungry baby's needs matter more. *Caring* can sound so calm and lovely that we lose sight of the demands on the person doing the caring itself. Once visiting hours are over, when help comes only if you have the temerity to sound the buzzer, we're left to feed and tend to newborns any which way we can with our exhausted bodies totalled by labour, major surgery or both. In the past, *matrescence* for many began by acknowledging the care needed by the post-partum mother. The old myth that colostrum (the highly nutritious and antibody-rich fluid which a pregnant woman's breasts produce before and after birth) was dangerous for babies, though less than ideal for the neonate, gave new mothers some respite straight after birth. Lying-in was not just for the very wealthy but went on quite far down the social scale, though the very poor and the enslaved had no such rest.

For those who couldn't afford paid help, families and parishes rallied round and husbands were expected to pitch in, even (at least in the imagination) in the holiest of families. In Matthew's gospel, Joseph contemplates a quickie divorce from Mary before Jesus's birth, but an angel reassures him she's still a virgin and it's all meant to be. A medieval retelling of that Bible story, written by John Mirk in the 1380s to help under-trained parish priests stuck for ideas for sermons, has the angel telling Joseph to stay put because he'll be needed as Mary's 'keper' and 'norse [nurse] to her child' when she gives birth in Bethlehem's worst-rated Airbnb. *Keeping* now sounds possessive or controlling, but among its many meanings in medieval English were the senses of looking after, watching over, nurturing and caring. Even Mary, often painted or sculpted as the epitome of devoted motherhood, could expect help, so Joseph would have to stand in as Jesus's nurse.

After birth came *infancy*, the first part of childhood when the baby needs 'tendre and softe kepinge, fedinge, and norischinge' according to our medieval encyclopaedia. Having their hands full, women in the past didn't often pause to jot down their observations about the daily round of caring and tending, thus failing to leave us an account of this work in their own words. Instead this love and drudgery, the oxymorons of bringing up baby, tend to break the surface when male authors have some other point to make. For all that the Renaissance educationalist Vives shamed mothers for employing nurses, when it came to consoling those who were infertile, he changed his tune: 'What joye or what pleasure can be in children?' he asks. 'Whyles they be yonge there is nothing but tediousnes'.

Likewise, the twelfth-century pamphlet written to persuade girls to aspire to be religious recluses rather than society wives was, as you might imagine, unenthusiastic about childcare. Babies wake you up at midnight, the author says, 'wanunge ant wepunge', whining and crying. You have to feed your baby 'se moni earm hwile', so many wretched times and, with its tiny stomach, 'se slaw his thiftre', so slow his thriving. Often, he writes, there'll be 'fulthen', filth, in the cradle and in your lap. Pre-modern poo explosions were a thing, clearly. Even if you shell out for a nurse, you're the one who has to worry about what she does and doesn't do. Yet, dialling down his rhetoric, he says he isn't blaming mothers for their own misery. For a moment he thinks in the first-person plural rather than the shouty second. These acts of care are what 'ure alre modres drehden on us seolven', what all of our mothers (or nurses) endure for ourselves. Messy, dull, unrelenting, sometimes wretched, and yet the making of each of our selves. That verb *drehden*, deriving from an Old English verb *dreogan*, has a spread of meanings which capture the demands of caring for a small human, part suffering and torture, part patience and stoicism.

If this anonymous writer found looking after infants mostly nightmarish, other authors found the work of caring to be something almost supernaturally marvellous. John Dod and Robert Cleaver, two Puritan preachers, co-authored a guide to virtuous conduct published in 1603. A marriage, they opine, needs love because love breeds patience with one another. To prove their point, they turned to motherly affection and in doing so described some of the demands that caring makes on you. A baby tests its mother's patience: it will often 'crie all night, and breake her sleepe, and disquiet her very much'. Despite those hallucinatory nights which break the binary of consciousness, awake-but-asleep, asleep-but-awake, 'she will not throw it out of doores, nor lay it at the further end of the house, but she useth [treats] it kindly, and will doe what she can to still [soothe] it'. Then, in this fairy story, mother and baby will in the morning 'be as good friends as ever before, and she feedeth it and tendeth it never a whit [little bit] the lesse for all the nights trouble'. If you'd no understanding of love, they write, such behaviour on the mother's part would seem inexplicable, a wonder.

Dod and Cleaver say cheerily that mothers forget 'all the nights griefes in the morning', but a decade and more on I've not deleted the memories of those *nights' griefs*. Was I coping or not coping? Perhaps *coping* doesn't have to mean serene maternal selflessness. Our modern verb *cope* comes from a medieval French verb, *couper*, which meant 'to come to blows' or 'to fight'. Its meaning enlarging a little, to *cope* soon meant to be a match for an opponent, to be able to hold your own. Somehow, holding my own, battling, I coped with nightly jousts of caring versus despairing, love against fury, tenderness fighting rage, until my sleep became my own again.

If Dod and Cleaver simply boggled at caring's amnesia, oblivious to the inner world of the exhausted mother, the more thoughtful Erasmus didn't take for granted what it took to make the stretchy bonds between carer and child. As well as textbooks for Latin learners, he penned a work that began as a jokey paradox, written while convalescing at the house of his friend Sir Thomas More in 1510. To prove that one could celebrate almost anything, Erasmus praised folly, humankind's tendencies towards foolishness, madness, even self-deception. Erasmus's book is a peculiar mix of satire, wit and strange truths. Early on, Folly, personified as a speaking figure, wonders how babies can 'supple the travaile [work] of their bringers-up and provoke the benevolence of such as tende unto them'. To *supple* means 'to make softer': how do babies soften the undeniably hard work of looking after them? The answer, she says bigheadedly, is evidence of the 'allurement of Folie', how attractive she herself is. We find irresistible those 'younge babes that we dooe kysse so, we doe colle [hug] so, we dooe cherisshe so'. Humans adore foolishness and so they adore babies' fondness and cuteness, giving them the care they need. Erasmus intuits what neuropsychology now explains: touch and gaze generate the bio-behavioural feedback loops which bond baby and carer, bodies made interdependent by the love hormone oxytocin. The gentle treatment babies need has to be *provoked* by these means, the hardness of the daily and nightly grind made supple by cuteness's soft-soaping.

Phrases like *motherly love* or *maternal affection* can be accurate descriptions of what mothers feel or do, but they can also insinuate that every mother should aspire to such selfless hands-on devotion. While Puritans like Dod and Cleaver recognised the hard work of bringing up baby, they didn't question their assumptions that mothers were particularly suited to the love and labour of child-rearing. Another Puritan divine, Thomas Taylor, said that the 'main duties of love', the work of caring for small children, are the 'special calling' of mothers. He thought that fathers should play their part on the domestic front, but 'while children be young', he said it was the 'proper employment' of their mothers 'to be about them, and among them within the house, whilst the fathers occasions for most part call him abroad'. Fathers go out while mothers stay at home.

Women's exclusion from education and the majority of public life left them handily available to care for their own and others' children. It's a 'tragic paradox' (to use the historian Eli Zaretsky's phrase) that what we value and what each of us needs – care, love, attachment, altruism – are some of the very obstacles used to barricade women into pokey housebound corners. These necessities can't be chucked out, broken up or taken to the tip. The duties of love required (though not always received) by every starter human have to be somebody's 'proper employment' if it isn't a child's parents, whether that be the past's paid or enslaved nurses or today's au pairs, childminders, nannies and nursery staff. Each of us needs the attentive care which keeps us safe, feeds and comforts us, gives us language and builds our brains.

This *proper employment* was often left to mothers and to other women who cared for children. Yet the past's vocabulary of caring and bringing up wasn't necessarily as gendered as it was in everyday life, especially when appearing in metaphorical language. Some of the earliest synonyms for *caring* and *nursing*, verbs like *bringing up*, *tending*, *cherishing* and the rare but lovely *nursle*, linked childcare to other kinds of caring. To *cherish* in medieval English meant not only to feel affectionate towards someone but also to treat them with kindness and take good care of them. When one spouse promises to *love and cherish* the other in their marriage vows, *love* is the feeling but *cherish* is the doing. *Tend* likewise is an abbreviated form of *attend* or *entend*, both verbs which mean to listen, to push the mind towards something or someone. Tending to a child or to someone who is ill, you *ex-tend* your concerns, stretching out your own thinking to work out what they need.

When I went back to my teaching job when my daughter was about one year old, I found her a place with a childminder who looked after a handful of children in her own home. The compound words *childminding* and *childminder* are inventions of the early twentieth century, but the verb *to mind* is first used in the fourteenth century, coined from the noun, the *mind*. To *mind* first means to remember (as it still does in Scottish vernacular English) or to think about something, and then to care about something. (*I don't mind*, we might say, or *do you mind?*) By the seventeenth century, you could mind shops or babies as well as thoughts and memories. When we're at work we rely on others to *mind* about what our children need. My childminder was sometimes helped by her own mother and I would often arrive at their house to find my daughter jigsawed half-asleep into the crook of a grandmotherly arm on the sofa. I was so grateful, especially on those days when I had relished every last second of being free from thinking about my toddler, that she didn't mind an unrelated infant calming herself by eavesdropping so very closely on the rhythm of her heart and breath. *Minding* and *not minding* the tending of someone else's needs proves much more important than some sentimental ideal of *mothering*.

Another Puritan conduct book, William Gouge's *Domesticall Duties* (1622), a written-up version of the popular sermons he'd given at St Ann Blackfriars church in the City of London, is scarily keen on discipline and teaching morals but also surprisingly eloquent on why such minding is vital. Children, it says, need *nourishing* in the form of food, clothes and protection, but also *nurturing*, educating and encouraging. The meanings of both these verbs, *nourish* and *nurture*, ripple out from our basic bodily needs into wider circles. *Foster* too, which is now a label for temporary state care, had these same stackable senses of feeding, looking after and educating. Metaphors which now slumber in Latin like marble knights laid out atop of tombs once made these links between the carer who cherished you as an infant and the person or place who nourished your mind. Your *alma mater*, your former school or college, is, literally, your bounteous mother. Your fellow pupils or students, *alumni* and *alumna*, are your fellow foster brothers and sisters, nurslings who were fed alongside you. Both *alma* and *alumni* derive from the Latin verb *alere*, 'to nourish'.

Nurse might also refer to a foster father or tutor, someone who nourished the mind rather than the body. In the 1410s, Margery Kempe, a middle-aged mum of fourteen children, reinvented herself as a holy woman after a series of mystical visions in which she talked intimately with Christ. We know about her because, with the help of the clerics to whom she dictated her life story, she authored the first autobiography in English. Along the way, she sought out spiritual advisers to guide her understanding of this midlife change of plan. One confessor played bad cop, testing out his suspicion that she was a sinful woman who'd found a new way to show off, but another unnamed religious recluse living in a friary in her East Anglian home town of Lynn was more encouraging. He told Margery he'd been provided by God to be 'your norych [nurse] and your comfort'. After two decades of caring for children, it was Margery's turn to be spiritually nourished.

Untethered from the messy business of milk and mushy pap, such imagery proved useful in the early history of the Christian Church. The Bible at times presented God's wisdom as motherlike and His love for humanity as parental or nourishing. Some early Church fathers made these metaphors much more particular. Clement of Alexandria, for example, imagined a God who 'nurtures us with milk flowing from Himself, the Word'. Sometimes these were mere similes, God doing such and such *just as a mother*. But God's wisdom was also called *mater nostra*, 'our mother' (so said St Augustine), reason itself being born from 'the womb or uterus of eternal wisdom' (per St Bonaventure). Christ too could be maternal, feeding Christians with milky love or nursing them with his blood through the Eucharist. Such metaphors wafted around monasteries' cloisters and across theology's dense pages until they arrived at the door of another East Anglian woman who perhaps took her name, Julian or Juliana of Norwich, from the church, St Julian's, where she lived in a small cell as a religious recluse. Margery Kempe recalls in her memoir many days sat in conversation with Julian in 1413, taking her advice about matters spiritual. After a near-death experience in 1373, Julian had had sixteen visions of Christ on the Cross. Over the next twenty years, she contemplated what she had seen and teased out mystical insights into the nature of Jesus's love, writing a book known as her *Revelations* or her *Showings*.

As earlier authors had done, Julian called God and Christ *mother*. The Benedictine nun who copied out the oldest surviving manuscript of the full version of Julian's work in the 1650s wrote *Moder* and *Moderhode* (i.e. 'motherhood') with a capital M. And Julian went further, making maternity transcendently divine, with human birthing and caring only a pale imitation of something yet more perfect. Christ is our 'very moder', she writes, our true mother, 'in whom we be endlesly borne and never shall come out of Him'. Christ is both perpetually pregnant and perpetually in labour, suffering birth-like agonies in His Crucifixion. For all her mystical hyperbole, Julian knew enough to conceptualise motherhood as something more than gushy images of nursing and loving. Having her visions aged thirty, it's possible that she'd been married and had children before becoming ill, perhaps losing her family to one of the fourteenth century's merciless waves of plague.

Julian expands motherly care into the abstract, isolating its distinctive qualities regardless of who does the caring, whether they are human or divine. Motherhood is, in its purest form, 'kinde love, wisdam, and knowing'. *Kinde love* is humanity's instincts for love and affection – so far so stereotypically maternal – but the rest of Julian's triad is more unexpected. Motherhood is wise and understanding, properties she justifies when she explains mothering's 'fair werkyng', its proper methods, as we might say today. Motherhood works best by cycles of observation and recalibration. A mother 'knowith the need of hir [her] child', knows what her child needs. Then, as the child grows, 'she chongith [changes] hir werking but not hir love', revising how but not why she cares. Caring, *motherhood* in

Julian's terms, is essentially dynamic, whether done by a parent, a teacher or two-thirds of the Holy Trinity.

I wish I had Julian's calm certainty that *mother knows best*, that *motherly intuition* or *instincts* are always wise and knowing. Phrases like these imply that knowing how to care for a child is somehow innate, part of the physical make-up of being a woman who might become a mother, but in truth it's mostly learned, the expertise which comes from repetition and close observation. Call it *carer's intuition* or *instincts* instead. Being closest at hand often gives you a good chance of being right. But sometimes – around midnight, say, clutching a coughing, red-hot child, dithering between calling the doctor and waiting till morning – I've felt like a TV guest booked in error. It might say 'mother' on the screen, but I'm not sure I have any relevant qualifications. Caring can drift from wise to foolish in every compass direction, too harsh, too uninterested, too spoiling, too anxious. It's not always *fair working*, but work-in-progress, a churn of dogma, doubt, mistakes and what seems to work, at least for now. Yet among the muddle, it has its logic.

Medieval religious writers used the rough outlines of child-care's ways of working to explain why things change, why you do things differently for different people or across different times. One noted how 'a nurisch [nurse] or a modir [mother]' isn't obliged to nurse or spoon-feed a child 'alwey and forevere'. Just as carers teach children to feed themselves, so priests should help their parishioners become independently virtuous. Another cleric wrote to advise recluses like Julian on how to avoid temptation and error in their contemplations. He warns that God tests those who've lived devoutly for many years with stronger temptations than those he sends to the newly godly. Just so the nurse or mother first milk-feeds, but then she 'withdraweth a litel and a litel the mylke and other delicacies', she gradually weans him from the milk and the mush. She changes her behaviour too, offering less of the drollery we lavish on babies and giving more firm instruction about manners and behaviour. She 'sumtyme spekith sharply, sumtyme threteneth him', sometimes tells him off or threatens him with punishment. A carer's love adapts continually as it tracks its moving target. Perhaps that's why I feel I'm often dancing on the wrong foot or one beat behind.

With such change and variety, it's no surprise that early English didn't settle on a single verb for parenting or mothering. Many actions done many times over and again require many words. Writing for midwives and mothers in the 1670s, Jane Sharp ran through the basics. You should 'shift the childs clouts often', seventeenth-century speak for changing nappies, as well as feed on demand and 'carry it often in the arms'. The heaviest lifting, I think, comes when one body soothes another to calm or rest, *lulling* or *stilling* or *soothing* or *comforting*. Trevisa's medieval encyclopaedia describes how the nurse 'hevith him [the baby] up and doun yif he squeketh and wepith', she carries him, heaves him, back and forth when he squeaks and cries. A carer is impelled to rhythm, bouncing, swaying, pacing, singing and bearing the weight of their dance partner for weeks, months, years.

Which of the two meanings of that strange biblical phrase, *a labour of love*, fits best here? Is it labour you do because you love someone or something, or is it labour you do because you love the work itself? And does love make this labour somehow easy? I don't think so. In the early 1540s, Edward Gosynhill's pamphlet *Praise of All Women* asked how any man dare criticise womankind when he's so indebted to them for care in his early life. If a man undertook 'suche labour', carrying a baby to and fro endlessly, he'd find his arms and shoulders soon failing. It's a twenty-four-hour occupation with little downtime: 'in her armes and in her lappe/Nyght and daye she must you wrappe'. And such women's work carries on overnight: 'Out of the bed her armes cast/The cradell to roke tyll they bothe ake'. She reaches over the bed's side to rock the heavy wooden cradle until her arms are sore. In the daytime, until the toddler's steady on its feet, she can neither 'rest ne sytte/But ever dandle you in sure holde', forever cuddling the baby and keeping them safe. In this one-sided poem, the division of childcare is profoundly uneven: 'Thus hathe the mother all the care,/All the labour'. An exaggeration, of course, but the majority of childcare, and caring for the sick and vulnerable, has for centuries been slid over to women's side of the table.

The labours of love, for whatever reason they're done, are emotional as well as physical. In medieval English, as well as meaning 'to subdue' or 'to tame', the verb *to daunt* could describe the action of soothing a child. It's not that you scare the infant into submission, but that your touch or movement or voice helps them tame their own emotions. Trevisa's medieval encyclopaedia explains that a carer, just like the baby's mother, mirrors its feelings: 'right as the modir, so the norse is glad [happy] if the childe is glad and sory [sad] if the childe is sory'. A carer, if she isn't waylaid by a hundred other competing demands, must be responsive, acknowledging and commiserating by turns, connecting with touch and attention. Infants in early English are often, as in Gosynhill's *Praise of Women*, *dandled* or *daddled*, verbs meaning not just holding safely but gently bouncing or amusing in some way. Other similar nursery-rhyme words – *fondle*, *foddle*, *feddle*, *faddle* – describe roughly the same thing: a baby in your arms, playing together those ephemeral games of faces and noises. Touch was also imagined to have health-giving properties in the past. Long before the need for vitamin D was understood, nurses were advised, once babies were released from their swaddling clothes, to keep their limbs straight by supporting them to stand and walk. Jane Sharp tells her readers to 'dance it [the baby], to keep it from the Rickets and other diseases'.

Carers of babies and infants loan out their minds and bodies like this in their charges' service, dandling, fondling, responding, soothing. Our speech changes too, diverting temporarily into baby talk, the specialised way of speaking which plays a key part in how young children gain their language. Trevisa explains that, because the baby needs to learn how to talk, the nurse 'whilispith and semisouneth the wordis'. His own strange verbs seem almost babytalk themselves, meaning to mispronounce, *whilispith*, and half-say, *semi-sound*. In wealthier households, mothers might teach children to read as well as to speak. Vives, in his book on women's education, says that if a mother has the 'skyll of lernyng', she should teach her children when they're small so that they can have 'all one bothe for their mother, their nouryse [nurse] and their teacher'. Perhaps only someone who wasn't himself likely to undertake this kind of multitasking could issue such a blithe instruction that mothers be *all one both* for their children.

Mostly uncaptured by the written record, realistic accounts of juggling work and care in English's past are hard to find. Just as Vives was concerned with the education of the elite, most job descriptions for nurses (or mums) are skewed heavily towards the lives of the privileged, like those who commissioned Trevisa's English translations at the end of the fourteenth century or bought Jane Sharp's *Midwives Book* in the 1670s. Families like these had the resources to employ nurses and servants to concentrate on the work of caring. Lower down the social scale, caring for babies and small children had to be juggled with running a house and often with moneymaking activities as well. For those enslaved, conditions were far harsher and caring responsibilities yet more difficult, though this truth was undermined by wilful misrepresentation. Jennifer L. Morgan's historical research has traced how explorers' accounts of African women with elongated breasts which supposedly allowed them to breastfeed babies over their shoulders while they were working the land evolved into a stock-in-trade trope of sexism and racism.[2] Sensationalised in illustrations and rehashed across the seventeenth century, this over-the-shoulder-nursing myth supplied 'evidence' of these women's supposed 'savagery'. Such a fantasy offered the flimsiest of disguises for eighteenth-century hypocrisy which idolised the commitment to motherhood of wealthy white women while enslaved mothers carried on their labour.

At least there's a genre of role-reversal poems which imagined some of what it was like for working mothers. Depicting their subjects with stereotype's wide and easy strokes, they entertained audiences with stories of what might happen if a husband and wife switched places. One from the fifteenth century begins by describing the busy day of a smallholder's wife. As we'll see in the next chapter on women's work, she has 'meche to doo', much to do. Things are made more difficult because she has many 'smale chyldern to keep', so many kids to look after. When her husband complains that dinner isn't ready, and suggests that his work in the fields is much harder than her days at home, she goes nuclear. Some of her truth-bombs expose the medieval peasant equivalent of what sociologists call the *double day*, *double duty* or *double burden*, or the *second shift*, combining work outside (or in her case, in and around) the home with unpaid caring work dealt out unfairly. While he lies in, she gets up after a long night of disturbed sleep with a baby, only to find the place in chaos: 'Whan I lye al nyght wakyng with our cheylde,/I ryse up at morow and fynde owr howse wylde'. She has to leave her children to cry while she makes butter and cheese. There just aren't enough hours in the day. As she asks in dismay, 'How wold yow have me doo mor then I cane?' Why would you ask me to do more than I'm able? When her boorish husband proposes a role reversal to test out her claims, she agrees at once. Maddeningly, the poem stops short just here, without revealing how her day at the plough and his in the house play out.

Jumping forward two and a half centuries, we can hear the thoughts of one working woman in her own words. Mary Collier was a Sussex girl who'd moved to Hampshire, making her living doing laundry, brewing and other manual jobs. Though she'd been taught to read at home, she was sent out to work young, rather than attending school, when her mother died. One day in the 1730s, when she was in her mid-forties, she read 'The Thresher's Labour', a poem by a farm-worker called Stephen Duck. Duck's poem, while enlightening about the harsh life of a male labourer, implied that women didn't work in the fields. Collier, who knew different, took him to task, drawing on her own experience and those of the women around her in a counter-poem, 'The Woman's Labour', published in 1739. As an advert for the book stated, prospective purchasers might be enticed by 'the Novelty of a Washer-woman's turning Poetess'. Collier's poem laments working women's sleep deprivation: 'we, alas! but little sleep can have,/Because our froward [grumpy] children cry and rave'. And her poem also proves that rural women do labour outside the home, being so willing to 'get a living' that they take 'babes into the field' while they gather corn. They work less efficiently, interrupting themselves in order to check on their children: 'often unto them our course do bend,/To keep them safe'. Collier is describing women's looping around the field, but it's a suggestive metaphor too for modern choices. Up against the obstructions which make combining paid work and caring responsibilities at home difficult, we often compromise and *bend our courses*.

Given Duck's outrageous omission of women's fieldwork,

why shouldn't Collier say something equally provocative? Her poem, tarter than a bowl of lemons, suggests that men's 'mighty troubles', the concerns about which they often complain, would suddenly disappear, or at least seem insignificant, 'Were you, like us, encumber'd thus with care', if they did the bulk of the caring. In the past, such encumbrance was a potential defence against misogynists' accusations that women were always up to no good. The medieval French-Italian writer Christine de Pizan, reasoning her way out of the internalised misogyny which causes her such self-doubt at the start of her *Book of the City of Ladies*, lists some of the works of mercy – looking after the sick, helping poor people, preparing corpses for burial – and notes that these are mostly women's jobs. It seems to her 'these be the werkes of women' (as her sixteenth-century English translator has it), the works of women. The pamphleteer Gosynhill likewise asks women's detractors just who looks after you when you're sick. A woman tends and cleans you, watches over you, finds you medicine and will 'in her armes bere [carry] you to bedde'.

Women in English's past, with other choices of routes through life mostly roadblocked, generally didn't have the luxury to forget their caring responsibilities, though some were accused of doing so. The Norfolk mystic Margery Kempe and her husband lived apart after she had pledged her life to God, in order to avoid any gossip suggesting they were still having sexual relations. As an old man, her husband had a fall down some stairs at his home. When she arrived on the scene, Margery's neighbours said reproachfully that she should be hanged because 'sche myth a kept hym and dede not', she could have looked after him and didn't. Earlier in her life, Margery had refused to be encumbered by care. She'd set out on pilgrimage to Jerusalem when her oldest child was about twenty and the thirteen others, if they survived infancy, were younger. Somebody looked after them, but not her. Now her ailing husband needed tending.

As with many decisions she made, she discussed things with Christ. Jesus tells her to take her husband home and 'kepe hym'; she responds that if she does that she won't be able to 'tendyn to thee as I do now', to pay attention to God's demands. There is only so much care and attention to go round. Yet the Lord sends her home to care for her husband for the rest of his life, a job which hands her 'ful mech labowr', very much toil. Her husband becomes senile and incontinent, his clothes needing 'waschyng and wryngyng'. This domestic work 'lettyd hir', impeded her, in what she calls her *contemplation*, her spiritual meditation. Margery reluctantly moves from one kind of tending to another, from attention to caring, refracting her single devout purpose into a spectrum of distractions and concerns.

The history of our language of caring shows there need be no automatic equation between care and motherhood, and yet the work of caring remains predominantly the *werkes of women*, as Christine de Pizan noticed. This division of labour is still hard-baked into our world, trackable across all kinds of uneven statistics. Its stranglehold makes me question my own instincts. Was it my nature to nurture, or have I been nurtured to nurture? Did I willingly choose to bend my course around the field or were my choices bent by larger forces? Today, in theory, we have much more choice about how much *nursing* of whatever kind we do. Yet the extortionate costs of care for babies and infants and, when children are older, the offset between school and work hours, as well as social expectations and conventions, do a good job of typecasting who does the caring for small children.

The encumbrances of care are even greater for the sandwich generation who look after younger and older relatives at the same time, and those who are family carers for the sick or for the disabled. In the time of Covid, we applauded those who tend to the vulnerable, the sick and the elderly, understanding once again how much our society relies on care. But, despite this brief appreciation in a time of national emergency, not much has shifted. Caring has to happen and someone, more often a woman, must do it. As Gosynhill in his pamphlet in praise of women wondered in the 1540s: 'Howe shulde this worlde contynued be,/Man, I meane, in his most need,/Were nat women?' How might this world carry on, at those times when humanity is most needy, I mean, if it weren't for women? How could we continue without someone doing the caring?

Six

INDUSTRY

Working Words

—

Nowadays most job titles – *firefighter, flight attendant, police officer* – are unisex. And in theory at least, every path is open to us, no prohibitions to hinder our progress. Why even bother, then, to glance over our shoulder at how the English of past centuries handled women workers? Yet like furrows worn in the tread of a stair or finger-marks grubbed on a newel post, history's sexist patterns have left their trace in words and in practice. Stereotypes of who used to do what still scaffold our assumptions. Doctors are mistaken for nurses, bosses for secretaries. At work I seem to have graduated from occasionally being mistaken for a student ('I am here to *teach* the class,' I remember bellowing through the lodge glass at a college porter) to sometimes being assumed to be an administrator or an assistant.

Gender-free job titles haven't yet produced a gleamingly gender-neutral society wiped clean of the smears of old-school sexism. Labels still matter because they decide what counts as work, often to women's disadvantage. Though words like *work* and *labour* are all-purpose and multifunction, some kinds of work like *housework* or *care work* are often done unpaid, while others

get the gold-star badge of *gainful employment*, compensated by
pay and status. Women did a disproportionate amount of this
unpaid work in the past, as they do today. Yet though women's
work has often been downplayed, it's nonetheless there to be
found in the history of our language, if you know where to look.
Even *economics*, the social science which offhandedly categorises
unpaid caring work as 'economic inactivity' or 'unproductive'
work, takes its name, ironically enough, from the Greek word for
the knowledge and skills needed to run a household.

This splitting of work and home is, in historical terms, a
pretty recent invention. Terms like *occupation*, *employment*,
industry and *business* (in its initial sense of being busy, *busy-ness*)
first described activity itself, any of the things people might do
in a seamless mix of work and home, before these terms become
particularly associated with paid employment done outside the
home. What was once a marker of status and wealth – that the
wives and daughters of the most privileged families didn't need
to earn money – evolved into a Victorian ideal that was pushed
much further down the social scale. Victorian values urged
that women should keep house while men earned wages. Wives
were allocated the *housework* (a noun which gains its current
meaning, the ouroboros of tidying, cleaning, washing, cooking,
only in the mid-nineteenth century) or *home-making* (its first
use in 1863), while husbands were reinvented as *breadwinners*
responsible for providing financially for their families. For many
households this ideal was an irrelevant pretence: poorer women
had no choice but to keep working in the nineteenth century
and many in the middle classes found socially respectable ways
to earn a living.

Privileged women's retreat from paid work outside the home
during the Victorian and Edwardian decades was, when you take
the longer view, the exception rather than the rule. To be sure,
the centuries before 1800 weren't some now-lost golden age for

what economists call *FLFP*, female labour-force participation. Women's work has generally been lower paid and lower status, belittled as low skilled and so linguistically entangled with the day-to-day feeding and cleaning that every human life needs that it's often hard to pick out. Men have dominated the nouns, monopolising job titles and professions, while women's labour has been more often captured by verbs: doing not being, because women were less willing, or able, to claim the occupational label that went with the work that they did.

To find out how women described their own occupations and employment, historians have had to turn detective. As we'll see, if you look in the right kind of historical source, most women publicly acknowledged what they called their *industry*, *labour* or *pains-taking* (a word which was a noun before it became an adjective, *painstaking*), seeing themselves as workers and earners. Even English's everyday honorifics – the nosy-parker drop-down alternatives of *Mrs*, *Miss* or *Ms* – were, for most of their history, shaped more by employment than by marital status. While women have often been pushed to the margins of the page, their working lives can still be found within the histories of many English words.

The women whose work was first captured in the earliest English writing were those enslaved through poverty, war, as punishment or because their parents were already enslaved. Until a century or so after the Norman Conquest, people were bought and sold as property within Britain's shores, their labour extracted from them under duress. At the end of the tenth century, as England was taking a breather during its turbulent on-off relationship with Viking invaders, a scribe somewhere in the south-west of England copied out two hundred and more pages of English poetry. This anthology was probably made for a monastic community of men or women; a century after it was assembled it was given by a bishop to the monks of Exeter Cathedral. Whoever chose the poems for this book liked riddles, little lyrics which make enigmas of everyday realities. One of these riddles sings in a voice which is both an animal and then, playfully, also that of various objects. The riddle's speaker, its answer to the question 'What am I?', is an ox, first a farm animal and then various leather items made out of its hide.

In the middle of this bovine-minded lyric, you find a woman working late at night, a woman who (according to the poet) is dark-haired, drunk and doing something or other to the leathery speaker of the poem with a groping hand. She's also called a *wale*, a term which in Old English could mean both 'a foreigner' and, more particularly, a Welsh person. Because so many captured Celts were enslaved, it also became one of the words for 'a slave'. Some readers of the poem see this *wale* as a craftswoman, busy boiling and drying leather to shape it into a box or case. Some think she's just a cleaner of filthy boots and shoes, feeling her fingers towards the toe-end just as I perch my daughter's school shoe on one hand while I brush with the other. Whatever she's doing, she's hard at it late at night. The poem, written to amuse its learned audience, doesn't much care about her, smirking at her fumbling fingers. A millennium and more later, we might have questions: why is she drunk, who really does the groping in the dark in her world? The precise job description of this working woman 'feorran broht', brought from afar, is hazy, but her labour is clear in the poem's catalogue of doing-words: she bends and presses, wets, heats and polishes this leather.

Other enslaved women whose work was recorded by chance in the oldest written English were put to different jobs. In the 940s, Wynflæd, a rich widow who owned lots of land and people in south-western England, made her will, a document that survives in a later copy. She freed some of her workers but others she passed on as property to her family. Old English agent nouns often had two forms, one ending with the suffix *-estre* for female doers of particular actions and one with the suffix *-ere* for male ones. So we can tell that Wynflæd bequeathed to her granddaughter two enslaved women, one a *crencestre* and one a *semestre*. Dictionary-makers aren't quite sure what a *crankster* did, perhaps operating some moving part of a weaving loom, but a *seamster* made seams, joining fabric to construct clothing.

This feminine suffix *-estre* acknowledges some of the work women typically did in Anglo-Saxon England. Your daily bread could be made by a *bæcestre* or a *bæcere*, the feminine or masculine suffix signalling whether the baker in question was a woman or a man. If you stopped for a beer after work in pre-Conquest England, your ale might be served by a male *tæppere* or a female *tæppestre*, depending on who did the job of *tapping* your drink (that is, pouring it by means of a tap in a barrel). And, more surprisingly, there could, as the mother tongue evolved, sometimes be a default female rather than a default male. The *-estre* form, used originally only for women, was chosen to translate some Latin words for working men if they were doing one of the jobs conventionally done by women in Anglo-Saxon England. And so, as language evolved, these forms, now ending in the spelling *-ster*, were used in the medieval English spoken in the north of Britain for men doing jobs previously done by women. Up north, *tapster*, for example, became the default term for whoever fetched your drink. These once-feminine forms were used for men in other occupations too: a *webster* weaves (*webbe* being woven fabric), a *maltster* makes malt, a *combster* prepares wool, a *hewster* dyes fabric (think *hue-ster*) and a *thakster* thatches.

In the medieval English spoken in the south, these *-ster* forms remained reserved for women but eventually by the end of the Middle Ages their gendered form was forgotten too. What was once a grammatical option for signalling women who did this activity gradually became gender-neutral. You could have *she/her* tapsters, *he/him* tapsters and tapsters of indeterminate gender. Once English had got used to the idea that *tapster* was a gender-neutral word, new words were invented by speakers who needed to specify that the bar-keeper in question was a woman. A new seventeenth-century word like *tapstress* could therefore be coined by adding a French-derived feminine suffix, *-ess*, to what was now considered the gender-neutral *tapster*, creating a new word for a woman bar-keep. *Seamstress* likewise has not one but two feminine endings tautologously squished in its second syllable, both the Old English *-stere* and the French-derived *-ess*.

We're now rightly suspicious of coinages like *tapstress* or *seamstress* which mark the doer as female as if they're the eyebrow-raising exception to the default and doesn't-have-to-be-said male. Marked by suffixes which came initially from French and Latin like *-ess*, *-ress*, *-trix* or *-trice*, or by modifiers ahead of the noun like *lady*, *woman* or *she*, words and phrases like these were generally invented sporadically to mock or marvel at certain types of working women, though some were more straightforward acknowledgements of women doing particular jobs. In today's English, agent nouns ending in *-er* or *-or* like *caterer* or *surveyor*, nouns whose final syllables were once-upon-a-time grammatically masculine, are appealingly unisex. Women performers often prefer to be *actors* and *singers* not *actresses* and *songstresses*, for example. Nowadays we mostly convert the default male into the gender-neutral, for not many of us are keen to announce ourselves as a *poetess*, a *lady doctor* or a *she-boss*. I've been lucky enough to be employed as a Fellow for some of my time in Oxford, a job title which would silence even the most mansplaining new acquaintance at a conference if I dropped it into conversation. (*Fellow*, by the way, comes to English from Old Norse, and was originally gender-neutral, meaning 'companion', 'associate' and 'co-worker' – once upon a time we could all be *fellows*.)

Though we don't think much of them now, the grammatically feminine forms of agent nouns can help us find the work that women did in distant centuries. As well as jobs done by both sexes, the grammar of the earliest English shows signs that particular types of work were customarily done by women. Today a person who torques and tortures bread dough would, I guess, be a *kneader*, but in Old English there was a different, grammatically feminine, agent noun, a *dæge* or *dige*. This job title was given first to enslaved woman in wills and then to female servants who not only prepared bread but did other household work too. It's a word which reaches modern-day English hidden in the past lives of other nouns. The widow who owns the farm on which Chaucer's talking chickens, Chauntecleer and Pertelote, live in his *Nun's Priest's Tale* is described as 'a maner deye', a phrase which might stump my students. Chaucer is saying that she's a dairywoman, making cheese and butter for sale as part of her living. The same root gives us *dairy* itself, the place where the *deye* or *deie* does her work, a *deie-ery*. And that same word, *dige*, also makes up part of our word *lady*. *Hlæf-dige*, an Old English word combining *hlæf* (the forerunner of Modern English *loaf*) and *dige* ('kneader'), eventually becomes our *la-dy*. Even the fanciest lady who lunches has, at least etymologically, a working woman fossilised within her.

That *loaf-kneader* could be a synonym for 'woman' was an assumption made far back in English's prehistory. By the time the word appears in the oldest written English, the title of *hlæf-dige*, 'lady', is reserved for the female head of a household (and also for queens and heads of monasteries), someone who commands her subordinates rather than doing the jobs herself. The lucky few had already been filtered out from the less fortunate many. A guide written just after the turn of the first millennium sets out what labourers on an agricultural estate should do, what they owe to the lady or lord on whose land they live and work, and what they can expect in return each year. Enslaved women field-workers are at the bottom of the heap, given rations because, living in the worst of hovels, they didn't have enough land to sustain themselves: eight pounds of corn, one sheep or three pennies at midsummer, beans in the spring. When it comes to the more specialised and higher-status jobs, the guide specifies just one woman worker while the rest are assumed to be men. The *cys-wyrhtan*, the cheese-maker, gets perks of the job rather than basic rations, a hundred cheeses for herself and most of the buttermilk to add to whatever she produced on her smallholding.

This eleventh-century guide concerns itself with the jobs of the fields and the farmyard, so it ignores most work indoors, the place where much of women's skilled labour was done. Only the cheese-maker's expertise, and the perks it gets her, are recognised here. By the thirteenth century, more guides to agricultural management were written, this time in French, the language of the Norman conquerors whose descendants now held England's landed estates. One treatise, already confident in the cliché that women thrive on multitasking, gives extra work to the woman who runs the dairy, the Norman equivalent of the Old English *daege* or *cys-wyrhtan*. She should also look after the hens, ducks and geese, and care for pregnant animals and their litters, and winnow the corn in harvest-time, helped by another woman. The dairywoman has her butter and cheese to make, but why shouldn't she juggle a few more tasks? Even if the manor doesn't have a dairy, the guide suggests in its oddly spelled Anglo-Norman French that it's handy to employ a woman to do these tasks, 'a plus leger coust ke hom', at a much lesser cost than a man. The author, who had himself managed farms of this size, knows without even having to think about it that women's labour is cheaper and more flexible.

This self-evident truth is the gloomy backdrop to whatever cheerful story one might tell about the majority of working women in Britain's past. The historian Judith M. Bennett, in her 2007 book *History Matters*, compares the average lot of women workers around the year 1300 with their counterparts four hundred years later and finds not progress but stolid stasis. Even as Britain's economy grew and grew, patriarchy's self-sustaining hive-mind lovingly maintained the social machinery which kept women at perpetual disadvantage. Economic historians Jane Humphries and Jacob Weisdorf have tracked over six centuries the wages paid to female workers who were hired casually by the day or through annual contracts.[1] These were (in the standard tactlessness of economic categories) 'unskilled' workers, not trained in a particular specialism but able to turn their hand to many kinds of manual labour. As wages started to increase from the middle of the fourteenth century, the two lines on their graph showing the daily pay of women workers, one line for those employed day by day and one for those on annual contracts, wobble and sometimes intertwine, yet both consistently track several pennies below the daily wages of male daily-paid workers. Our French-speaking bailiff was right: women workers are cheaper. The pay of women casual workers almost caught the men's around the year 1400, when half the population had been killed by waves of the Black Death and labour was scarce, but it quickly fell back.

By looking at the language used to describe working women, Humphries and Weisdorf also flag up some surprising discoveries from their dataset. A good proportion of casual workers were listed by marital status as 'wives', suggesting that married women were not so tethered by housework and childcare as we might think. Rather, thanks to their husband's contacts, married women often gained opportunities to work. Many women did jobs that a careless historian might categorise as 'domestic' work, underselling the physical effort demanded by pre-industrial cleaning and scouring. A medieval sermon-writer chooses washing clothes as his metaphor for how best to cleanse yourself of your sins and, in passing, sets out the laundry list of labour required: the laundress first soaks the clothes or linens in alkalised water, then she 'draweth hem owte [drags them out], turneth, betes [beats], and washes hem [them], and hangeth hem up'. Other women worked on building sites and in lead mines. When a Cheshire port town built a new harbour in the 1560s, they paid daily wages to 'mayds in the craine', not, as it turns out, some grim Pornhub sub-genre but the young unmarried women who worked 'in the whele', turning a treadwheel which powered a crane lifting stone blocks. For all the talk of the weaker sex, women were out and about doing physically and mentally demanding work.

Because women were often listed according to their marital status rather than their precise occupation, researchers have had to hunt in other types of written records to find women's work. Jane Whittle and Mark Hailwood – economic historians seem to come in pairs like TV sleuths – have turned to court documents written between 1500 and 1700 from five counties in the south-west of England to find out more about what work women did.[2] Their method of detection is ingenious, finding out not the 'official story' from tax returns, parish registers and the like, but analysing the work which people said they were doing when events occurred about which they later testified in court. Women, they've discovered, were involved in every part of the economy, not only agricultural and household labour, but manufacturing, buying and selling.

This mass of data does also show patterns of occupational segregation, some jobs done predominantly by women, others more by men. Such segregation seems more a matter of custom and practice than rhyme and reason. In farming, most of the groundwork was done by men but women did most of the weeding. For jobs like sowing, harvesting and animal husbandry, men and women did them in roughly equal proportions. In textiles, one of England's big businesses in the Middle Ages and Renaissance, the split was more clear-cut. Women did much of the prep work, cleaning, combing and spinning wool, while men did much of the finishing, the dyeing, fulling and weaving. When it came to making clothes, men generally made the outer clothing and did the leatherwork, while women made undergarments and decorative accessories and trims. The entrepreneurial business of making, selling and buying food, drink and other commodities was split more evenly, though men and women tended to trade in different sorts of stuff.

Some of the rationale for these differentials in who did what job is lost in the mists of time, but much segregation was thanks to more obvious sexism. From the Middle Ages onward, women were mostly excluded from regulated trades and crafts, those of the guilds of masters and apprentices banded together into companies and protected by royal charters and warrants. Guilds were also known as *misters* or *mysteries*, a word which comes from a muddle of the Latin words for *ministry* and *mystery* (in the sense of 'secret knowledge'), with a dab of *mastery* clouding the waters as well. Though they were partly social clubs, supporting the families of members in life and praying for their souls in death, these companies were, at heart, fraternities which controlled who could do a particular craft or trade in certain items and how and where certain commodities were bought and sold. They offered like-minded men the chance to network, share knowledge and together lobby local and national government.

In many guilds, a widow could carry on her husband's business, and wives and daughters enjoyed some of the benefits of guild membership, but women couldn't just pitch up and ask to join any old company.

Some women did, exceptionally, find ways to make money from skilled work in professions whose names now seem beautiful and mysterious. In the fifteenth century, London had a thriving community of *silkwomen* and *throwsters*. Throwsters twisted silk filaments imported by Italian merchants into thread and yarn. *Silkwomen* used these threads to make ribbons, laces, hairnets, tassels and trims for sale. This was no cottage industry of women doing piecework in their odd quiet moments, but a very profitable trade in its own right. In 1455, the *silkwomen* petitioned Parliament to ban cheaper imports which were undercutting their own products, arguing that this industry funded 'many good Housholdes'. More than a thousand trainee girls and women, according to the petition, had been put to 'lernyng the same Craftes and occupation'. Yet despite their expertise and the scale of their businesses, these workers didn't or couldn't protect themselves as successfully as the craft frat boys. Silk work was never formally recognised as a city guild, and its workers thus remained more vulnerable to competition.

Though a few women earned their livelihood in lucrative and specialised industries, their preclusion from major trades and crafts meant that most women's making and selling were concentrated in less-regulated sectors with much competition and hence low wages and profits. Medieval and Renaissance English, like a crowded farmer's market, is stuffed with compound nouns in which the second element is *-wife* or *-women*. You could buy from an *apple-wife*, *egg-wife*, *oyster-wife* or *tripe-wife*. Healthy eaters might prefer to seek out a *kale-wife*. Dictionaries also list *book-women*, *herb-women*, *butter-women* and *cake-women* among a jumble sale of others. I suppose that I'm a kind of

book-woman – that compound nicely describes my ad hoc
combination of study, teaching and writing. Or, reaching back
even further, I'd like to be a *lærestre*, a term combining that Old
English feminine suffix *-estre* with *lar* (the ancestor of our word
lore), meaning 'teaching', 'learning', 'knowledge'. A *lorester* or a
lorestress would do very well as a job title.

These miscellaneous *wives* and *women* sometimes travelled
to market to sell their own home-made produce, but they also
made money by huckstering or forestalling. A *huckster*, the *-ster*
suffix preserving huckstering's history as an activity often done
by women, was a hawker or a peddler selling goods going from
place to place rather than in a fixed shop or stall. *Forestalling*
meant arriving early and buying stock from sellers before they'd
set up their stand and before the market opened to the public. If
you *forestall*, you're literally making a move before someone's set
out their wares. A stall-owner might be grateful to sell a certain
amount early in the day or to do a bulk deal at a guaranteed
price, even if it was strictly against market rules. Forestallers
and hucksters often made their skimpy profits by subdividing
what they bought into smaller quantities which the very poor
could afford. Or, like walking-pace Deliveroo, they offered the
convenience of bringing goods to you.

Women traders also bought and sold lower-quality or less
desirable products not covered by local government regulations.
Even so, other traders and local authorities often complained
about them, not only what they did but how they supposedly
behaved. *Fishwife* is shorthand today for an outspoken, sweary
woman, a nickname which derives from complaints about one
group of these hand-to-mouth entrepreneurs. In 1590, the City
of London proclaimed that the fishwives of Billingsgate, the
capital's biggest fish market, were apparently guilty 'not onely
of lewde and wicked life and behaviour themselves' but also
of enticing the young 'to sundry and wicked actions'. Popular

culture of the time represented these fishy street criers as gossipy, shouty, lewd, crude and abusive to sensitive souls, especially bookish men. Poor dears, threatened by women armed only with cheap herring and the gift of the gab. By the eighteenth century, the real or imagined speech of Billingsgate fish-sellers had a life of its own, becoming, as *Billingsgate-Rhetoric*, a nickname for slangy, exaggerated, jargon-filled talk.

Whether by time-immemorial custom or habit's mind-numbing force, through official regulation or sneering stereotype, women were usually muscled out to the edges of the working world where it was harder to make a living as the first precarious gig workers. Their job titles record something of these lives in the margins, as do the histories of words like *spinster* and *singlewomen*. Things were particularly tough for those who were single, as many women were for some or all of their lives. When you think of Shakespeare's going-on-fourteen Juliet, or Lady Margaret Beaufort giving birth to Henry VII in 1457 at thirteen, you might fear that most women in the past were child brides, but in reality the average age in the Middle Ages and Renaissance for a woman's first marriage was her mid-twenties. Before setting up home as part of a married couple, many women from poorer families were taken on as servants. In service, you were employed by someone else in return for bed, board and wages, doing whatever household, workshop or agricultural tasks you were given. Hard work, I'm sure, but service did give young people a chance to save some money and perhaps enjoy some freedom away from their family home.

The job titles of these not-yet-married young women were often compound nouns ending in *-maiden* or *-maid*. Some of these occupations – *bower-maids* and *handmaidens*, *milk-maids* and *dairymaids* – sound as if they belong in a medieval romance or a pastoral idyll, but others like *kitchen-maid*, *wash-maid* or *shop-maid* show that what these girls did was generally much more mundane. A few of these compounds survive today in names for low-pay, low-status jobs done by women: *barmaid*, *chambermaid* and *housemaid*, for example. At the bottom of the pile was the *drudge-maid*, such the woman who was paid fifteen shillings plus bed and board for six months' work in that role in 1620. Its etymology mysterious, *drudge* is a word that pops up like a mushroom at the start of the sixteenth century to describe a person, often a woman, doing menial, unappealing work. A French–English vocabulary list printed in 1530 gives *drudge* as an interchangeable synonym for 'a woman servaunt'. From *drudge* comes *drudgery*, the boring work that someone has to do to make life liveable for all of us. Sir Thomas Elyot, in his 1538 Latin–English dictionary, glosses a *drudge* as the person who 'doth in the howse all maner of vile service, as swepe or clense the house, carie wodde to the kitchen, and other like drudgery'. *Drudgery*, with its echoes of *trudge*, *sludge* and other grungy words, might do today as a more truthful name than the blandly minimalist *housework* for the jobs that need doing over and over.

Medieval women in service often switched employers at the end of a six-month or annual contract in hope of better working conditions, perhaps escaping drudgery or something worse. For a minority, the independent but more precarious life of casual work and daily wages appealed. But local authorities were suspicious of women not living under the supervision of an employer, a father or a husband, as well as those who moved around in search of higher wages. A year after the Black Death had first scythed through England's population, Edward III and his government worried about just who would bring in the harvest. Their solution was the 1349 Ordinance of Labourers which decreed that any man or woman (*homo et femina* in the Latin text) who didn't make a living through craft or trade, who wasn't already employed or who didn't have private income, could be required to work for any employer. Over the next decades, more women than men were pressed into service in this way. Women were less able to challenge officialdom and their lower wages made it harder to make ends meet in other ways.

As the Ordinance's wording spells out – no default male here – poorer women's participation in the workforce was needed and demanded by those in need of cheap labour. Women who weren't married were particularly vulnerable to such compulsions. In medieval England, unmarried working women were common enough to gain their own legal designation, giving English some early names for single career girls. At the start of the fifteenth century, judges and lawyers agreed that extra information should be added to legal documents because so many Christian names and surnames were shared. These *additions*, giving your social status or trade, would distinguish two people of the same name.[3] The legal eagles decided that the all-one-word term *singlewoman* was an appropriate label for unmarried working women. One Sibilla de la Bere, for example, is described as a 'sengilwoman' in a 1431 document. *Singlewoman* was soon joined by *spinster* as a generic term for a working single woman. A spinster was, to start with, a woman who spun wool with a spindle or a wheel, work which was not very well paid. A Renaissance farming guide warns that 'a woman cannot gette her lyvynge honestely with spynnynge on the distaffe, but it stoppeth a gap', it fills in when needed. Though spinning was often the work of poor single women, in the sixteenth century you could have married spinsters and male spinsters too.

A word's meaning often moves crab-wise, one circle in a Venn diagram encroaching on the next through some real or invented connection. *Spinster* eventually replaced *singlewoman* as the legal term for an unmarried woman thanks to the overlap between unmarried women and the poorly paid spinning work many of them did to try to keep financially afloat. *Singlewoman*, having started off as the legal term for an unmarried woman, also became something much more stigmatising, a label for a woman who earned her living selling sex. In 1598, the Tudor antiquarian John Stow published a guide to London describing its medieval buildings, landmarks and some of its history. Relying on testimony from 'ancient men' (who, dare we suggest, perhaps bought sex in Southwark's brothels before they were shut down by the government in 1546), Stow writes that 'these single women', the women working in the stews south of the Thames, were banned from church services while they lived their 'sinnefull life'. Even in death, they weren't allowed a Christian burial if they hadn't repented and been readmitted as Christians. If no repentance came, 'there was a plot of ground, called the Single womens Churchyard, appointed for them, far from the Parish Church'. One kind of disapproval segues into another: a poor single woman working for her living, not supervised by father or husband, was, in this line of thinking, not so different to a seller of sex really.

Other overlaps reveal similar assumptions about the lives of women at society's margins. Job titles for low-status workers, especially jobs done by single women within a large household – *chamberer* (a chambermaid), *lavender* (a laundry woman) and *wench* (a young female servant) – were sometimes used as synonyms or euphemisms for women who sold sex. Low-status women workers were seen as sexually available, whether by force, necessity or choice. These moralising overlaps might tell a kind of truth too. Ruth Mazo Karras, who has studied the history of prostitution in medieval England, explains that women who came to the sex trade did so 'more or less voluntarily', not trafficked or directly threatened, yet they were often 'coerced by economic necessity and lack of alternatives'.[4] As well as the poorest workers and unmarried women, the *spinsters* and *singlewomen*, Karras finds migrant women without a support network of friends and family nearby, and young female servants exploited or tricked by employers.

We know a bit about their working conditions because, in two port towns and in a borough just south of London's city walls, brothels were legal in the later Middle Ages. In a fifteenth-century list of rules to guide those who inspected and regulated the Southwark stews (as these brothels were called), there's some desire to make sure that women weren't held there against their will and to offer assistance to those who wished to leave this trade. But the guide is mostly concerned with controlling the lives of the women who worked there, their behaviour and dress, when and where they could come and go. The rule book some-times calls a woman working in the brothels a 'syngle woman' but also relies on paraphrase, describing her as 'a woman that liveth by hir body', a woman who earns her living through her body. This is the plainest of speaking in comparison with today's tight navigation between, on the one hand, words like *prostitute* or *whore* which stigmatise or moralise women who sell sex, and, on the other, phrases like *sex work* which sanitise, euphemise and overlook this trade's harm and exploitation of those at society's frayed edges.

These overlapping meanings, some based on observation and some on prejudice, let slip something of the lives of the poorest single women. At the other end of the social spectrum, many single women, in the little rituals of everyday conversation, once overlapped with married women, at least in linguistic terms. Nowadays strangers fish for the right title: are you *Miss*, *Mrs* or the sometimes reluctantly hissed *Ms*? Given that men's marital status is not up for examination like this, it's fun for me to parry the question with 'Dr, actually'. But for most of its life in English, as Dr Amy Louise Erickson has discovered, Mrs was an honorific title given to women whether they were married or not.[5] In the past, if they were thought to warrant a polite term of address, both married women and single women were called Mrs, the speeded-up, said-out-loud *missus* version of *mistress*.

Mrs could be a marker of wealth and reputation, but it could also signal that you were somebody's mistress, in the sense of giving orders to servants or junior employees. Some unmarried women from wealthier families found routes around the obstacles authorities devised to hamper women from trading independently. By the 1700s, as England's consumer economy burgeoned, single women were running shops and making fashionable new styles of clothing (an industry outside the male-dominated trade of tailoring) as well as gloves and hats. Some were teachers in girls' schools or governesses, and a very few found their way into traditionally male occupations. These women would by courtesy be a Mrs rather than a Miss, even though they remained unwed.

Miss, like Master for a boy, was the title for a young girl whose social status meant she would become Mrs, whether married or not, when she came of age. Both Miss and Master come from the same medieval pairing of *maistresse* and *maister* which give us Mrs and Mr, the juvenile versions appearing as different pronunciations of those same words. Only from the 1740s was Miss used for an adult woman of a certain social status who was unmarried. Copying a French fashion, Miss was repurposed to distinguish marriageable daughters from servants (who, if they had a certain degree of status or seniority, were also Mrs Whatnot) and from tradeswomen (who were also Mrs So-and-so whether married or not). Hence those staples of TV period dramas, *the Misses What's-their-name* in over-emphatic frocks, unmarried adult sisters joined at the hip and speaking in chorus in the pursuit of eligible bachelors. Not until the mid-nineteenth century, though, were the dominant meanings of Mrs and Miss used to reliably separate married from unmarried women. This forgotten history of Mrs, its associations of respect and business sense, makes me feel a little foolish for spending the last fifteen years avoiding my married title wherever possible.

If a single woman of a certain social standing could be a Mrs, a married woman could be a single woman, at least in limited circumstances as a legal fiction. A married woman running a business might have to choose between two now-mysterious words: was she *covert* or *sole*? In English common law, as a sixteenth-century dictionary for trainee lawyers explains, when married 'the wife is called a woman covert'. Not some secret service agent but literally a 'covered woman', a woman whose legal identity was subsumed into her husband's. A book on women and the law published in 1632 says lyrically that once married a woman is 'clouded or over-shadowed', legally eclipsed, her selfhood lost like a stream feeding into a larger river. A wife was subject to her husband's authority, her property becoming his, unable to enter into legal agreements in her own right. This stranglehold of coverture lasted long into the nineteenth century until campaigners set about dismantling it.

Yet well before Victorian reformers got going, there were workarounds. The flipside of coverture, if a practice which curtailed married women's autonomy can have a shred of silver lining, was that it was clear that single women *did* have legal independence. A married businesswoman might thus apply to be treated as if she were single for legal purposes. In London, Bristol and some other towns from the fourteenth century onwards, tradeswomen could register themselves as trading independently of their husband as a *soul marchaunt*. Sole trading had some advantages – especially if you didn't want your finances entangled with those of a feckless spouse – but also drawbacks.[6]

Sole merchants were supposed to trade without exploiting their husband's contacts, networks and protections.

Many women who ran moneymaking enterprises of their own thus decided not to register as *sola* and remained within the coverture system, finding other ways around its constraints.[7] Plenty of wives used pre-nups and post-nups and other legal instruments to keep some control over their own property in marriage. Married women could make contracts relating to household 'necessities' (which could be interpreted pretty widely) with their husband's agreement. By the eighteenth century, such agreement could be generally presumed, according to a book published in 1777 on *The Laws Respecting Women*. And, in other matters, a wife might act as her husband's agent, the person to whom he'd handed over his authority. A woman in a fifteenth-century court case said she acted 'undre [under] the commaundement, authoritie, privilege and libertie of hir [her] said husband as many other poure [poor] women doon [have done]'.

In some cities and towns where there were many merchants' households, there was a *gise* or custom which allowed wives to make valid contracts 'by the sufferaunce of their husbands in th'absence of them', that is, by permission of their husbands when they are absent. A 1607 legal dictionary says that a wife can't sign a contract without her husband's 'consent and privity [i.e. his knowledge]' or, as its author, a Cambridge law professor, tellingly qualifies, 'at the least, without his allowance and confirmation'. That *at the least* suggests a certain amount of wriggle room: was prior approval needed or would after-the-fact agreement do?

Privileged women must therefore often have made decisions and given orders while their husbands were away on business or diplomacy, at court or Parliament, on pilgrimage, crusade or military service. Sometimes this meant inventing a new word to capture their new roles. Margaret Paston, for example, a Norfolk woman who'd married into the family whose correspondence is some of the oldest surviving private letters in English, had to organise the defences of some family properties in her husband's absence. In one letter of 1465, she informed her husband, then at another location, that she'd chosen a particular manor house in which to be 'captensse', a word she'd likely invented and which her secretary didn't seem to know how to spell. Margaret was preparing to act as *captainness*, a female captain, a woman leading the defences of her property against the Duke of Suffolk who might try to take it by force in a dispute over land ownership. A covered woman, as far as legal theory was concerned, but one in charge of her own fortifications.

We needn't, then, underestimate the day-to-day decision-making powers of married women in the past. Today being a *housewife* is sometimes felt to contrast with her supposed opposite, the *working woman*. This invented rivalry annoys everyone: the woman working at home without pay or recognition and the woman working outside the home who nonetheless does the housework. But the history of *housewife* is rather different. This title originally said more about *what* a woman did than her marital status. A *hus-wif* was the female counterpart of a *hus-bond*. In the oldest English, a *bonda* or a *hus-bonda* was a man in charge of his own home rather than being in someone else's service. *Husbandry* described the skills needed to manage a household and, by extension (as many families lived on the land), the practicalities of running a small-holding or a farm. *Animal husbandry* is thus a perfectly respectable branch of agriculture rather than being something against public decency laws.

Housewifery likewise summed up the jobs women customarily did in these rural households, processing crops, preserving food, brewing ale, gardening, directing servants and looking after farmyard animals. It wasn't just a word for work we might loosely call 'domestic', but a name for the means by which a woman at the joint head of a household might earn money. Before she career-changed midlife into a medieval mystic, Margery Kempe also ran her own businesses. Alongside producing her fourteen children, she was 'one of the grettest [greatest] brewers' in her Norfolk town of Lynn. Then, after brewing ale proved tricky and not very profitable, she decided on what in her fifteenth-century autobiography she calls a 'newe huswyfré', a new housewifery. This turned out to involve a mill, two rented horses and an employee so that she could grind flour for a living. No mere cottage industry.

From enterprises like this grew the cliché of the busy woman, running a household and earning a living without so much as a flimsy office partition between the two sides of her life. It's a stereotype that many of us know all too well as we get phoned by school or nursery mid-meeting or carry on answering emails while launching traybakes at the oven. I admire, and fail to emulate, those men of my acquaintance who fortify the boundaries between work and home as doughtily as Margaret Paston, the *captainness*, defended her manor house. You can catch a glimpse of another plate-crammed-full housewife in one of the plays performed annually in medieval Wakefield. In towns and cities, guilds and fraternities funded street theatre presenting the whole of Christian history in a day, Creation to Last Judgement, with key scenes from Christ's life in the middle. The Wakefield play re-enacting the shepherds' Christmas visit to the Holy Family in the stable begins with a comic skit which blurs the boundaries between the Yorkshire countryside and Bethlehem.

In the play a local scoundrel, Mak, steals a sheep from the Nativity shepherds' flock. His wife, Gill, volunteers to hide it by pretending it's a newborn baby and that she's in labour with its twin. This ruse, she thinks, will deflect the shepherds when they come in search of their stolen property. It's a neat dramatic touch of parody: a sheep tucked up in a baby's cradle, just before the audience meets Jesus, the Lamb of God, peacefully sleeping in an animal feeding-trough. Despite her quick thinking, Mak says Gill is lazy (another cliché-to-be, this time of the idle homemaker who doesn't really *work*), but she's having none of it. 'Why, who wanders, who wakys, who commys, who gose? Who brewys, who bakys?' she asks. Who's on the go, who's up early, who heads out and comes back, who brews, who bakes? He's the troublemaker and she has to deal with the rest. Who should come, who should go, who should stay, I think to myself as my husband and I bicker and barter over every last free day in the family diary. His job takes him all over the globe while I, for now at least, trace much smaller circles in my daily routine. At least he engineers racing cars rather than steals sheep.

Housewives of the past, it seems, were notoriously busy. The sixteenth century's publishing boom included books of advice on managing farms and smallholdings. Though John Fitzherbert mainly offered tips and plans for farming husbands, he couldn't resist addressing a chapter or three of his 1523 *Boke of Husbandrie* to rural housewives. He admits that he doesn't have 'the experience' of women's 'occupations and warkes', but he can't resist a quick skate on mansplaining's thin ice: 'a littell wil I speke, what they ought to do, though I tel them nat [not] howe they shulde doo'. I feel stressed just reading sentence after sentence, paragraph after paragraph, of the jobs he thinks a housewife *ought to do*. Sort out the house, the children, the dairy-work, organise food for everyone, direct employees, do the washing, the gardening, grow flax and hemp, harvest crops, winnow corn. And, what's more, be on hand 'in time of nede to helpe her husbande to fill the mucke waine or dounge carte, drive the ploughe, to loode hey, corne, and suche other'. Women were not necessarily the frailer sex when it came to loading manure or crops onto wagons. Sensing our panic, Fitzherbert acknowledges that sometimes 'thou shalt have so many thinges to do, that thou shalt not well knowe where is best to begin', offering advice on how to order a to-do list. As another husbandry guide observes, bad weather sometimes gave farming husbands a day off 'but huswives affaires hath never none ende'. *Never none end* for the woman of the household.

The reality of women's working lives, their industry and business, pushed back against the sexist slogans favoured by sermon-givers and authors of conduct books. A husband, in this simplified view of the world, *went abroad* to earn a family's income while a wife stayed close to home, spending and saving the household resources with care. These divisions give us words and phrases like *keeping house* and *house-keeping*, the money handed over from a wage to run a household. Yet sixteenth-century writers knew that contributions to household finances didn't divide neatly into laborious earning and easy spending: 'Though husbandry semeth to bring in the gaines/Yet huswiferie labours seeme equal in paines,' says Thomas Tusser in rhyme.

It's clear too that housewives often went out and about as part of their working lives. Fitzherbert's book tells them to head to the mill with their wheat and to the market with goods to sell. Such trips gained female householders a reputation as skilled negotiators and managers of money. Another Paston family correspondent told his brother jokingly in a 1473 letter that if he could recoup a certain price for timber felled on disputed land, he 'woll seye that ye be a good huswyff', *he'll say you'll be a proper housewife*. The art of *housewifery* was something to be admired.

The same sense of effort and expertise also appears when working women, especially married women, were allowed to speak for themselves, choosing their own designations. In many official documents, women's occupations are ignored in favour of the multiple-choice marital question of maid, wife or widow.

But other courts were interested in women's job descriptions. Alexandra Shepard, Professor of History at the University of Glasgow, has analysed over three thousand witness statements made between 1550 and 1728 by women.[8] Those giving evidence had to answer questions about their creditworthiness, establishing their financial and social status and thus their credibility. They described their 'worth', what assets they had, how they maintained themselves or earned a living. From these records, Shepard finds that two-thirds of married women, when asked, said that they maintained themselves 'by my labour', 'my industry' or 'of herself', *by her own efforts*.

Marriage was thus by no means an end to a woman's working identity. The physical demands of pregnancy, childbirth, nursing and caring certainly made an impact, as did the expectation that women were responsible for the practical needs of day-to-day life. But the availability of servants and live-in employees in households even quite far down the social scale meant more hands to help with childcare and drudgery. The court statements number-crunched by Whittle and Hailwood, revealing what witnesses happened to be doing when events about which they were testifying occurred, likewise find little evidence that married women were particularly responsible for housework and childcare. Women did most of this work, but it didn't dominate their lives, and married women often delegated these tasks while they pursued other more profitable jobs. Perhaps they wouldn't have shared the guilt that some of us mothers feel nowadays, the irrational sense that time at work is time that could or should really be spent on children and homemaking.

Shepard's research also finds that women were far more likely to describe how they earned their living by verbs rather than by occupational titles. A handful might claim to be a *sewster* or a *laundress*, say, but on average six times that number would say they sewed or washed for a living. More women than men were happy to say that they switched jobs depending on what was available; many men probably did this too but in court they picked a particular job title. Wives and widows were more likely to claim an occupation than single women, marriage bringing them more rather than less chance to establish their working identity. And many widows continued or expanded their own work or took on their husband's business after his death. The historian Jane Whittle has paired up seventy-five Early Modern probate inventories (a list of a deceased person's belongings) of husbands with those of the widows who outlived them. She finds, from the clues these matched sets of belongings give, that widows ran farms, managed businesses or carried on their trade very profitably, often increasing their wealth and possessions. Yet while nearly two-thirds of men are given an occupation by the person who wrote out the inventory, only a single widow, a shopkeeper, is accorded the same.

Searching for women's work in the language of the past is like opening the many little doors and drawers of an antique cabinet or bureau. Some drawers are almost empty: women's work is under-reported or not easily sayable in certain forms of words. But behind the right doors, thanks to inventive historical research, women's past labours are there to be rediscovered. Much changed, of course, as the Industrial Revolution tore up and rewrote what the jobs advisor at my school, trilling his rs, called the *world of work*. New opportunities came but many of them demanded long hours out of the home in an office or a factory, and plenty of women, lumbered with care work and household tasks, weren't able to capitalise as easily as men and childless women. Higher up the social scale, men kept tight hold of profitable occupations for themselves and clubbed together to gatekeep certain professions. Marriage bars in some employments meant women had to choose between family and work. Middle-class women, happily or reluctantly, became the angels

and goddesses of the home, their serenity and divinity sustained
by the poorer women they employed to help them.

From this low ebb, the tide has slowly turned. Now most
women work outside the home and many of us build careers
without having to give up on marriage or a family. A *career* was
originally in French a 'racetrack', a 'gallop' and only later, metaphorically, an uninterrupted progress through life, an ascent
towards the top of your profession. Going full tilt, racing ahead,
giving full horsepower to your work and ambition is easier to
do, let's not forget, if someone else deals with the drudgery of
everyday life and looks after those family members who need
care. Many of the handicaps and hurdles that impeded women's
working lives have been thrown aside, but plenty remain to
hamper our progress, not least the scarcity and beyond-belief
expense of the childcare needed for parents to carry on their
careers. But though words can only do so much, at least it's easier
these days to name our jobs and our professions, to say what we
are, owning the nouns as well as doing the verbs.

Seven

GHYRLES AND HAGS

Words for Ages and Stages

—

In language at least, we never really escape from girlhood. Women of any age might enjoy a *girlie lunch*, a *girls' night in* or a *night out with the girls*, each of them full of *girl talk*. These phrases, even as they infantilise, capture what might be most enjoyable about time without partners or children, hours spent with friends as if we're back at school. *Girl talk* is sometimes dismissed as trivial gossip but it also contains the truths women tell each other when men aren't listening. Sometimes images of girldom are more-or-less synonymous with stereotypes of femininity, though the doubling-up of a term like *girlie girl* shows that not every girl is *girlish*. From there it's only a short hop-step to presenting girls as the opposite of whatever conventional masculinity imagines itself to be. Some phrases try to shame men and boys by telling them that they're *crying* or *throwing like a girl*, or being a *big girl's blouse* or a *girlie swot*.

Yet English also once turned to girlhood to find names for those of us who roam far beyond the boundary of behaviours supposedly 'appropriate' for women. In this chapter, along with middle-aged *old maids* and elderly *hags* and *crones*, we'll meet

medieval *damsels sauvages* and Renaissance *roaring girls* who leap
over the barriers and break free, at least for a while. These wild
girls are the ancestors of more modern figures like the *riot grrrl*,
that punky feminist growling and baring her teeth, strong, angry
and independent. *Girl power* was the 1990s slogan for a woman
being assertive, prioritising her own needs rather than pleasing
men, valuing her friends over romantic relationships. The *career
girl* is an older creation, a phrase coined in the 1930s when working women in certain professions were given the choice between
married life and their jobs. More recently we've had a whirlwind
romance with the sweetly named *girl boss*, an entrepreneur successful in business yet unthreateningly feminine.

When I was younger and conversations about puberty were
more cloak-and-dagger, girls having their first period were often
told with solemn ceremony that they were now *becoming a woman*.
A strange message for young adolescents often many years away
from other aspects of adulthood. *Nubile*, a word which now rings
as many alarm bells as a dodgy uncle at a family party, was originally a description for girls who had gone through puberty and
hence, in the centuries during which a British girl could in theory
be married at twelve, were thought ready for marriage. Girls who
are physically a good way advanced through puberty yet much
younger than the age of sexual consent are still today sometimes
called *mature*, a euphemism which blurs the sharp line society
draws by means of that fixed age of consent to protect every girl.
Slippages like this sexualise girls prematurely, the verbal equivalent of men in vans shouting at teenagers in school uniform. The
language of ages and stages, past and present, has much to tell us
about how society treats us across our life cycle.

It's funny, given its origins, that *girl* has become English's go-to
word for women of all ages. Its roots are mysterious and none

of the proposed theories for its etymology really convincing. Its spelling – do you prefer *gurle*, *gerle*, *garle* or the quirkier *ghyrle*? – took a while to settle down, as if medieval scribes weren't sure what to make of it. The first appearance of the word in the written record comes from a poem written around the year 1300 which describes a crowd of 'gurles and men' bustling in a London street, meaning a group of boys and men or, more gender-neutrally, a throng of children and adults. And, for several centuries afterwards, *girl* could mean a child of either sex. In one medieval play, the infant boys whom evil King Herod wants murdered in the Nativity story are called 'knave gerlys', male girls.

The first example we have where the word unambiguously refers to female youth doesn't come until the 1530s. Back at the start of our language, Old English had to manage with workarounds, saying, for example, a *wife child* or *maiden child*. Yet even with these paraphrases on offer, there's a deficit in vocabulary when it comes to the dividing up of women's lives. Dr Daria Izdebska's research shows that there were more Old English terms for different ages and stages in the lives of men and boys than there were for women and girls.[1] Not much of a surprise, given that most texts were written by men who defaulted to their own life experiences.

Women in English's first centuries thus had fewer words of their own and the words they did have were multitaskers. The Old English *mæg* and *mægden* (this latter word the root of *maiden*) might describe a child, a teenager, a young woman or an unmarried adult. *Meowle*, rather than being an Anglo-Saxon Catwoman prototype, could mean not only a younger, unmarried woman but also a woman or wife, as did *ides* and *fæmne*. Context was all. But this verbal flexibility didn't last for ever. When these nouns were turned into abstractions like *fæmhod* or *mægdenhad* (like the modern word *maidenhead*), they concentrated their meanings in the concept of 'virginity' rather than on the age of 'girlhood' itself. That's no surprise given that the Church was enthusiastically in favour of chastity, not just the Virgin Mary's miraculous motherhood but also the purity of religious women who chose celibate lives as nuns or recluses. Such pious girls and women were, in one way, going against the social grain, rejecting marriage and children in favour of prayer and contemplation. But the equation of *maidenhood* and *maidenhead*, of girlhood and virginity, begins to narrow the path of girlhood, starting to hedge girls in.

As well as praising the Blessed Virgin, the medieval Church was keen to tell the life stories of the superheroes who'd played their part in establishing Christianity in Britain. In these legends, male saints have a normal childhood or, if they were precociously saintly, they're shown being pious while their friends do familiar boyhood things. But (as Professor Joyce Hill points out) stories of Anglo-Saxon female saints-to-be skip over childhood and go straight to admiration of their chastity and purity.[2] Perhaps the monks who wrote these hagiographies weren't sure what girls really did to amuse themselves. When we do get glimpses of girlhood, it's only to reinforce the difference between a *good girl* (that coaxing, head-patting phrase which tells a girl she's fitting in with society's expectations of her) and the less virtuous rest.

At the end of the eleventh century, a monk named Goscelin compiled the biography of a saint who'd lived four centuries earlier. Seaxburh was an East Anglian princess who, having first married the King of Kent, became, once widowed, the head of the religious house at Ely until her death in 699. Even though she would go on to marry and have children, her piety was unmistakable in her childhood. Seaxburh (in Goscelin's Latin) was a Bible-reading child who wasn't 'lasciva' or 'garrula', not playful or talkative. Inventing details of her girlhood in efficiently circular fashion from the advice Church leaders gave about how girls destined for a life in the Church should behave, Goscelin recounts that Seaxburh didn't smile at floppy-haired boys or handsome suitors, nor, most importantly, did she 'egressa cum Dinah', go out and about like Dinah.

Of all the anecdotes the Hebrew Scriptures put at the disposal of Christian moralists, this story was one of the most consequential for girls. As recorded in Genesis Chapter 34, a man called Shechem raped Leah and Jacob's daughter Dinah. About twelve years old, Dinah had set out by herself one day to see local women, perhaps those who had dressed up for a special occasion. For Christian thinkers coming to this bit of Israelite history a-brim with motivated reasoning, Dinah's ordeal could be made into a warning. Though Shechem attacked her, it was Dinah's own 'wandering curiosity' (to quote a medieval commentator on the Bible), a doubly damning amalgam of her mental and physical adventuring, which supposedly put her in danger. In the words of a fifteenth-century poem, Dinah was to blame because she 'went owte to see thynges in veyne', she went out to explore her world for no good reason. The story also appealed to Protestant reformers like Luther and Calvin who cited it as proof that girls shouldn't venture out without their parents' permission and without a chaperone. Being curious and outgoing was dangerous, staying out of sight was safer.

These be-good-or-else threats made to girls in the past set up home inside the meanings of words like *shamefastness* and *modesty*. The Old English adjective *sceamfæst* and its noun, *sceamfæstness*, summed up the character of person who's serious, shy, humble and cautious. The *fast* part (just as we might say that something is *fixed fast*) suggests someone whose behaviours are constrained, limited by the desire to avoid shame. *Modesty* and *modest* arrive in English in the early sixteenth century, giving another word for someone reserved, restrained or self-effacingly cautious. *Shamefastness* was not, it's true, always seen solely as a feminine quality. In a fifteenth-century English translation of a sexy Italian story, a servant blushes and blanches by turns when a princess declares her love for him. The author explains that 'yong men of nature beth [are] ever shamfast'. Yet the concepts of shame and modesty were mostly put to use policing the clothing, speech and behaviour of girls and young women. As male attention swings its spotlight towards them in their teenage years, it's girls who are told to shrink back into their shells. The guide to learning French published by John Palsgrave in 1530 has, as one of its illustrative sentences, a proverb which says the quiet part out loud: 'It is good to bolden a boye in his youth and to acustome a gyrle to be shamefaste'. Boys have to be made bold and girls have to get used to being modest.

The mould which society made for stamping out replicas of *young ladies* and *good girls* was long in the construction, its unforgiving shape formed from words like *honour* and *shame*, *chastity* and *modesty*. Yet some girls, real and imagined, resisted its forceful limitations. In the Middle Ages, bookish types made lists of collective nouns of birds and animals, things like *a murder of crows* or a *shrewdness of apes*. These catalogues soon gained satirical and creative extras, witty flourishes and sparks of invention. In some lists, a group of girls or young women was said to be a *rage* or a *lure* of *maidens*. A *lure* was both the bait used to bring trained birds of prey back to their handler and also the collective noun for the raptors themselves, *a lure of falcons*. A *rage* can be a spell of madness, anger or fierceness, as it is today, but in medieval English *rage* also meant 'playfulness' or 'lustiness'.

Along with a *rage of maidens*, you could also have a *rage of colts*, young male horses high-kicking with energy. These nouns make me think of the many-legged, several-headed creatures I sometimes see on the loose: gaggles of girls cantering at speed through the shopping centre while laughing at something on their phones. Or that sleepover girl band of my daughter and her friends who keep up an unpredictable soundtrack for hours – yelps, whisperings, giggles exploding like fireworks – until, like some medieval falconer, I shush them up for the night. Not every girl fits these archetypes, I know. Some of us are more like the Church Fathers' description of the ideal childhood companion for a devout princess like Seaxburh, a girl 'serious, sombrely attired and with the hue of melancholy'. Yet even these kinds of maiden might rage once in a while, albeit quietly and with a Gothic twist.

If only girls were free to fly and kick in whatever way best suits them. True freedom from stereotypes is hard to be sure of in a man-made language. Though these collective nouns are fanciful and fun, they also insinuate that girls are playful because they're frisky, ready for sex. At the same time that they were told to be chaste and demure, maidens were imagined to be particularly driven by lust. In ancient medicine and medieval morality, adolescence was a time when sexual desire grew and sometimes ran rampant. The mid-sixteenth-century 'book of secrets' written by the Dutch doctor Lemnius, read first in England in Latin and then published in an English version in 1658, theorised that, once girls no longer needed calories for the physical growth of puberty, their spare energy built up into 'venereous imaginations', what we would call sexual desire.

With their blood up, girls are thus 'easily allured to copulation' by their suitors, he continues. If their parents are slow to marry them off, says Lemnius, these young women take matters into their own hands and elope with their lovers. Renaissance writer Robert Burton, in his rambling, really-needs-an-editor book about depression that sprawled in its sixth edition to half a million words, rehashed this theory in a section on lovesick-ness and uncontrollable desires. He slavers that girls of fourteen and older 'do offer themselves' to men and 'some plainly rage', some undoubtedly flirt and frolic and run riot. In your dreams, dear Robert.

Such thinking partly explains the not-at-all-shamefast young women you can sometimes find in the pages of medieval romances. In these stories, girls are lovesick and eager while young men are unexpectedly hesitant and cautious. A princess called Rymenhild, in a tale written in the thirteenth century, falls madly in love with a foundling, a young man with the uncompromising name of Horn. She summons him to her bed-room and makes the first move. Embracing him, she kisses him 'so wel so hire luste', just as she liked. She offers to wed him on the spot, but Horn knows he'll need to become a knight to stand a chance of marrying into royalty.

Girls and young women in these romances are by no means just helpless damsels in distress in need of rescue by a knight. Borrowed into English from French, damsel was a word for the posher kind of unmarried women. Some damsels do turn up at Camelot in a state, demanding that King Arthur's Knights of the Round Table make good on the oath they've made to help women in need. But there are other damsels who are venge-ful or spiteful or who wield magic spells or weave deception. In the ultimate fanboy's account of the Arthurian universe, Sir Thomas Malory's Morte Darthur written in the 1480s, Sir Gawain's little brother Gareth has the quest that earns him his knighthood micromanaged by a woman named Lynet. She's a damsel sauvage, a wild, undomesticated maiden who commands, instructs, humiliates and harangues. In the past's fantasy fiction, some girls and young women freewheeled and roamed, seemingly unaware that they were supposed to be meekly still and quiet.

To be a girl in English's past was to wade unsteadily in these cross-currents, the forceful flow of what moralists thought you should be and the eddies of frothy escapism. Girls were paradoxically everything at once. And so, once established as a word for younger females at the start of the sixteenth century, *girl*'s missing etymology was retrospectively invented along various sexist lines. Rather than admitting their own ignorance about its mysterious origins, dictionary-makers suggested that *girl* might have been derived from the Latin word *garrula* (meaning 'talkative') because girls are known for their excitable chatter. Or it might derive, so they speculated, from the Italian word for a weathervane, turning this way and that with the wind, because girls' emotions and decisions change so quickly. In reality it was society which twisted and turned on the subject of girls, its mixed messages pointing in many different directions.

In the guide to raising girls requested by Katherine of Aragon, first wife of Henry VIII, Spanish academic Juan Luis Vives does recognise that young women just can't win in this culture. If you say very little, Vives writes to Renaissance girls, people think you're stupid, but if you talk a lot, they think you're 'light' (as the 1520s English translation has it), trivial or superficial. If you say silly things, they'll say you're 'dull witted'; if you say clever things 'thou shalte be called a shrewe'. A *shrew* was a disparaging name for a woman who didn't conform to the expectation that she be quiet and subordinate, as in the *Taming* of Shakespeare's Katherina. Carrying on, Vives says you can't be too reserved in case you're thought to be proud or rude. If you sit 'with demure countenaunce', with the kind of meek humility Renaissance conduct books advised for girls, 'thou arte called a dissembler', you're told you're just pretending to be good as gold in order to disguise your so-called natural tendencies towards raging and lust. You can't glance or laugh in case someone claims you're flirting with one chap or another. Vives's solution, convenient for his constrained view of girlhood, was to stay at home and avoid engaging with this impossible weathervane world.

Not everyone was listening to Vives, though. At the same time that academics and preachers prescribed how girls and young women should behave, the English language coined plenty of new names for those who didn't go along with such choking strictures. Though *tomboy* at first described a young man whose behaviour went beyond what polite society thought acceptable, it was soon used in the sixteenth century for rebel girls too. Dictionary definitions hint at how such girls might transgress: their energy, their movement, their loudness, their boldness and impudence. Sir Thomas Blount's *Glossographia*, a dictionary of tricky words published in 1656, defines a *tomboy* as 'a girl or wench that leaps up and down like as a boy'. John Kersey's 1702 *New English Dictionary* says that 'a girl, or wench that ramps up and down like a boy' might be called either a *tomboy* or a *tomrig*. Verbs like *ramping*, *romping* and *rigging*, informal and slangy words whose meanings are far from exact, described how unruly youths roamed around in public, mucking about and having fun, giddily enjoying what moralists said were vices. As many young people didn't marry until their mid-twenties, usually working in service and living away from home, their behaviour, real and imagined, was often a source of concern.

These *ramping*, *rigging* verbs had equivalent nouns which, as the decades went on, were used more for girls than boys. Joseph Scott's *New Universal Etymological English Dictionary*, published in 1755, explains that a *ramp* was a 'hoidening, frisking, jumping, rude girl' (a *hoiden* or *hoyden* was another word for a lively lass) while a *romp* was a 'rude, boisterous, awkward girl'. If girls were supposed to be silent, still and submissive, it wouldn't have taken much to be labelled impolite or overactive. As well as lists of tricky words and interesting etymologies, the book-buying public of the sixteenth and seventeenth centuries also lapped up dictionaries of slang, books of words from regional dialects and guides to the vocabulary of *canting*, the coded speech of the criminals and ne'er-do-wells. John Ray's 1691 book of rare and unusual words reported that a *harry-gaud* was a name for a 'Rigsby, a wild Girl'. A dictionary of underworld cant published in the same decade said that a *hightetity* (like the more familiar *hoity-toity*) was another name for 'a Ramp or Rude Girl'. A 1746 collection of dialect words from Lancashire glossed a *mey-harry* as a 'a robust Girl that plays with Boys'. It seems there were enough girls who flouted norms to need words to name them, or at least enough parents and preachers who wanted disapproving words for telling off bumptious, boisterous girls.

As well as *ramping* or *romping*, young people having fun during the Renaissance might also be *roaring*, hence why you might once in a while hear someone described as *roaring drunk* today. Not someone doing lion impressions in a state of intoxication, but *roaring* in another sense: lively, riotous and revelrous, like the *roaring twenties*. A *roaring boy* was a stock figure, recognisable from everyday life but also a stereotype found in plays or poems. He was a loud and aggressive young man, identifiable on stage through his exaggerated banter, famous for drinking, smoking and fighting. He delighted in every behaviour Puritan moralists criticised, so much so that you might suspect that roaring boys were conjured into being by the magic words of disapproval alone. And, if you could meet a roaring boy on stage or in a London tavern, you might, more rarely, also encounter a young woman doing the same things. The most famous of these was the real-life Mary Frith, known by her nickname Moll Cutpurse, the inspiration for the title character of a play by Middleton and Dekker called *The Roaring Girl*. Like a reality-TV star today, Moll was the talk of the town, a notorious minor celeb with a colourful life. She wore men's clothes, swore, smoked and visited pubs, up to her neck in minor crimes and dodgy dealings.

The Moll of *The Roaring Girl*, a play first staged between 1607 and 1610 and then printed in 1611 when she was around twenty-five, is a cleaned-up version of the real-world Mary, more caped crusader than underworld crook. But she still baffles expectations. A snooty, snobby conservative dad says of the play's Moll, 'It is a thing/One knows not how to name'. Ignoring society's customs turns her, in his mind, into a nameless, genderless *it*, yet at the same time, as the title of the play confirms, she's very definitely a *girl*. Professor Jennifer Higginbotham, who has studied the language of girlhood in the seventeenth century, finds that women were called *girls* precisely when they were being unruly, rebellious or unconventional.[3] To be a girl was to break the mould. And there wasn't just one kind of mutiny. *The Roaring Girl*'s prologue imagines various audience members arriving for the play, each anticipating what 'he would of a roaring girl have writ', what he'd particularly like to hear about these unconventional women. The playgoers are keen to discover 'what girl this roaring girl should be', what type she'll be, because 'of that tribe are many'.

Moll Cutpurse, it seems, wasn't a one-off but one of a crowd. According to the play's prologue, there were uptown wealthy roaring girls, as well as those who fought and stole and those who lived by selling sex. Yet as the seventeenth century went on and Puritan values were mainstreamed, this fashion for cross-dressing rebellion faded away. The image of the *ramping, romping, roaring girl* endured mostly in dictionaries, plays and stories in the words for girls who refused to meet society's expectations. Mary Wollstonecraft, in her 1792 *Vindication of the Rights of Woman*, was certain that 'a girl, whose spirits have not been damped by inactivity, or innocence tainted by false shame, will always be a romp'. What society called *romping* might just refer to the way that many girls would want to be if they weren't squashed down by ideas of modesty and shamefastness.

Though waiting to marry until their mid-twenties gave many girls and young women a spell of time in which to roar and ramp as much as they dared or were allowed, society generally assumed that a maid would eventually become a wife. Despite these expectations, around a fifth of women remained unmarried, some by choice and many because of circumstance and lack of opportunity.[4] Not every woman streamed along the pipeline from maid to wife to widow. In the later Middle Ages, as far as can be gathered from surviving records, between one-third and two-fifths of English women were either unmarried or widowed, the percentage still higher in towns where moneymaking opportunities were greater. In the sixteenth and seventeenth centuries, despite the Protestant promotion of companionate marriages and happy families, the number of women who remained single grew and grew. By the end of the Middle Ages, as we've seen, the English language had terms like *singlewomen* and *spinsters* for working women who weren't yet or would never become a wife. A century later *spinster* had become the standard legal term for all unmarried women. Blount's *Glossographia* explains it as a term of 'Law-Dialect', appended to the names of 'unmarried Women, as it were, calling them Spinners'. Blount's explanation seems puzzled that all non-married women, even the posh ones, were thus designated *spinsters*, but this belittling label has stuck fast in English.

Towards the end of the seventeenth century, public commentators became more and more worried about the fate of these unmarried women. At first, these concerns were well meant and practical: plans, for example, for communities in which single women could live and work, with education and training provided to give them skills to support themselves. Yet as Professor Amy M. Froide has discovered, unmarried women were soon blamed for their failure to make a match, characterised as disagreeable, unattractive and unlovable.[5] With new industries and trades giving some women more economic opportunities and marriage being potentially less attractive, British society quickly recalibrated its views of spinsters, meeting them not so much with concerned pushback as the sort of shoving designed to stop social change in its tracks. Singlewomen and spinsters were rechristened *old maids*, a more mocking phrase than the equivalent term for men, *bachelor*, originally a word for a man in the early stages of his career as a knight, student or tradesman.

All too aware of this name-calling, some writers argued that how unmarried women might be labelled depended on how they behaved. The clergyman Richard Allestree, a royalist rewarded for loyalty during the English Civil War with cushy jobs in academia once the monarchy was restored, found the time to pen accessible advice books on 'how to be good'. In a work called *The Ladies Calling* published in the 1670s, he set out how women could live their best lives (or, rather, their best lives according to the limited life-goals of Christian morality). One chapter offered advice for unmarried women young and old. If what he called 'superannuated virgins', a phrase not much kinder than *old maid*, behaved with the utmost 'gravity and reservedness', then, he suggested, they might just persuade society that they'd made a devout and virtuous choice to remain unmarried. Such women could hope, said Allestree, for 'at least the reverence and esteem of Matrons', to be treated with as much respect as *matrons*, a term used, as we'll soon see, for married women of a certain status. But, if single women enjoyed a social life and kicked around with younger friends, they deserved to be mocked as 'the most calamitous creature in nature'.

Some women, unsurprisingly, were spooked by the invention of this old-maid bogeywoman, frightened in case they ended up a laughing stock or a *calamitous creature*. The philosopher Mary Astell, in her bestselling, trailblazing work on female education, *A Serious Proposal to the Ladies*, which whizzed through four editions between 1694 and 1701, reported that women often panicked and married some 'idle fellow' because they were 'terrified with the dreadful name of Old Maid'. But other women weren't to be coerced by heavy-handed fear-mongering. The writer Jane Barker remained unmarried from her youth in the 1670s, when she swapped verse with other would-be poets and got her brother to teach her Latin, until her death in 1732 after a lifetime of managing her family property and looking after younger relatives. In her early twenties she wrote a poem titled 'A Virgin Life'. She hoped, so the poem said, to stay in this 'happy life', unafraid of 'being called Old Maid'. Other relationships, those of family, friends, creativity and religious faith, were as valuable to her as any marriage might have been.

With her piety and her studies, Jane Barker was the sort of spinster whom Richard Allestree thought might earn the honorary title of *matron*, even if she never married. *Matron* was used in English from the fourteenth century as a word for a married woman, usually one in middle age and with a certain amount of social status. That usage lingers on when a married woman is called a *matron of honour* rather than a *maid of honour* if she's chief bridesmaid at a wedding. It also lives on in the job title of a senior nurse, because a *matron*, in the sense of experienced capable woman, was once the sort of person who'd be put in charge of a hospital's female staff and its everyday running.

In the past, the human life cycle was divided, at least in theory, into equal-sized chunks. Writers usually defaulted to the generically male – the schoolboy, the lover, the soldier and so on – but in Thomas Tusser's mid-sixteenth-century handbook for farmers there's a rare exception: a ladies' life-course in doggerel verse. Given their sexism, it seems these lines were designed to give husbands material with which to wind up their wives. From the ages of fourteen to twenty-eight women are, according to Tusser, nothing more than their youthful beauty, admired like a precious pearl. From twenty-eight to forty-two, their beauty starts to 'swerve', to totter or give way. He's stretching for a rhyme there because he tells us next that from forty-four to fifty-six women face two extremes: 'for matrons, or drudges they serve'. In middle age, women were either matrons, taking advantage of the economic opportunity and social status that marriage might bring, or mere drudges, those poorer and often unmarried women who did menial jobs for low pay.

For Tusser, there's not much else to say, not many identities for middle-aged women to inhabit. Even now, once our girl-hood's only rhetorical, there's a dearth of words for middle-aged women and they aren't exactly celebratory. There are our job titles, of course, and the labels given to us by relationships, *parent, partner, child*. Many of us are still sorted into approximate categories: *school-run mum, career woman, housewife, working mum, wine mom* and the rest. Even our calendar age is rendered embarrassing, best avoided in polite conversation, something that shouldn't be asked about or admitted to. And other words aren't particularly kind. Adjectives like *mumsy, frumpy, dowdy* or *matronly* scorn middle-aged bodies just doing what ageing bodies do. They make it sound like we're settling into being part of the furniture, as lumpy as soft furnishings that have lost their shop-fresh bounce. In our forties, fifties and beyond, we're told we mustn't *let ourselves go*, that peculiar turn of phrase that implies that our selves are no more nor less than our youthful appearance. Keeping up with fashion and meeting beauty's standards, so this logic goes, are the way to hold true to yourself.

As I tip past the midpoint of life, my self feels to me in no danger of letting go or leaving, however slapdash my daily grooming and style choices get. In fact, my self seems more firmly fixed, more robust and less self-doubting. Many women in their midlife and beyond find themselves in this exasperating paradox. We're more confident in our expertise and experience, yet find at the same time that the public world often overlooks us, even as it admires the same qualities in older men. Once our resolve and resilience have been thickened up by all that life throws at us, bad and good, society finds us more invisible, less audible. Such dismissive treatment stings, but it has its freedoms. If the eyes looking around the room care little about me, I likewise care less and less about what they might think. Perhaps we might reclaim a little of *matronly*'s former meaning, not its signalling of marital and social status but its articulation of the respect that a woman in middle age might accrue through whatever kind of long service they've enjoyed, endured or survived.

What metaphors and words are there to give shape to this long stretch of middle life? This language of ages and stages has far too many *girls* and not enough words for the later decades of women's adult existence. In bodily terms, between the point when periods begin, the *menarche*, and when they stop, the *menopause*, we are, in doctor speak, technically living through our *menacme*, a word that sounds not so much empowering as mechanically dubious. These nineteenth-century medical terms bring with them a set of assumptions, a story arc we mightn't agree with and which our lives mightn't match. *Acme* is the ancient Greek word for the highest point of something, its fullest growth or greatest flourishing. This vocabulary insists that what matters are fertility and reproduction, that these years are our prime. They act out a long-standing metaphor which compared the life cycle of the human body, especially that of a woman, to the changing of the seasons. Puberty was a time of ripening, followed by a period of fertility and then an autumn and winter of decline. In another 'book of secrets', an early encyclopaedia which made its way, via Latin, from ninth-century Arabic to medieval English, spring is said to be like a young person about to get married, while summer is a person in their prime. Autumn is compared to a middle-aged woman feeling the cold. Winter, in portraits which are equal parts sexist and sympathetic, is 'an old woman broken with age', having lost her strength and beauty. In one version, this winter woman is 'acremet for eld', crumbled through ageing. If appearance and fertility are all that is valued in women's lives, the ageing crone becomes the epitome of physical decline.

Whether starting to crumble or still floridly flourishing, the majority of us will arrive, sooner or later, at what past speakers of English euphemistically called the *change of life* (a phrase first recorded in the 1760s) or the *turn of life* (a phrase from the 1820s). These names for the menopause imply that we might metamorphose overnight, our lives suddenly swerving down a side road too narrow for a three-point turn, too twisty to reverse back onto the highway. If we ditch these idioms, we're left with the medical terms – *perimenopausal, menopausal, post-menopausal* – which bring with them a wrong-headed hint of pressing pause on life within their syllables. While periods may splutter and end, life goes on and we're not stopping yet. Happily, as with so many other aspects of gynaecological health, the menopause is now emerging from the medical shadows. We're not so embarrassed any more to acknowledge that we've reached that stage, speaking up about problems and demanding better information, assistance and accommodations.

I hope these conversations will produce new vocabulary for this stage in life. There aren't many menopausal words to revive from the history of English. The earliest medical books mention the spread of ages at which menstruation begins and ends, but don't give much more information. The first medical study devoted to the menopause as a particular topic, addressed to fellow doctors in 1774 by John Fothergill, a Yorkshire farmer's son turned physician, had to be titled by paraphrase: 'Of the Management Proper at the Cessation of the Menses'. In fact it was the perimenopause which was described more eloquently in past centuries. A book published in 1670, full of advertorial content designed to sell the author's pills and potions, said that some women require medical help when Nature starts to drop hints that change is afoot. Women's bodies alert them to what's about to happen 'by their Courses [i.e. their periods] dodging them', by their periods becoming unpredictable, like a hunted animal evading its pursuers. By the start of the nineteenth century, this idea of an elusive menstrual Scarlet Pimpernel gave the perimenopause a now-forgotten nickname. An 1803 textbook for midwives records that the period before the menopause is 'called the dodging time by many women'. It *is* a *dodging time*, baffling in many ways, not least the question of which bodily troubles are an effect of ageing to be gracefully accepted and which other symptoms might be rebuffed by means of Hormone Replacement Therapy.

The medicine of past centuries was itself somewhat baffled by the menopause. Some experts discussed it in a low-key way. Others presented it as a source of worry and ill health.[6] A few described physical symptoms that we would recognise today. That women's bodies were innately dysfunctional was the only consistent theme, even as arguments pulled in different directions. If menstruation was the body's way of expelling toxic waste products, then women's well-being might worsen when periods ceased. But if the workings of the misbehaving womb were finally being quelled in older age, then perhaps health improved as menstruation ended. There was such disagreement that when John Fothergill wrote his 1774 essay 'Cessation of the Menses', he first hung out to dry the 'various and absurd opinions' surrounding the subject. Though older theories meant that some women were 'naturally alarmed' by the menopause's approach, he said reassuringly that there was no need to fear. He steps away from any dogmatic account of women's experiences of the menopause. Some see no 'alteration' in their health, he reports, some find their well-being improving and others encounter problems which he and his fellow physicians can treat.

Given the long tradition of disparaging women in the autumn and winter of their lives, such neutral assessments of women's ageing like Fothergill's were few and far between. One medieval training exercise for those learning the rhetoric needed to dress up letters or poems was to write in extravagant praise of youthful female beauty: the lily-white skin, the red-rose lips, the 'middel smal' as one poet describes a tiny waist. For contrast, students also imitated model descriptions of aged ugliness, which presented older women as dirty and diseased, runny and rotten. Some poets, bored with the clichés of youthful beauty and inspired by these crueller portraits, wrote verse in praise of more mature ladies. They mostly mock, but sometimes they do shift the dial just a little from disgust towards appreciation. One fifteenth-century poem compares an older woman to an overripe quince left on a tree. As her time has gone on, she's become 'a thyng that all men have forgotyn', a thing which everyone's forgotten. Exercising his poet's privilege to decide what's nice and what's nasty, he relishes how she's large and loud, her complexion multicoloured rather than uniformly pale. She's even 'bawsyn-buttockyd', badger-bottomed, whatever that means. In among the rhetorical high jinks, he calls this imagined woman

'My lovely lewde masterasse', my lovely lewd mistress. Not a flattering portrait, but there's something about his appreciative tone which I like.

Other older women invented by medieval writers were not even *jolie-laide* lovely (that elegant French way of describing unconventional beauty) but indisputably *loathly ladies*. This name for ugly older women was coined at the start of the nineteenth century when authors of historical novels raided past English for archaic, medieval-sounding words. *Loathly ladies*, like modern-day *cougars*, were often older women who pursued younger men. Once a young knight is under her control, by agreeing to marry her or by putting his fate in her hands some other way, the *loathly lady* sometimes magically transforms, revealing herself to be a pretty young woman who's been cursed to live as a hag. Here the real sorcery is the wishing well of fiction: embody your fears in another figure, all the things you don't want to be, and then magic them away at the end by turning her into something easier to deal with. But not every writer was quite so obvious. When, in *Sir Gawain and the Green Knight*, our hero arrives at a remote Peak District castle for Christmas, he sees an unnamed *loathly lady* after dinner. Apart from sneering at her saggy cheeks and her bleary eyes, Gawain and his unsuspecting readers don't think much of her. But the poet teaches us a lesson at the end of the story: watch out for the thing which everyone's forgotten, the quince left on the tree. Once Gawain has failed in small but significant ways both of the tests to which he's agreed, the *loathly lady* is revealed to be Morgan le Fay, his aunt. She's mistress-minded the affair to test King Arthur and his Round Table knights.

Medieval English does have a scatter of respectful names for the oldest women. Both men and women might be called an *auncien*, as Morgan is in *Sir Gawain*, someone who is wise and venerable thanks to their age. But, for the most part, the stigmas and slurs addressed to older women grew stronger and crueller over time. They might be labelled as *old trots*, *veckes*, *hags* or *crones*. *Crone* was in the sixteenth century used both as a farming term for an older female sheep and as an abusive name for an elderly woman. Lexicographers suggest that *crone* may derive from a French word, *careine*, the same root which gives us *carrion*. Whether ovine or human, in this way of thinking no-longer fertile females are (etymologically at least) walking corpses, mere carcasses. One of the first books to investigate the language of England before the Norman Conquest, published in 1605 by an Anglo-Dutch author called Richard Verstegan, notes that *crone* is a word for an old ewe which is 'applied in anger upon an old or elderly woman'. Verstegan points out the disparagement, but not everyone cared to be so precise. In Robert Cawdrey's 1611 *Table Alphabetical*, *crone* was glossed simply as 'an old prating [talkative] woman'.

The growth of this vocabulary suggests that English society found much to dislike about older women: their bodies, their talk, any power or influence they might have. Under this pressure, once-positive words slid downwards from neutrality into misogyny. *Beldame* was originally a polite medieval way to address an older female relative, a nurse or some other matronly woman. Like the *grand* in *grandmother*, *bel* starts off as a marker of respect. Yet a 1699 dictionary of fashionable slang said that *beldame* was a nickname for a 'scolding old woman', while the 1735 *New English Dictionary* glossed *beldame* as 'a decrepit, or ugly old woman'. In the seventeenth century, *beldame* was used both for an old woman and for a witch. These overlaps assume that age and malignity come hand in hand to women. Similarly, in the Renaissance *hag* was not only a mean nickname for an ugly old man or woman, but also, as in Shakespeare's 'secret, black, and midnight hags' in *Macbeth*, a word for a witch.

Witch itself was first used in the Middle Ages as a word for an occultist of either sex, before becoming increasingly a word for a female magic-worker. As an accusation, it could be a dangerous word for women. The notoriety of certain witchcraft investigations and prosecutions – North Berwick in 1590, Pendle in Lancashire in 1612, or Salem in New England in 1692–3, for example – makes you fear that an older woman could hardly roll her eyes in the past before she was accused of being a witch and swiftly hanged or burned. In the puritanical world of Reformation Scotland, from 1563 to 1736 four thousand people were accused and two and a half thousand executed. But those extremes aren't the whole history. In most areas of England during the nearly two centuries from 1560 to 1735 when witchcraft legislation was in force, trials were relatively rare (averaging out to one person per county every two years), authorities mostly cautious and the conviction rate on average just over 20 per cent.[7] For every witch-finding pin-pricker, there were many voices who feared that accusations of witchcraft were too lightly or maliciously made.

These days *witch* has undergone reclamation, becoming a self-appointed symbol for those of us who find ourselves labelled *difficult* or *nasty women*. There's long been suspicion that authorities found witchcraft a useful means of squashing women with authority, status or expertise. Feminist historians once argued that witch-accusers targeted midwives and women healers in particular, a narrative disproved by more recent studies. There's no evidence of any top-down cunning plan to rid the world of *cunning women* or to put midwives out of business so that male medics could benefit. In fact, *wise wives*, as they were sometimes called, might be as much appreciated as attacked. As well as being titillated by witches, Renaissance playgoers and book-buyers were fascinated by *wise men* and *wise women* who earned a living through rudimentary medicine, fortune-telling, sage advice and the sort of white magic which didn't do much harm.

Perhaps they weren't so very different to today's alternative ther-
apists and life coaches. The title character of Thomas Heywood's
play, *The Wise Woman of Hoxton*, first performed around 1604,
begins one scene cheerfully complaining about how much hard
work it is to be someone like her, 'a woman ... wiser than all
her neighbours'. A capable and insightful woman is always in
high demand.

It's true that women, and especially older women, were
over-represented among those accused of witchcraft in the
English-speaking world (though in some other countries men
were in the majority). The prejudices tangled up in witchcraft
can't easily be teased out into one single-stranded story: they're
a mass of threads which pull themselves ever tighter. In the
sexist logic of the time, women's supposed mental and physical
weaknesses made them more vulnerable to devilish interference.
Historians have found that women who deviated from gendered
expectations, those outspoken or hot-tempered, for example,
were more frequently accused. But not every accusation sought
to knock a proto-feminist off her perch. Sometimes accusations
targeted the vulnerable, a parish's impoverished and needy,
those more likely to be women. Older and poorer women often
worked as cheaply paid carers and helpers, coming and going
from different houses, and thus were easy to suspect when some
misfortune occurred. At other times accusers seem to have been
jealous of older and more comfortably off neighbours, those who
might be called *matrons*. Some persecutions came about (and
this may sound familiar in light of today's culture wars) because
different generations didn't see eye to eye on what constituted
virtuous behaviour.

When writers sceptical about the truth of witchcraft paid
attention to who was accused and who confessed, they sometimes cast a brief light on the lives of women at the margins of
society. Robert Burton, though no fan of the ageing female body

in his vast 1621 book on the causes of melancholy, described how old women who are 'poore, solitary, and live in base esteeme and beggary', despised and forgotten by society, are particularly susceptible to what we would call depression. Their lurid confessions of witchcraft come about, Burton thinks, because their elderly 'braines are crazed'. Thirty-odd years earlier, another author was even more questioning. Reginald Scott, a middle-class man from Kent with a day job as a surveyor and engineer of dams and flood defences, published a *Discoverie of Witchcraft* in 1584, a detailed sceptic's exposé showing that witchcraft just didn't exist. Those accused were innocent, he wrote, the events surrounding their prosecution explicable without any need for sorcery. He points out that they are disproportionately old women who are 'lame, blear-eyed, pale, fowle, and full of wrinckles; poor, sullen, superstitious'. Sounds like most of us after a bad week, I fear. Such women fall out with their neighbours with curses and cross words. When misfortunes then inevitably happen, they blame her or she blames herself and confesses. A witch is not necessarily wicked or wanton, but the result of society's dislike of older women and their habits.

Whether we're scapegoated as a witch, disparaged as a hag or written off as an old maid or mumsy matron, the language of ages and stages isn't often on our side. Yet some of this same vocabulary could also inch us towards equality. As eighteenth-century modernisers argued that education ought to allow many more than a select few to realise their full potential, they gave new impetus to the argument that it wasn't women's weaker minds which held them back but their useless schooling and lack of training. The writer Mary Hays, in her 1798 book *An Appeal to the Men of Great Britain in Behalf of Women*, skewered in block-capped outrage the enforced dependence and learned helplessness created by women's limited education and opportunities as nothing more than 'PERPETUAL BABYISM'. Her friend Mary Wollstonecraft likewise argued that what society valued in adult women – weakness, sensitivity and docility – was ridiculously infantilising. There was nothing very enlightened, she pointed out, about a world in which men 'try to secure the good conduct of women by attempting to keep them always in a state of childhood'. Instead she proposed that daughters as well as sons should be allowed to strengthen their minds and bodies so as to mature and develop. Some of our first steps towards equality were taken by means of these radicals' encouragement to live not as everlasting children but, once we come of age, as grown women.

Eight

FORS

Naming Male Violence

—

Now we turn to words for the traumas that are perpetrated against many women. Women are much more likely to be the target of physical or sexual violence than they are to be its perpetrators. Words like *violence* and *force* most obviously describe physical attacks and the threat of such assaults, but already by the fourteenth century, *violence* was also used to name wrongful or unjust treatment, attempts to menace or control: what we might call an abuse of power. Much of what is aimed particularly at (many) women by (some) men is exactly this kind of show of force, targeted, intrusive, imposed. Street harassers disturb the peace selectively, usually picking on younger women and teenage girls. Voyeurs force their way into privacy, while flashers (or their contemporary reboot, the senders of unsolicited dick-pics) shove their genitals into view. Gropers intrude into personal space, hands fumbling for private parts. Harassers at work impose their sexual aggression on junior employees. Stalkers force their obsession into every corner of someone else's life. Rapists *force themselves* (a euphemism that for once tells the plain truth) on the unwilling, the unconsenting. Domestic abusers use their brute force on the people closest to them.

Here I think the language of the past can help us piece together what underpins the rotten thinking of abusive men. Just as there is nothing in women's nature to determine how they should live their lives, so nothing in men's nature destines them to target women with these particular forms of violence. *Not all men*, as the saying goes, are responsible for this epidemic. Yet a minority of men *are* responsible, licensed by what our culture encourages and what it doesn't sufficiently inhibit. Some of the fixtures and fittings of Christian marriage, transmitted in evasive phrases like *conjugal debt* and *reasonable chastisement*, have provided fake justification for marital rapists and domestic abusers. And the past must undoubtedly plead guilty to the role it's played in getting what we now call *rape culture* up and running. Myths about what is and isn't rape, which still hinder the successful prosecution of rapists today, have their beginnings in the ambiguous histories of words like *ravishment* and *seduction*. Storytellers and poets since the beginnings of English have been oh-so-fond of rape stories. The wooing and pursuing of women in medieval tales of courtly love is, when push comes to grab, pestering, coercion and harassment. But it's not just us who can see how dubious the logic of courtly romance is. Some poets blurred the lines between love and abuse, but other writers in the past focused much more sharply on violence and coercion.

Once upon a time, police forces called a husband's murdering of his wife an *isolated incident* to reassure a local community that no one else was at risk, before feminists objected to the implications of this choice of words. When domestic abuse leads to two British women per week being murdered by their partners, these incidents cannot be considered random or isolated but part of a predictable pattern. So too is the prevalence of *intimate partner abuse* or *domestic violence* targeting women part of this pattern. Those phrases should be impossible oxymorons but are in reality all too familiar. They do at least reveal the paradox that the person closest to you might prove to be the most dangerous. Someone able to make it through the day without hitting their boss or strangers in the street comes home and assaults their life partner. While women (if the court records and popular culture of the past are anything to go by) were often verbally and sometimes physically abusive, the majority of the targets of spousal abuse were female and the majority of perpetrators male, then as now.

Perhaps some wife-beaters took undue licence from the twin-tracks of legal coverture and Christian marriage which handed a husband authority over his wife supposedly comparable to that of a parent over a child. As the head of the household, it was his duty to *chastise* or *correct* his wife if she (in his opinion) stepped out of line. But the degree of discipline permitted was nowhere spelled out, leaving a fertile acreage of grey areas. A husband was thus left to decide what was *reasonable chastisement*, that anodyne phrase once used to justify wife-beating and still sometimes pressed into service when a parent's right to punish their child physically is under scrutiny.

The little early medieval book which warns posh young girls away from childbirth and childcare also paints a pessimistic picture of what it might be like to end up married to an angry, violent man. The author tells his readership of privileged girls that, once an aggressive, noisy, frightening husband returns home, 'alle thine wide wanes thuncheth the to nearewe', every one of your large rooms will seem to you to be too narrow. At worst, he'll 'beateth the ant busteth the', beat you and pummel you. Not every husband, we hope, but it was enough of a reality to scaffold a recognisable stereotype and to populate the records of many court cases. In the medieval job-swap poem, where a peasant and his wife trade roles for the day, the husband is 'an angry man', quick to fly into a rage. He's always 'chydyn and brawlynge', chiding and shouting, behaving like someone 'that oftyn wyl be wrothe with ther best frend', like someone who'll often be angry with their best friend. Verbs like beat, buffet and batter leave nothing hidden in the shadows, their brute force on show.

Yet wives didn't just have to put up and shut up, and husbands could be publicly shamed. Legal records from the Middle Ages onwards show local communities stepping in to protect women, formally and informally.[1] If a husband was found to have treated his wife with what courts called *cruelty* or if he was demonstrably a threat to her life, the Church courts could order that they lived apart, *a mensa et thoro*, separate 'in bed and board' as the legal phrase went, though divorce was out of the question. And while in theory a husband's decision-making was sovereign, in practice authorities knew that women were often abused. Those with a captive audience packed in under their pulpits often reminded their congregations that husbands must exercise self-control and that *chastisement* wasn't an open invitation to wife-beating.

Most of the Puritan instruction books for household and marital harmony said that it was neither lawful nor moral to beat your wife. As Gouge's *Domesticall Duties* argues, if a husband and wife were 'two in one flesh' (the phrase which Adam says when he first meets the woman cloned from his own rib in Eden), who 'but a frantike, furious, desperat wretch will beat himselfe'. Only an idiot would beat a part of his own body. A neat bit of logic, though one which seeds the convenient idea that a wife-beater is a lunatic, chaotically incapable of any self-control, rather than a bully who ring-fences his violence for those closest to him.

Academics who offered up intellectual underpinnings for

violence against women could thus expect some criticism. The Oxford scholar William Gager spent his career writing Latin plays and poems to entertain visiting VIPs. In the summer of 1608, as an academic in his mid-fifties, he gave a public lecture during the university's end-of-term celebrations. These public talks were on provocative and contrarian topics, subjects that seemed inconsequential and amusing to Oxford's academic men. Based on responses to his speech, the text of which hasn't survived, Gager seems to have argued that it was legal, if not exactly admirable, to beat your wife. A younger academic, William Heale, swiftly wrote and published a pamphlet rejecting each and every argument which Gager might have used. Heale calls the case for lawful wife-beating 'a monster of opinion'. In sixty-odd pages, he bolts through every argument against Gager's thesis which he can find, historical, scientific, legal, moral, philosophical. 'What appearance of virtue can it be for a man to beate a woman?' he asks, whether that woman is his wife or not. Heale is adamant that violence targeted at women is neither 'valour', 'wisdom', 'justice' nor 'temperance' – it's something that 'the world hath proclaimed a shame'.

An ambitious greasy-pole climber like Samuel Pepys certainly felt ashamed when he hit his wife. Late one night, a week before Christmas in 1664, Pepys was angry with Elizabeth about some household mishap. She answered crossly and he (as his diary tells us) 'did strike her over her left eye such a blow, as the poor wretch did cry out and was in great pain'. He confessed himself 'vexed in his heart' at this, because Elizabeth soon had a blue-bruised shiner 'and the people of the house observed it'. His servants knew what he'd done but either he or Elizabeth wanted to keep her injury from public knowledge. On Christmas Day, Pepys went to church without her; on Boxing Day he excused her absence from a dinner party 'by sicknesse'. Whatever *reasonable chastisement* was, Elizabeth Pepys's black eye was something which would have been *proclaimed a shame*, in William Heale's phrasing.

Violence within marriage was acknowledged to be sexual as well as physical. During most of the history of English, being married created an ongoing, irreversible *implied consent* (a loathsome phrase) to sex. Appalling, and yet not some ancient common-law principle long since disowned. This legal opinion stayed with us, at least in theory, until it was finally overturned in Britain by the Sexual Offences Act of 2003. A husband couldn't (according to the law) rape his wife. Generally hidden from sight, marital rape thus appears in the oldest English only in the darkest hints. One medieval medical book describes what we would call *birth injuries* after labour. Women suffering from prolapses, where organs in the pelvis bulge into the vagina, often can't bear to have penetrative sex. But, says the writer, 'summe tyme they be constreyned to suffer, wyl they nyl they'. Sometimes they'll be forced to endure sex whether they want to or not. Likewise, the twelfth-century pamphlet written to put girls off getting married so that they might consider becoming religious recluses says that a wife must put up with whatever a husband wants to do in bed 'wulle ha, nulle ha', will she, nill she, whether she wants to or not. *Willy-nilly* (as that little bit of rhyming grammar becomes in Modern English), a married woman's non-consent counts for nothing.

Though prosecuting marital rape was an impossibility, the crime of rape appears indisputably in the earliest legal language. Medieval court cases about abductions and disputed wardships (that is, who had the right to control the affairs of an underage heir or heiress) which use words like *raptus* and *ravisement* have misled some to think that rape (in our modern meaning) was considered as merely a property crime in the written law's first

centuries, with fathers, husbands and guardians considered
the 'victims'. In fact, that was never true. From English's very
beginnings, the victim of rape was the woman who had been
attacked. Yet some of the first legal definitions and discussions
of rape also ushered in some of the myths that still hinder
prosecutions today. In the earliest English accounts we can see
that not all rapes were considered equal. The particular circumstances or status of the victim played a part in deciding what
had happened.

Old English did have a specific verb meaning 'to rape',
niedhæman. The verb hæman means 'to have sex' and nied
'force' or 'violence', so the two sandwiched together meant 'to
force someone to have sex'. Just as we might sometimes write
non-consensual sex (a phrase which, if you think through its
oxymoronic implications, might be quietly put aside) instead of
rape, Old English sometimes also combines verbs which mean 'to
have sex' with words which signal the use of force. These phrases
appear in the law codes formulated by Anglo-Saxon kings to set
out fines due from those who committed particular crimes and
the compensation due to their victims.

These codes are as much politics as policing, making manifest
a king's power, his aspiration to have a safe and secure realm.
In King Alfred's law code, put together in the 890s during a
quiet week when he wasn't fending off the Vikings, every level
of men's sexual harassment and violence is addressed. A man
should be punished if he gropes a nun's clothes or breast 'butan
hire leafe', without her permission. Depending on the social
status of the targeted woman, religious or not, there are similar
specific penalties for unwanted touching, for what we would
nowadays call sexual assault, and for rape itself. The compensation due is usually to be paid to the woman in question. This
might be pure theory, just easy words. Without doubt, there were
many rapists who went unpunished and many women who saw

no justice done. Yet the world view offered by Alfred's famous *domboc*, his book of laws, is one where women's safety matters.

The Normans, though they violently displaced England's ruling elite, took on many of the Anglo-Saxons' laws and models of good kingship. The first book setting out the legal customs of the royal courts, written in Latin in the 1180s, states plainly that rape is when 'a woman charges a man with violating her by force'.[2] So far, so unambiguous, but not all rape was treated the same. In another similar book from the 1230s, a more substantial guide to English common law, the 'loss of members' is punishment for the rape of a virgin. Some other severe but unspecified punishments, it said, were due to men who raped married women, widows and nuns, and also to those who raped a woman who cohabited with a man or to someone who raped a woman earning her living by selling sex. 'All of whom', says the royal justice who wrote this treatise, 'the king must protect for the preservation of his peace, though a like punishment will not be imposed for each'. This sliding-scale of differing punishment depending on the social status of the victim is appalling to our eyes, but, at least in theory, almost every woman had protection.

In practice, prosecutions for rape were rare and contained within the narrowest of parameters. The 1230s law guide runs through what a raped woman should do: ideally she must report the attack straight away to local authorities, showing the evidence of blood, injuries and torn clothing. This was the original *hue and cry* (from the Anglo-Norman law term *hu e cri*): a victim of crime had to make an outcry to local law officials to demand that their assailant be pursued. Here deep-seated expectations were seeded as to how a raped woman should behave in order to be believed. Even worse, because of the ancient medical theory that a woman's orgasm released the second 'seed' needed for conception, medieval courts were unlikely to convict a rapist if a woman became pregnant. In the thirteenth and fourteenth centuries, church courts were more interested in policing sexuality and protecting virginity than prosecuting rape. Punishments were much easier for a judge to write about than for women to rely on in everyday life.

Myths like these made prosecuting rape difficult for women, as did the muddle that language gets itself into in this semantic field. As with their equivalents in Latin and French (*raptus* and the verb *rapere* in Latin and *ravisement*, *rapir* and *raviser* in French), the English words *rape*, *ravish* and *ravishment* meant several things at once. In addition to naming the modern offence of rape (and also the physical abduction which might be needed to accomplish such a sexual assault), they could also describe the illegal removing of someone else's property or the taking away of a person who was under someone else's supervision. Wives and children were, by society's default-setting, under the control of husbands and fathers. If an orphaned heir or heiress was a minor, they would have a family member appointed guardian or, if the family held land direct from the Crown, someone would be appointed by the king. These wardships were desirable roles because they brought with them income from the estates in question as well as the chance to arrange a socially and financially advantageous marriage. They were given out as royal favours, bought and sold, and offered as collateral on financial loans. With so much at stake, matters relating to wardships often became disputed and sometimes violent. *Rape* and *ravishment* could thus refer to cases where someone had been abducted (but not sexually assaulted) against their will in order to be married. And yet confusingly those same words could also be used in cases in which someone was very happy to elope against their guardian's wishes. These overlapping meanings often muddied the waters around what was and wasn't rape.

*

Similar muddy thinking and ambiguous language can also be found in the first literary representations of male violence targeting women. English's first sexual aggressors appear in legends of saints and virtuous women, sourced from the Bible or from the history of the early Christian Church and updated thanks to the Anglo-Saxon genius for storytelling. These women, in various extraordinary ways, fend off attackers whom we might today call *predatory*. *Predatory men* is the standard phrase nowadays for those aggressors who pressure other people into sexual activity despite their unwillingness, when they don't or can't consent. It's a cliché which too easily winnows out the bad guys from the rest. It's harder to tell in practice who's predatory and who isn't. *Predatory* for us evokes images of creatures hunting, carnivores driven by uncontrollable hunger to pursue their prey. It hints that such men are more beast than human, excused by some primeval urge impossible to suppress. Definitely not the nice guys hanging out all around us. Except, given the statistics, some of the nice guys must be the very same men who predate. To my surprise, *predation* started off as something done by humans before the sense of the word was extended to animals. The Latin *praedatio* means 'to plunder' or 'to pillage', turning up without warning and taking something that doesn't belong to you. Predatory men aren't animals but thieves.

In describing their villains' intentions, the authors of these saints' legends featuring English's first predators choose verbs which mean 'to sully' or 'to defile', words which imply that something pure has been corrupted, something clean dirtied. *Defile* is just an altered spelling of the more self-explanatory *defoul*. One poem retells an Old Testament story of a woman's killing of her would-be rapist in self-defence. The poem comes to us in the same now-lightly-toasted manuscript (thanks to a fire in the eighteenth century) as the more famous epic *Beowulf*.

Beowulf the hero slays the monster Grendel with his bare hands; Judith beheads her predator, saving herself and her home town too. The Bible's Judith is an all-action widow but in this Anglo-Saxon version she's a young unmarried woman. Holofernes, a warlord, has her brought to his tent because he plans to *besmitan* her, a verb you could modernise as *be-smut*, literally meaning to 'pollute' or to 'desecrate'. The smut's all his, but words like *defile* and *besmitan* are the ground zero of victim-shaming language, expressions which cross-contaminate the blameless target of sexual violence with the dishonour and shame of her attacker. Holofernes is an Assyrian Harvey Weinstein: rich, powerful and, usefully for Judith, very drunk. She takes no chances, pressing her concealed weapon, a sword, to his neck.

As French culture dominated after the Norman Conquest and new fashions were imported from the Continent, sexual predators like Holofernes were reclothed in the new outfits of courtly love. The tradition was encouraged in part by the rediscovery of Ovid by medieval academics in the twelfth century. Ovid's verse guide on how to be a lover, *The Art of Love*, is a plentiful fountain of predatory self-justification. This handbook (in the words of Thomas Heywood's English version from the 1610s) advises young men to take kisses 'ungiven', ignoring anything a woman might do to 'resist'. Here is the germ of the myth that women are always *playing hard to get*, that their reluctance is mostly pretend, *token resistance*. Worse still, Ovid scare-quotes women's refusal and reluctance, converting it into what they supposedly want: 'They term it "force", such "force" comes welcome still,/What pleaseth them, they grant against their will.' Women call it 'force', Ovid says, but it isn't really, because they secretly desire it. A handy way for men to write off their own force and coercion. A woman's *no* to a proposition or a sexual assault can be unilaterally reinterpreted, according to Ovid's guidelines, as a *yes*. If this was the poem which got Ovid exiled to the shores of the Black Sea in 8 AD, far from Rome's high life, then good riddance to him.

Inspired by Ovid's bad advice, medieval courtly love provided a good part of the clichéd script of romantic courtship that still holds true today: a devoted lover yearning for a woman he's fallen in love with at first sight. Love was often unrequited to start with and thus a lover had to overcome obstacles through persistence. The object of a lover's affection – not a subject, or a person, but, tellingly, an *object*, a woman who could just as easily be a sculpture or a treasure-box as a person – was expected to be reluctant, her unwillingness or lack of interest interpreted as resistance to be chipped away. The *pastourelle*, a style of poem popular in France and imported into medieval England, shows what could happen to this courtly love logic in the wrong hands. In these poems, a man bumps into a woman, sometimes a shepherdess, in an isolated spot. We hear his words and thoughts as well as her replies. The male speaker *propositions* the woman or *makes a pass* at her, as those shady euphemisms from 1920s American slang might have it.

What exactly is being proposed in these countryside propositions? At best, it might be an offer of casual sex to be freely taken up or rejected. But it's often not so simple, for men in *pastourelles* sometimes don't stop asking. Things can escalate from flattery to bribery, from menace to rape. Though *sexual harassment*, unwanted sexual behaviour at work or in public, was picked out as a nameable problem by academics and campaigners in the 1970s, *to harass* has been a resonant verb in English since the early sixteenth century when it was borrowed from French. A 1611 dictionary gives a long gloss for the French source verb, *harasser*: 'to tire or toile out, to spend or weaken, wearie or weare out by overtoiling; also, to vex, disquiet, importune, harrie, hurrie, turmoile, torment'. To be a victim of harassment is, in many varied ways, to be wearied, vexed and disquieted by unwanted sexual advances.

The women in these *pastourelles* are, indisputably, harassed. In the oldest English example preserved in a manuscript from the 1330s, a man encounters a beauty in a wood. Getting ahead of him, she says not to bother with a 'henyng', an insult, an indecent proposal, we might say. Ignoring her, he offers fancy clothes and a life of luxury in exchange for sex. Though he promises to be faithful, she worries out loud that he'll love her and leave her. We hear her self-doubt: should she take her chances with this posh chap or risk a life married to some abusive oaf? These seem to be her only options: she'd have to be a shape-shifting 'wicche', a witch, she says, to escape these choices. The poem ends without a decision. Another medieval English *pastourelle* has a man disturbing a woman reading a book in a meadow. He begs to be her lover, but she resists firmly and he grows angry. As it turns out, his clothes tell her that he's a priest who ought to be celibate. Perhaps that's what gives her the confidence to tell him to get lost at the end of this particular version.

But not every man takes no for an answer. In another *pastourelle* copied down in the 1520s, a man meets a woman out riding. After a proposition and then the offer of a gold ring, he grabs her round the waist, forces her down and rapes her in a prolonged ordeal: 'Twys or thrys . . ./He wolde nott stynt yet'. Two or three times, says the poem with little sympathy for the woman in question, he wasn't done yet. Sometimes a near-miss, sometimes an assault. Like these women in their medieval meadows and glades, we don't know what a proposition might turn into, how things will play out. If we want to turn the proposer down, we quickly gamble: do we make a polite demurral, a feisty refusal, or just run for it? It's uncomfortable to be put by these poems into the mind of a predator. One speaker notes the response he provokes: 'With a cri gan sche me sey,/Sche wolde a-wrenchin awey,/but for I was so neye'. This means something like 'she saw me with a gasp: she'd have changed her route except that I was already so close'. Yet he presses on regardless. Some men feel a woman's fear and do what they will anyway.

Medieval stories and poems like this took for granted that men often sexually harassed women, not just posh-boy knights and squires but also university students and junior priests. Geoffrey Chaucer turned clerical misbehaviour like this into stories which shine a light on what's at the heart of such harassment. In the tale told by Chaucer's Miller on the road to Canterbury which ends with arseholes and nether beards, the eighteen-year-old Alison, married to a much older tradesman, is surrounded by young men who harass her. Absolon, a trainee priest, uses his job of taking holy incense around the parish as an excuse for 'many a lovely look' at married women, especially Alison. She's also pursued by their lodger, an Oxford student called Nicholas. One day, when her husband's at work, Nicholas grabs Alison 'by the queynte', by the pussy, as the forty-fifth President of the United States has taught us to say. This medieval student parrots the script of courtly romance: I'll die of unrequited love if you won't sleep with me. But at the same time he grips her 'harde by the haunchebones', tightly by her hips. If you're that fancy, she says, 'do wey youre handes', get your hands off me. Despite her initial refusal, he persists and she agrees, 'atte laste', in the end, to sleep with him. From here the story freewheels to its climax of arse-kissing. Yet it begins, unmistakably, with an example of what Victorian law-makers eventually criminalised as *indecent assault*.

When it comes to rape, that staple of medieval storytelling, Chaucer is similarly sharp-eyed. The Wife of Bath, once she's finished regaling the rest of the pilgrims with details from her many marriages, starts her own tale with a scene straight out of a *pastourelle*. A knight meets a young woman out walking and rapes her 'by verray force', which means something like 'by dint of his sheer physical strength'. There's similar bluntness in another of Chaucer's stories, his retelling of one of Ovid's legends. Tereus rapes Philomela, his wife's sister, 'by strengthe and by hise myght', by his strength and his power. Both men rape these women 'maugre hir hede', as Chaucer's medieval turn of phrase has it, meaning something like despite whatever she as an individual might think or do. Sexual violence happens *maugre our heads*, whatever we wear, wherever we go, however we behave. No matter whether we *fight* or take *flight*, *flop* or *freeze*, or what Rape Crisis's alliteration calls *friend* (that is, either to yell for help or plead with your attacker), it's never our choice or our fault. As Chaucer exclaims after narrating Tereus's rape, 'Lo, here a dede of men'. Look, he says, this is what men do. Not all men, but some of them, too many of them.

My admiration of Chaucer's keen-edged articulations of male violence is balanced by some nagging doubts. In May 1380, a woman named Cecily Chaumpaigne testified that she released Chaucer from any legal liability regarding anything 'de raptu meo', anything relating to my rape/abduction. Cecily was in her thirties, seemingly unmarried, the younger daughter of a well-to-do merchant. When medieval court documents use *raptus*, *ravisement* or *rape*, those terms with a cluster of different meanings, they usually supply extra details to allow you to work out which type of offence was at stake, but here the nature of the *raptu* was unspecified. Historians have therefore speculated about whether or not Chaucer should be cancelled for his own medieval #metoo moment. But this year more evidence has been found in the rug-sized parchment rolls and pillowy bundles of documents preserved in Britain's National Archives.[3] Six months before Chaumpaigne absolved Chaucer, they had been named as co-defendants in a legal action brought by one Thomas Staundon. Staundon accused Cecily of quitting her job as his servant without permission before the end of her contract. She had gone on to work for Chaucer, and he in turn was accused of not sending her back to Staundon when asked. Quitting service and poaching someone else's servants were both forbidden by the Statute of Labourers, introduced after the 1348 Black Death to combat rising wages caused by the lack of workers. It's therefore much less likely that Chaucer abducted Cecily or sexually assaulted her, and much more likely that her testimony was part of a legal strategy to counter Staundon's accusation. It seems to have worked, for the case was never prosecuted.

Even in the light of this new evidence, I worry that Chaucer and his words are, as we now say today, *problematic*. In some poems I teach to my students Chaucer unpicks what other writers euphemise about male sexual violence and coercion. But other works by him are unteachably rapey and misogynist, especially given that (according to a 2021 survey) 60 per cent of female students at British universities have been sexually assaulted during their time in higher education. Whoever's voice we think is speaking in another of the *Canterbury Tales*, whether you attribute it to Chaucer or his character the Reeve, the words on the page say that two Cambridge undergrads enjoyed a 'joly lyf' – we would say a good time – the night they took revenge on a miller by means of his wife and daughter. In the cold morning light of our modern day, their *good time* is one rape by deception and one rape in which a woman is asleep and can't consent. Not so jolly, it seems to my students and me.

Another medieval writer was much more clear-sighted and careful with her language. Christine de Pizan, writing in French about five years after Chaucer's death, fumed at the ideology Ovid's *Art of Love* had disseminated. It infuriated her (in the words of the 1521 English translation of her *Book of the City of Ladies*) that 'many men say that women wolde be ravysshed, and that it dyspleaseth them not, thoughe they saye the contrary with their mouthe'. Whatever women say, however much they protest, in this way of thinking, they aren't unhappy to be *ravished* and they secretly desire it. That can't be accurate, can it, asks Christine. Her inner sense of what's right and true, personified here as a wise figure who answers her questions, says that rape for women is usually a 'grete sorowe above all other'.

To prove her point, Christine and her inner voice remember the famous story of a sexual attack which shocked the inhabitants of Rome so much that they overthrew their royal family in 509 BC in favour of becoming a republic. Sextus Tarquinius, son of Rome's king, tricked his way into the bedroom of a noblewoman, Lucretia, when her husband was away. First Tarquin offered 'grete promyses, gyftes' if she'd have sex with him, all of which Lucretia refused. Then he 'menaced her' with his drawn sword, threatening death. Then, 'another grete malice', a threat to accuse her falsely of sleeping with someone else. Grimly sure that his word would be believed over hers, she 'suffred his strenghe', as the English translation of Christine's book says. To a would-be rapist, one type of *strength* is as good as another, menace, blackmail, malice or physical domination. Unable to live with what had been done to her, this 'grete outrage' as Christine calls it, Lucretia killed herself.

The word which Christine's first English translator chooses for her French verb *efforcer* is 'ravish'. This lie which many men exploit, the lie that 'femmes se veulent efforcier', becomes, in English, 'women wolde be [i.e. 'wish to be'] ravysshed'. *Ravished* might seem an odd word choice to a modern reader, but, in 1521 when her translator chose this word, it could mean 'to be raped', as well as 'to be abducted'. The notion of being physically taken away from a guardian had also led to *ravished* becoming a metaphor for being spiritually or mentally transported by some sort of strong emotion. These different senses of the same few words risk the confusion of seduction and abduction, ravishment and rape. An anonymous legal guide with the promising-sounding title of *The Lawes Resolutions of Womens Rights*, published in 1632, seems as if it might offer helpful clarifications. But the historian Helen Barker warns that *Lawes Resolution* might well be a bit of book-trade speculation, a genre hybrid combining the popularity of useful books on the law with the ever smoking-hot topic of women's status in society.[4] Its author (who might have been a lawyer called Thomas Edgar) was both entertaining and error-prone, privileging juicy rhetoric over accuracy and explanation. He does seem to separate out 'two kindes of rape', which he says are both confusingly called *ravishment* by lawyers and the public alike, but there's no guarantee that this distinction was understood by judges and juries.

One kind is 'rape by abduction', elopement against a guardian's wishes or kidnap for the purpose of forced marriage or sexual assault. The other kind he describes as 'a hideous hatefull kinde of whoredome in him which committeth it, when a woman is enforced violently to sustaine the furie of brutish concupiscence', whether she's abducted or not. This author (if not the letter of the law) is sure that the harshest punishment should be intended for a man who 'being himselfe overcome with concupiscence, overcommeth a woman hand to hand, by length of breath, and strength of his owne sinewes'. *Hideous* and *hateful* is the man who feels his own sinews strain as he overpowers his target, who knows his stamina will probably outlast the struggle of the woman he's raping and carries on regardless. The *whoredom*, one of those catch-all disapproving words for immoral or illegal sexual activity, is all *in him*. But even in his phrasing this author can't stop himself drifting towards excuses. A man who *overcomes* a woman is himself supposedly overcome by *concupiscence*, by animal desire. Easier to imagine a *brutish* half-animal, half-human monster, than accept the reality of the guy who thinks himself entitled to sex, undeterred by the law and not bothered by the consequences for the woman he targets.

A century or so later in 1716, William Hawkins, one of the fanciest barristers in the increasingly fancy world of Georgian England, published a guide to English criminal law in four plump volumes. Some of Hawkins's words about sexual violence are crisp and clear, a vast improvement on medieval and Renaissance muddles. A man rapes a woman by having sex with her 'by force and against her will'. The offence is 'not any way mitigated' if the woman 'at last yielded to the Violence, if such her Consent was forced by Fear of Death, or of Duress'. *Duress* is legal-speak for constraint or compulsion. 'Nor is it any excuse', Hawkins continues, if a woman 'consented after the Fact', or if she was a 'common strumpet', or if she became pregnant. Hawkins calls this last idea, that pregnancy signalled consent, 'very questionable', a feeblish understatement but better than nothing. His own grasp of *consent*, though, is questionable from our twenty-first-century perspective. Hawkins, while he insists that it's no excuse or mitigation, says that if a woman shuts down, as many of us would do if attacked, she has somehow *yielded*. A man's threat can produce something Hawkins calls *consent*, for want of another way to describe it. From such imprecise thinking comes the mistaken myth that the absence of protest, if a woman freezes rather than fights, means that somehow she isn't being raped.

The second edition, published in 1764, of the very authoritative-sounding *New and Complete Dictionary of the Arts and Sciences* gives exactly William Hawkins's definition of rape. But its entry for *rape* also has a second strand. It outlines 'another kind of rape, called rape of subordination or seduction'. A man who *rapes by seduction* leads astray a young unmarried woman 'either to uncleanness or marriage, and that by gentle means, provided there be a considerable disparity in the age and circumstances of the parties'. This dictionary entry is evidence of the medieval and Renaissance stereotype of the lustful woman giving way, like the sun's polarity reversing itself, to the archetype of the sexually voracious man, the *rake* or *libertine*, a perhaps older, perhaps richer man preying upon a younger, naive, inexperienced woman.

Characters like these star in some of English's first novels, seducing a woman by *gentle means*, perhaps with the help of drink or drugs, by isolating her or by dazzling her with wealth or sophistication. Sometimes men rape by brute force or menaces, but sometimes they rape by taking advantage of what this dictionary, in its decorous afternoon-tea definition, calls *considerable disparity* in social status, wealth or power. We might think of *seduction* as being on the right side of the line, a flattering, exciting pursuit. Sometimes it is. But we should be suspicious that the age-old, oft-told story of a dominant man seducing a submissive woman, the standard set-up of pornography and romantic fiction alike, establishes disparate circumstances as the very model of what's supposedly sexy. The notion of *rape by seduction* concedes that consent is contextual and power rarely in balance.

Dictionary-makers do their best to sort the different meanings of complicated words like *rape*, *ravishment* and *seduction* into separate compartments, their various senses tidily numbered and nested. But it's not always so easy to seal one from another. Some of rape culture's myths are propagated as one sense leaks from its holding pen through metaphor or association. We talk now about *rapture* or something being *rapturous* or *ravishing*, or being *rapt* (which, if you think about it, is just the past tense of the verb *to rape*, akin to *dreamt* or *slept*). Perhaps I'm worrying too much about the etymological fallacy, that mistaken idea that a word's root still determines something of its contemporary meaning. Yet though these words have headed off down separate

roads, something rather like Ovid's wilful conflation of force and
pleasure still lingers like a stink.

These legal niceties and dictionary definitions were probably
not much help to women in the sixteenth or seventeenth centuries who had been assaulted. Not many *common strumpets* (as
Hawkins calls them) could in reality successfully serve justice
on men who raped them. A woman, especially a poorer woman
living at society's margins, risked being disbelieved. Accusations
of rape might backfire: she could be treated as if she was latterly
lying about an encounter to which she had at the time consented. Women tried informal tactics, complaining to rapists'
families and their communities, sometimes gaining out-of-court
settlements. Given the harsh punishments for rape, they pursued
the lesser crime of physical assault where courts might be more
likely to convict. They sometimes coordinated their reports to
strengthen their case against a serial attacker. But legal records
don't give us easy access to first-person accounts in women's
own words. When cases came to court, women's testimonies
were cut to fit a very conventional pattern. Women's accounts of
what led up to their attack make clear the *dicktatorship* of men's
sexual aggression, the menacing threats, crude propositions and
offers of money, as well as duress and brute force. But the rapes
themselves dematerialise into formal euphemisms, oft-repeated
phrases which stand in for the trauma itself: so-and-so forced a
woman to have *carnal knowledge against her will* or so-and-so was
determined *to be naught* with a woman (*naught* means 'wicked',
'immoral', the sense from which our more lightweight modern
sense of *naughty* evolved). We have no way of reaching the first-
hand testimony of these targets of men's attacks.

As well as recording his domestic violence, Pepys's famous diary
lets us eavesdrop on the words that a predatory man might say

to himself under his breath as he tells the story of his life. Day by day, month by month, the pages of his journal record his pursuit of the wife of William Bagwell, a shipbuilder he'd met during his work with the Royal Navy. First she's a pretty woman he fancies, someone he wants to get to know better. He's not put off by her husband, her religious faith or what he calls her 'modesty'. He flirts with her and then propositions her. It's hard to know exactly how to characterise this relationship, looking outside-in and only hearing one side of the story. Over the course of six years, Mrs Bagwell, whose first name might been Elizabeth like Pepys's wife's, regularly met him, making the most of his connections in return to advance her husband's career. But, at least at the start, Mrs Bagwell didn't want to sleep with him, if Pepys's version of events is true to life. In November 1664, having gone with him 'with much ado' to a shady pub, she was 'troubled' at what Pepys wanted. Despite her 'many protestings', Pepys writes that eventually 'I did arrive at what I would', in other words he got what he wanted. Three months later in February 1665, their 'struggling' left him with 'a mighty pain in my forefinger of my left hand' the next day.

Whatever relationship came about between this man and woman of disparate circumstances, Pepys presents the sex they had as one-way traffic: 'I had my way with her', he says, 'I did what I would'. Though he wrote his diary in a shorthand system to keep its entries hidden from casual glances, he often doubles up the disguise and slides into other languages, French, Spanish and Latin, when describing his aggressive pursuit of sex with Mrs Bagwell. On paper, as Pepys sets them down, these are predatory assaults: she was *vaincue* ('defeated'), *contre sa force* ('despite her resistance'). He gets what he wants *neanmoins en fin* ('nevertheless, in the end'). Like a tourist in Paris who's forgotten half his schoolboy French, Pepys garbles that *'Je faisais* whatever *je voudrais avec* her', I did whatever I wanted with her.

Pepys places himself as the agent, the person with the force and control. Mrs Bagwell is a mere grammatical object, the less-than-fully-human *femme*.

Like the puzzle of the diary itself, hidden in code but left for posterity to find, it's hard to know what to make of Pepys's language. Sometimes he baldly states the facts of his domination, sometimes he blurs matters in multilingual paraphrase. The long afterlife of Ovid's rape myths, as well as the sometimes ambiguous meanings of words like *ravishment* or *seduction*, perhaps gave Pepys and men like him just enough of a fog in which to hide from their own self-scrutiny. But these mists have long since cleared. Women are getting louder in their demands that male violence targeted at women and girls is not only punished after the fact but stopped at its source.

We're fed up too with the extra *safety work* (as the sociologist Professor Liz Kelly has named it) of shaping our lives with this danger much in mind. Now we want society to say out loud what licenses and enables it, what lets some men blind-spot their violence and sexual aggression. William Gouge, the seventeenth-century Puritan preacher, called husbands who launch 'furious and spightfull [spiteful]' attacks on their wives 'heads too heady', heads of the household who are too headstrong. Such men, in English's past and now in its present, fuel themselves with a heady mix of (on average) greater physical strength and a culture that hands them a ready-made set of excuses for their actions. I wonder what language breaks the surface of their consciousness, which grammar frames the harms they do? The philosopher Marilyn Frye offers the image of a birdcage to explain how all forms of violence aimed at women create systemic oppression.[5] A bird might easily evade a thin wire or two, yet enough wires overlapping construct a trap which contains it in a certain space. Just so, many incidents, things major and minor, build the cage of male violence targeting women. We know all too well what it's like to live inside this birdcage. Now it's time to hear from those who build it, wire by wire. Let them find the words.

Nine

CUSTOM AND TYRANNY

Finding Feminism's Vocabulary

—

Century after century, as English went from an immigrant language to a tongue imposed and exported far around the globe, the lot of women didn't change much and demands for equality were rare. It's therefore no surprise that we've had to wait the longest time for a feminist vocabulary. Most of the terms in our toolbox have come lately and in a sudden rush. Some were coined in response to the women's rights campaigns of the nineteenth century: both *womanism* and *womanist* (two early synonyms for *feminism* and *feminist*) as well as *feminism* and *feminist* themselves. *Sexism*, initially used in the 1860s to refer to the state of being male or female, takes on its modern meaning in the first half of the twentieth century. *Misogyny* is, for most of its life in English, a rare dictionary term, more a historical curiosity than a real-world word. It doesn't seem to be much used before the poet Lord Byron (how very on-brand of him) chose it to describe his dislike of women's company in an 1823 letter. You'd thus be forgiven for thinking that medieval and Early Modern English wouldn't have a great deal to contribute to a feminist vocabulary.

Yet there was much important groundwork to undertake before equality could be demanded in law, in suffrage and political representation, at work and at home. Women and their allies had to rewrite what stood in for reality, putting the not-yet-said into words. Today we have a quick shorthand of feminist words and concepts to describe a society set up to discriminate systematically against women. But imagine trying to think your way outside of this system when every source of authority in your world approved of it. This chapter explores some of the words that unlocked this new way of thinking. After getting to grips with the meanings of *patriarchy* and *gender* then and now, this chapter investigates some of the words which presented this state of affairs as 'natural' or 'legitimate', as well as some of the terms and ideas which teased femininity apart from femaleness strand by strand. It also rediscovers the first English words used to make the argument that limiting the lives of half of the population was a socially constructed artifice rather than a justifiable social order. With these foundations in place, the first English-speaking feminists could demonstrate that men's dominion over women was an illegitimate oppression. Feminism needed such baby steps before it could take great strides towards equal rights.

Let's start with the histories of those two words, *gender* and *patriarchy*, which now expose in a flash what for so many centuries was presented as wall-to-wall actuality. In their contemporary meanings, they draw back the curtain, showing exactly how treating women as second-class citizens was made to seem natural, self-evidently the right and proper order of society. *Gender* has been in English since the Middle Ages, borrowed into medieval English from the French *gendre* or *genre* meaning both a 'kind', 'sort' or 'class' and, more specifically, the two kinds of human needed for reproduction. *Gender* also labelled the classes of nouns which 'agreed' with particular forms of adjectives, determiners, possessives and pronouns. The use of *masculine, feminine* and *neuter* as names for such classes supposedly goes all the way back to the philosopher Protagoras in fifth-century BC Greece. For many centuries, *gender* trundled along doing these linguistic jobs, needed for its grammatical meaning as well as occasionally turning up as a synonym, half-fancy, half-playful, for *sex* in the sense of male or female. It appears, for example, in a 1474 will which leaves property to a son and his heirs 'of the masculine gender'.

Jumping forwards, *gender* is now the name we give to a society's assemblage of assumptions about masculinity and femininity. *Gender* wasn't, though, used in the first set of words which coaxed this social process out into the light of day. Nineteenth-century physicians and psychologists, when outlining their often barmy and usually prejudiced theories of how a person's identity was formed, used phrases like *sex rôle* or *social-sex role* to describe the parts an individual might play, willingly or unwillingly, in life and society. These phrases arrive in English as the theories of German and French experts were translated and discussed, often with *rôle*'s circumflex still in place like a souvenir hat from a holiday. The anthropologist Margaret Mead, in her 1935 book *Sex and Temperament in Three Primitive Societies*, chose the word *rôles* to describe the different norms for men and women in three regions of Papua New Guinea which she had studied as part of her fieldwork visits.

The switch to *gender* comes about thanks to 1940s psychologists who speculated about how babies and toddlers built up their sense of who they were. In publishing their theories, they turned to the prim-proper and squeaky-clean word *gender* to push back against the Freudian model of psychosexual development in which the forming of an individual's personality, at every age from baby to adult, was driven by sexual libido. Madison Bentley, a psychologist at Cornell University, defined *gender* in 1945 as 'the socialized interpretation of certain biological differences between male and female', a gloss not so far from today's working definition. Bentley also deployed an equivalent verb to explain how, as teenagers, girls and boys were further *genderised* by the pressure to conform to society's norms of 'manly and womanly modes of dress' or 'masculine and feminine sports, tastes, demeanor, and occupation'.

In the following two decades, the concept of *gender* was extended and developed by psychiatrists who studied both the experiences of transgender people and of people with differences or variations in sexual development (these current terms replacing earlier labels such as *disorders of sexual development* and *intersex* which some people with these conditions reject). Their studies teased out how what these psychiatrists called *gender role* or *gender identity* – how you were treated by your family and by society, which social norms you adopted, your understanding of who you were – didn't automatically correspond to the anatomy with which you were born. The artist, teacher and activist Kate Millett saw these studies as proof that women's 'role and temperament, not to mention status, have, in fact, essentially cultural, rather than biological, bases', as she wrote in her bestselling book of 1970, *Sexual Politics*. Women's typical social roles and society's normative expectations about women's behaviour and personality weren't the natural consequences of female anatomy or physiology, something lodged in women's brains or deriving from their bodies, but were 'evidence of the overwhelmingly *cultural* character of gender'. Millett used the older language of psychology and anthropology, terminology like *role* and *temperament*, but also popularised the newer word *gender*.

Uncoupling *sex roles* or *gender* from the fact of being female was vital for feminist thinking. Conversations can be tricky when the word *woman* might both describe the cultural baggage loaded into our laps from the moment of our birth *and* name the category of people selected for that treatment. Writing twenty years before Millett's *Sexual Politics*, the French philosopher Simone de Beauvoir used *femme* ('woman') without an article such as *la* ('the') or *une* ('a') to mean something like 'woman as an·institution, a concept, [and] femininity as determined and defined by society, culture, history'.[1] Constance Borde and Sheila Malovany-Chevallier, making the first full translation of de Beauvoir's book *Le deuxième sexe* (*The Second Sex*) in 2011, thus translate her famous observation 'On ne naît pas femme: on le devient' as 'One is not born, but rather becomes, woman'. The fact of being female shouldn't in itself set in motion any particular destiny as to how we might be expected to think, what work we might be expected to do or what lives we might live. It's civilisation, the conventions and customs of society, which produces what she calls the creature *woman*, formed by expectations and assumptions about gender roles and norms.

The word *gender* nowadays risks complete burn-out in our contemporary English under the pressure of constant and sometimes contrary multitasking. Once *sex* started to be used in English to mean 'sexual intercourse' around 1900, many speakers wanted to avoid that word in other contexts. *Gender* has thus increasingly been used as a polite synonym for 'sex' (in the sense of the two types of human needed to reproduce our species) at the same time as it has become the shorthand term for the socially constructed expectations attributed to those same two types. It's thus become almost a contronym or Janus word, a word whose meanings have forked and are now in some senses opposite. As an adjective, *gender* is also pretty busy these days. Activists campaign to lessen the influence of *gender norms*, the cultural baggage of *gender expectations* and *gender stereotypes* allocated to girls and boys as they grow up. *Gender expression* sums up the cues of appearance and behaviour which society codes as 'masculine' or 'feminine' according to its current set of assumptions. *Gender identity* names the inner sense some people have as to how they should best be categorised within society's system of gender.

As *gender* has doubled back on itself, my feminist students often change tack and blame 'the Patriarchy' for past and present sexism. *Patriarchy* is another word which Kate Millett brought to prominence in her book *Sexual Politics*. From Greek via Latin, *patriarch* starts its life in English meaning 'the male head of a tribe' or a particular type of senior bishop. In the seventeenth century, *patriarchy* was used to describe the legal system of inheritance passing down the male line and also, more broadly, male control of families. A 1680 book written by a barrister named William Lawrence said that this was just how things were meant to be: 'Patriarchy was the first form of Government instituted in Families by God and Nature'. Lawrence, one of those who was keen to make Charles II's illegitimate Protestant son his heir rather than the king's Catholic brother, thought that such paternal authority trumped everything, even the Church's laws about marriage and legitimacy. Ironically enough, Lawrence's own paternal authority hadn't proved particularly successful. His marriage had broken up ten years earlier because of what a near-contemporary biographer called 'a discontent arising from his wife', a 'red-hair'd buxom woman' (one suspects *buxom* here has its more modern meaning of 'plump' or 'busty' rather than its original sense of 'obedient', given the mysterious *discontent*). Three hundred years later in her groundbreaking book, Kate Millett expanded *patriarchy*'s meaning to cover not just men's monopolising of the obvious levers of legal and political power, but the engineering of an entire society to guarantee that most control is in the hands of men most of the time.

*

For the majority of the history of the English language, patri-archy's social engineering was presented as the ideal state of affairs. Such ideology was tricky to overturn when the 'truth' that female equalled feminine was supposedly demonstrated by the derivations of words themselves. Long-standing expectations that girls and women should be submissive, quiet and unobtru-sive were thought to be carved deeply into language. Isidore of Seville's Dark Ages encyclopaedia said that the Latin word for 'woman', *mulier*, was derived from *mollities*, meaning 'softness'. His justification for this etymology begins plausibly enough, noting women's on-average less muscular bodies. But *mollitia* has other connotations too, those of weakness, voluptuousness, and susceptibility to external influence. Isidore concedes that it's a stretch to get from *mollities* to *mulier* – you have to change a whole letter from *o* to *u*, he admits – but it's too good a fit with sexist assumptions for him to resist. Conveniently neat, don't you think, that this one-dimensional view of women as feminine, weak-minded and oversexed was encoded in their Latin name?

Though Isidore's etymologies are long-forgotten, our gender norms still expect women to be bendy and pliable, fitting in around everyone else's needs, comforting and caring. If you don't cooperate, you risk being labelled a cold-hearted bitch. The messaging never stops: help your mother, look after your partner, be a supportive friend or colleague, *be kind*. I daren't count how many times I haven't helped myself but have given my time to someone else instead. Sifting nature from nurture feels almost impossible from inside the gender-dome in which I've grown up and lived my life. Is it really me who likes being maternal, vaguely domestic, a boon to others? How much of that would be me if I'd been left to my own devices, entirely unaware of what I ought to do according to gender's rule book? Some days I shadow my husband's every move (or lack thereof), trying to copy his knack of seeing the world mostly through his own eyes rather than anticipating what everyone else might need. I can't keep it up for long.

It's hard to escape a pattern which is presented to you as your very destiny in life and backed up by words themselves. Even the term for the very first woman's purpose in life could play its part. Eve was said to be created by God for the role of being Adam's helper. I wonder what Adam needed help with? There can't have been any housework in Eden, can there? Some fruit-picking, perhaps, but not the apples on *that* tree. Or did God mean help with reproduction, as Adam couldn't do that by himself? The first version of the Genesis story in English poetry, perhaps made as early as the eighth century, chose the word *fultum* to describe Eve's original purpose. *Fultum* in Old English does mean 'help, support, solace, comfort', but it can also mean 'military support' or 'armed reinforcements'. Maybe God thought Adam needed an army to back him up? I wish that word had caught on as women's job description: not a bit-part helper but a force of nature, an army of woman.

By the time of the medieval and Renaissance English Bibles, translators had settled on the more familiar *help* or *helper* to describe Eve's purpose in life. But in the middle of the seventeenth century, Eve gets rebranded as Adam's *helpmeet*, that sickly-sweet description used for the ideal Protestant wife and mother, a handy appliance which every Early Modern home should have. It turns out that *helpmeet* is a grammatical misunderstanding, a word which was never meant to be. *Helpmeet* is spawned by English translations of the Bible verse in Genesis Chapter 2 which say that God made Adam 'a help meet for him'. *Meet* in this sense means 'fitting' or 'suitable', i.e. she's an appropriate assistant. The phrase got sandwiched into a single word by the addition of a wayward hyphen, a *help-meet* becoming a *helpmeet*. Whatever its origins, *helpmeet* made it clear that women were supposedly intended to be ancillary, not the boss but the assistant, not centre-stage star but supporting actress. And, after Adam and Eve's disobedience in eating the apple, God said that husbands should have power over their wives by way of punishment for Eve. Women were not only helpers but subordinates.

Words like *mulier* and *helpmeet* seemed proof that women were intended for the second-class status of femininity. To be female, these words propose, is to be feminine. For most of English's history, adjectives and adverbs like *wommanish* and *mannish* (and later *womanly* and *manly*) prescribed the behaviour supposedly natural to or appropriate for the noun from which they're formed, *woman* or *man*. *Feminine* and *masculine*, borrowed into English from Latin and French in the Middle Ages, first referred to grammatical gender but then became elegant ways of saying 'female' or 'male' as well as 'womanlike' or 'manlike'. These double duties make a tight fit of sex and gender, one so neatly stacked atop the other that you might believe they're one and the same. A French book of advice written by a nobleman for his three daughters in 1371 was, like Christine de Pizan's *City of Ladies*, translated into English and printed for Tudor readers. This knight tells his girls it's in their very nature to be modest and empathetic, weepy and sensitive. If a woman flunks these expectations, 'she is mannisshe and not womanly'. By the same logic, to be fierce or bold is 'a vice in womanhode', a sign you're doing *womaning* wrong.

Yet those same words, when used for someone whose adjective doesn't match their noun – masculine women or feminine men, say – created the merest thread to pull in gender's reality-creating 'logic'. They opened up the smallest fault line, just as the thinnest ridge tells your fingers where to peel the Sellotape, though they also usually came accompanied by explanations which tried to paper over the cracks appearing in gender's rationale. One such wrinkle can be found in the shifting meanings of the word *virago*. When that Latin word first parachutes into English, appearing in medieval versions of the story of Adam and Eve, all women are, mythologically at least, *viragos*. Though the Book of Genesis calls Eve Adam's helper, the first description Adam himself gives her is rather more self-centred. As the familiar King James version goes, Adam says 'she shall be called woman, because she was taken out of man'. The fourth-century polyglot St Jerome, who produced the version of the Latin Bible which remained the standard text for over a millennium, had to find a suitable translation for this name which Adam first gives to Eve.

In Hebrew as in English these two words are connected, *ishah*, 'woman', derived in both substance and name, from *ish*, 'man'. In Jerome's Vulgate Adam thus doesn't call his spare-rib personal assistant *mulier*, the Latin word for woman. Instead Jerome's Adam says she should be called *virago* because she's derived, physically and etymologically, from a *vir*, 'a man'. Jerome's choice of word, *virago*, gives *vir* a feminine suffix, creating a word a bit like *man-ess* or *man-tress*. Adam's handy helper, his all-mod-cons *manette*, gets a name that connects her with manly qualities like *virtue* and *virility* which also derive from *vir*. It's only after the disappointing business with the serpent and the apple that she's renamed Eve.

Though Eden's First Lady is soon rechristened, *virago* survived in English as a term for a woman who is brave and strong, often one who succeeds in famous feats, fighting wars, killing foes or founding cities or nations. The first English (well, strictly Scots) version of Virgil's epic, the *Aeneid*, completed in 1513 by an Edinburgh churchman, uses *virago* to name a nymph who disguises herself as a warrior so that she can help her brother on the battlefield. For readers who don't know what that word means, Gavin Douglas, the Scottish translator at work here, glosses this exotic term in his next sentence. A virago, he says, is 'a woman exersand [exercising] a mannys offys', a woman doing a man's job.

Medieval medical science also offered a bit of wiggle room in gender's tightly nested stack of thoughts. According to ancient authorities, a baby's sex depended on which seed, the 'colder' female or the 'hotter' male, won out in a gestational tussle. Thanks to the pneumatic movement of 'heat' around a woman's body, the position of the foetus within the womb might also influence its character or personality. Henry Daniel's textbook from the 1370s explained the basics. If the sperm lodges on the right-hand side of the womb, it gains more 'heat' and the baby will be male. If it sticks on the left, the baby will be female. But what about if it ended up nearer the middle, just offset one way or another? If it's on the left but not so very far from the right, Daniel says you'll get 'a bolde sturdy woman'. Who wouldn't want to be bold and sturdy? But *bold* in medieval English could mean not only 'brave' and 'strong' but also 'shameless', while *sturdy* could mean both 'valiant' and 'robust' but also 'rebellious'. What sounds empowering is meant to be a no-win situation. Qualities which would be admired in a man were seen as disruptive if a woman demonstrated them – an ingenious double bind. This early science imagined the possibility of gender-non-conforming women, but squashed them back down as undesirable outcomes.

The bold sturdy women and viragos found on the pages of medical theory and history books were proof that women weren't always the soft, subsidiary helpmeet, even if these exceptions were conveniently explained away. In the real world too, women's evident intellectual and practical abilities challenged sexist world views. Sometimes commentators had to backtrack and eat their words if their patriarchal theories went too far. William Gouge's 1622 conduct book, *Of Domesticall Duties*, is famous for its neatly nested and very quotable summary of patriarchal order: 'a familie is a little Church, and a little common-wealth', each governed by paternal authority which guides, protects and disciplines. Yet in his third edition, Gouge had to row back quite some distance. He said he needed to make a 'just apology', a well-deserved mea culpa, to those he'd offended by the first two editions. He didn't want them to write him off as 'an hater of women', he said.

Like a public figure called out on social media today, Gouge said some readers had misconstrued his meaning as being much more hardline than he'd intended. He had set out the 'utter-most', the outer-most, what we would call the extremes, of a husband's supreme authority and a wife's duty to obey. Some readers had interpreted these theoretical extremes as representing how things should work in everyday life and thought him completely unreasonable and impractical. In the preface of this third edition, Gouge thus tried to introduce some nuance into his earlier argument. A husband, though he had total dominance in theory, ought in practice to make his wife 'a joint governor of the family with himself'. *Joint governor* sounds much less patriarchal, though someone like Gouge wouldn't have dreamt of letting women govern much at all in the public world. But, at least within the family, husbands were to share their authority.

Renaissance progressives ingeniously flexed their thinking like this to take account of the capabilities of real-world women without letting patriarchy's grip loosen much. Their words, though, sometimes let slip more than they might want to say about the real causes of women's subordination. The schoolmaster Richard Mulcaster, for example, was aware of the intellectual achievements of a small number of wealthy women whose privilege allowed them to study and learn, not least the accomplishments of Queen Elizabeth I to whom he dedicated a book in 1581. In a chapter on the education of girls, he leaves exact details to parental judgement, but suggests reading, writing, singing and playing music, and perhaps languages too, as fitting subjects. Nevertheless he's careful to set limits. He isn't saying, he reassures his readers, that girls should go alongside boys to grammar schools, for this would be a practice 'not used in my countrie'. Likewise there's 'no president thereof in my countrie', no precedent in England for women attending universities. Because of the 'difference of their calling', the different roles of men and women expected and enforced in society, he advises that girls' education should be much more constricted.

Mulcaster justified the restriction of girls' access to learning not on the basis of their nature but as a matter of precedent and tradition, how things are done in one country but not necessarily in another. As words like *precedent* enter the discussion, something important shifts. If the limits placed on women were shown to be merely social tradition rather than divinely ordained decree or biologically determined inevitability, then they might eventually be changed. Some Renaissance writers spelled this out very plainly, though more as an academic exercise than a firm plan for women's liberation. In 1509, at one of the leading universities in what is now modern-day France, a new young German faculty star, Heinrich Cornelius Agrippa, delivered his inaugural lecture. His talk on women's equality was dedicated to Margaret of Austria, a thirty-year-old princess so capable that her father, the Holy Roman Emperor, had appointed her governor of the Low Countries. Unfortunately, thanks to complaints about some of the more esoteric aspects of his research, Agrippa was swiftly cancelled and his academic tenure denied. It thus took him twenty years to publish a version of this lecture called 'On the Nobility and Superiority of the Female Sex'. Agrippa's argument was that women were in fact men's superiors. His little Latin book ran to several editions across the next hundred years and was translated into several European vernaculars, including into English by David Clapham in 1542.

Agrippa starts his argument at first principles. The difference between the sexes, what he (in Clapham's translation) calls the 'two kyndes', is nothing more than the 'sondry situation of the bodily partes', the two halves of the whole needed for the reproduction of the species. Clapham's choice of phrasing in his translation, the *sundry situation*, the different arrangements and positions, isn't so very far from Simone de Beauvoir's answer in a 1976 interview when she was asked to define *woman* in her own right.[2] 'Woman', she said, 'is a human being with a certain physiology, but that physiology in no way makes her inferior, nor does it justify her exploitation'. Agrippa might have agreed with de Beauvoir's two conclusions, at least in theory. A woman, he wrote, 'hathe that same mynd that a man hath, that same reason and speche'. In terms of their souls, he says that both 'naturally have equall libertie of dignitie and worthynesse'.

Then, as if it's the most obvious explanation in the world, he puts forward a potted history of women's subordination. He, like Mulcaster, cites precedents, but Agrippa's are examples from the ancient world when women were supposedly on equal footing with men. Over time women's original 'libertie' was, he theorised, 'forbydden by lawes, abolished by custome, extincted [extinguished] by education'. Their rights removed, women were subdued 'as it were by force of arms', by social pressures equivalent in strength to physical conquest. What we would call patriarchy comes, says Agrippa, not from 'divine necessitie or reason, but by custome, education, fortune'. The subordination of women wasn't natural or reasonable – it was an unjust society manufactured by denying women education, by imposing repressive laws and by men taking advantage.

*

Paying attention to what was hiding behind the curtain, Agrippa spelled out as plain as day that patriarchal society was neither divinely intended nor rationally justifiable but merely a mishmash of opportunism and coercion. Such exposure, for all its frankness, changed little for the average woman. Agrippa's lecture-cum-book was academic show-offery, an upturning of conventional wisdom so theoretical that readers could enjoy its intellectual fireworks without ever thinking of applying it to the real world. But there was one word in Agrippa's historical expla-nation, *custom*, which, though it sounds dull to modern ears, was a vital concept for feminist thinkers. *Custom*, borrowed from French into English, first described any habit or tradition and then, in more specialised senses, something so long established that it had taken on the force of law, particularly a payment to your feudal lord or a tax (hence one of the modern meanings of *customs*, checks and taxes on imports and exports).

As Renaissance readers pored over the Greek and Latin Classics and travellers' tales brought evidence from other cul-tures, it grew ever clearer that there were very few universal social norms and that much of what Britain took for granted about its society was mere custom. Some explorers encountered or heard tell of women who 'Shoot, Runne, Leape, Swimme, as well as the men' (as English readers were told in accounts of tribes in what is now modern-day Venezuela), real-life versions of the fabled Amazons. Others found islands 'where the women travel [travail, i.e. work] and labour as our men do in England, and the men keepe house' (so said the merchant Ralph Fitch who toured around South East Asia in the 1580s). Other socie-ties could do things differently and yet both cultures could seem inevitable and natural to those living within them. 'Custome is a second Nature, and no lesse powerfull', said John Florio's 1603 translation of essays by the French philosopher Michel de Montaigne.

One obvious custom concerned differences in how men and women dressed and wore their hair. These gender norms had the backing of the Bible which said that cross-dressing was 'abominable'. Preachers complained about women whose hair was *shorn* or *polled*, cut short like a man's. In the first decades of the seventeenth century, there was a fashion for women to crop their hair and wear men's clothing, a fashion which the king and his bishops decried. Amid this controversy over cross-dressing, a couple of enterprising writers dashed off pamphlets about this new style. The pamphlets' titles swapped over the usual gendering of Latin demonstrative pronouns to give nicknames for women who behaved and dressed more like men and men who behaved and dressed more like women: *hic mulier* ('this grammatically masculine woman') and *haec vir* ('this grammatically feminine man'). The first pamphlet is certain that the cross-dressing women of London are 'monstrous' and 'deformed' – a recycling of Aristotle's old ideas. But the second pamphlet is a dialogue rather than a diatribe, a debate between a representative *man-woman* and *wommanish man* (as the Latin is translated in the subtitles). For her part, *hic mulier* defends the cross-dressing which Moll Cutpurse and other roaring girls had made so notorious.

As *hic mulier* points out, women wearing what have traditionally been men's clothes is 'offensive' only 'in as much as it is a Stranger to the curiositie of the present times, and an enemie to Custome'. It's not wrong, but merely unfamiliar. In fact, she says that '*Custome* is an idiot', at least when it came to prescribing what women should wear, where they might go or how long their hair should be. Her questions about custom hang in the air unanswered while the second pamphleteer ends this little book by fudging his way back to usual arrangements. *Hic mulier* agrees that if Jacobean men were more manly, she and her fellow cross-dressers might wear more conventional dress. A damp squib of a conclusion – I prefer the swaggering of the hands-in-pockets girl who announces that custom is just plain idiotic.

Gender is the very epitome of a social custom: something long-standing, hard to escape, familiar and traditional, yet arbitrary, irrational. It has certainly taken its *toll* (the equivalent word used in Old English before *custom* arrived from French) on women over the centuries. As women in the past started to describe what custom does, they felt out the edges of patriarchy like a crayon finding the shape of something under a piece of paper. Some were inspired by the Enlightenment's progressive philosophy which left no accepted idea unchallenged. Taking nothing for granted, philosophers analysed how society had developed and how human life might be made better. The Cartesian method, named after René Descartes, used reason to set aside any unpersuasive bit of assumption, prejudice or custom until you were only left with truths.

For the French philosopher François Poullain de la Barre, women's inequality was a prime example of humanity's often faulty reasoning and over-reliance on precedent and tradition. His 1673 book, *De l'égalité des deux sexes*, was translated and published in England in 1677 under the title *The Woman as Good as the Man*. Poullain said that the gender hierarchy which sees men as superior and women inferior is 'nothing but Prejudice, formed in us by the appearances of things'. Gender extrapolates from the way things seem now to create an idea of how things have always been and should always be. Because women were limited to helping and caring roles in the period in which Poullain was writing, society, he wrote, assumes that they're 'uncapable of anything else'. As women seem to accept the situation, 'being born and bred in dependence', men assume, says Poullain, that they're in the right. But the arguments for male superiority are nothing more than an 'odd Medley of always confused Notions'. And experts who claim innate or essential differences between

men and women, says Poullain, aren't paying enough attention to which difference comes 'from Custom and Education,
and ... which comes from Nature'. After many centuries, says
Poullain, society therefore can't imagine 'how matters could be
other-wayes; it appearing impossible to alter'. Feminism's task
was to persuade society that there could be *other ways* and that
alteration was indeed possible.

Though the notion of *custom* exposed how the holding-back of
half of humanity was specious and unjustified, real change for
women would need stronger, more demanding and denunciatory
language. Feminist writers soon began to make use of the vocabulary of political theory and reform. Judith Drake, who worked
alongside her doctor husband treating women and children as
an unlicensed medical practitioner, went even further in her
explanation for the limits placed on women. In 1696 she published *An Essay in Defence of the Female Sex*, two years after the
philosopher Mary Astell launched her *Serious Proposal* arguing
for women's education and the founding of all-women colleges.
In her *Essay*, Drake made men's subordination of women a story
of politics and power. It was fear that women would rule them
and jealousy of 'the Abilities of Mind in our Sex', she thought,
which made men 'slavishly depress' women far back in the mists
of time. With a certain amount of optimism, she speculated that,
'in the Infancy of the World', women were men's 'Equals and
Partners in Dominion', power shared between them in the pre-
historic past. But driven by suspicion and envy, men eventually
forced women into 'a Subjection Nature never meant'.

Following a century in which one British king had been executed as a 'tyrant, traitor, murderer' and another king had been
deposed, monarchs no longer ruled as a result of divine right
but understood their powers to be built 'upon the foundation of

parliamentary limitation' (as Daniel Defoe put it in 1705). As political theorists grappled with how best to restrain a sovereign's power, women borrowed their words to describe custom's iron grip on their lives. At just fourteen years old in 1686, a girl named Sarah Fyge had published a feminist response to yet another misogynist poem. Her father was not best pleased at this, sending her to live with relatives and then arranging a marriage for her against her wishes. In 1703, aged thirty-three, she ignored her husband's disapproval and published a collection of poems. In one verse, 'The Emulation', she calls custom a *tyrant*, a cruel and unjust ruler who uses force to oppress his subjects and to command obedience. If *custom* is such an illegitimate sovereign, Fyge asks, just why should women obey its 'impositions', the excessive burdens which tradition and socialisation piles up on women? She explains that men use customs like these to exclude women from the arts and sciences. If women are handicapped by lack of learning, men effortlessly look as if they ought to be in charge.

Reading these women's treatises and poems, you can hear their tone hardening and their vocabulary sharpening. Women no longer minced their words but alternately mocked and denounced inequality. The historian Catharine Macaulay starts off gently in one of her *Letters on Education* published in 1790, noting how difficult it is to let go of long-held ideas. But to argue that 'Nature intended the subjection of one sex to the other' was, she said, building up a head of steam, ridiculous, a proposal more full of 'contradiction and absurdity' than a brain-bending argument from the very worst medieval logician. Macaulay's *absurdity* and *contradiction* were words that snagged in the mind of Mary Hays. Like her better-known friend Mary Wollstonecraft, Hays was a campaigner for radical social change. In 1798, in her anonymously published *Appeal to the Men of Britain*, Hays said with uncompromising candour that the gendered socialisation which shapes women's minds and controls their behaviour was 'perhaps the most completely absurd' system which human nature had dreamt up in a moment of madness, 'if indeed a bundle of contradictions and absurdities may be called a system'. Such glorious snark, giving patriarchy's dangly bits more and more of a well-deserved kicking.

Good fun though pointing out the absurdities of gender's rackety shack of contradictions could be, feminism also needed a language to claim equal treatment for women. The Age of Revolution gave women more terms by which to make these claims for greater equality. Early feminist voices shared with other reformers the vocabulary of dissent, revolution and abolition. The terminology of political radicalism could be usefully redirected to matters domestic: the religious tenet that a wife should obey her husband was, for example, relabelled as 'male despotism'. *Despot* was first used in English, borrowed from French, in the early sixteenth century to mean 'the chiefe or soveraigne Lord of a Countrey'. But a supplement to Samuel Johnson's famous dictionary published in 1801 noted that *despot*, with its newer meaning of a ruler who governs tyrannically, was now a much more popular word because 'the French revolutionists have been very liberal in conferring this title'. Women too found many customs to label *despotic*.

Mary Hays's *Appeal* also said that women had been 'shackled and enslaved by a thousand absurd prejudices'. If modern men really wanted progress, she said they should begin with 'the gradual emancipation of women', just as society should simultaneously accomplish 'the gradual emancipation' of every human. *Gradual emancipation* was one of the legal mechanisms by which slavery was phased out in some American states from the 1780s onward. Hays drew on the language of abolition and took her metaphorical shackles from the reality of enslavement, an appropriation which makes us cringe today.

In the nineteenth century, women became well versed in political organising, learning its methods and its language from abolitionists and other social reformers. African American women in Salem, Massachusetts, founded the first Female Anti-Slavery Society in 1832, and other Anti-Slavery Societies soon followed elsewhere. Women petitioned legislatures, gave public lectures and went on speaking tours, campaigning for the abolition of slavery, for workers' rights and for property rights for married women. Perhaps the most famous of these activities was the 'convention to discuss the social, civil, and religious condition and rights of woman' (as it advertised itself) held at Seneca Falls, a town near New York, in July 1848. The convention's 'Declaration of Sentiments' (*sentiments* here meaning 'opinions about what is right' rather than anything more weepily emotional) set out what it called the 'facts' about men's 'absolute tyranny' over women.

This Declaration rewrote the resonant clauses of the American Declaration of Independence to include two extra words: 'We hold these truths to be self-evident; that all men and women are created equal; that they are endowed by the Creator with certain inalienable rights'. Not just *all men* but *all men and women*. As the historian Judith Wellman points out, this wording failed to spell out whether African American, Indigenous and immigrant women were included in that small but significant word *all*.[3] *All women* didn't necessarily mean every woman, as the later actions of some of the organisers of Seneca Falls made clear. Parts of the suffrage movement, in the words of the author and activist Sally Roesch Wagner, 'used racism as a tool' in their quest to achieve the vote for some women but not others.[4] Claiming *rights* doesn't automatically make you right-thinking.

This small meeting was not necessarily very influential in its own time, but over the next fifty years it was transmogrified by some of its participants into a vital founding moment for American feminism.[5] Its resolutions read like a blueprint for demands which women would make in many countries over the next century and a half. But history is always more complicated than myth. Not everyone present at this meeting, for example, agreed with its ninth resolution, a demand for voting rights for women. Some abolitionists felt that voting would legitimise the prejudice already written into the Constitution; some Quaker pacifists did not want to elect a government that might wage war on their behalf. It took the intervention of Frederick Douglass, an abolitionist famous for his persuasive powers of rhetoric and oratory, for this resolution to pass.

Rights is my last word in this chapter, perhaps the most important woman's word of all. Political theorists in the Age of Enlightenment were not entirely clear about whether women had the same *natural rights* (the precursor of what we would now call *human rights*) as men. But plenty of women saw what these terms and arguments could do. Mary Wollstonecraft published first the *Vindication of the Rights of Men* in 1790, defending revolution and reform against those who supported traditional models of society, and then two years later her *Vindication of the Rights of Woman*. In a letter which prefaced this second *Vindication*, addressed to a French diplomat who had suggested that women needed only a limited education for a limited domestic life, Wollstonecraft accused him of seeking to '*force* all women, by denying them civil and political rights, to remain immured in their families groping in the dark'. To be *immured* is to be confined, imprisoned, walled within a fortress, left without enlightenment. Women would need patience as they chiselled their way towards the light. Such political and civil rights wouldn't come easily – the nineteenth-century establishment found a hundred and one reasons to hold back social reform – but more rights would eventually come, though in reality emancipation and liberation for every one of us remain a work in progress.

One eloquent advocate for all women's rights was the anti-slavery campaigner Sojourner Truth. Having escaped from enslavement herself in 1826, she was targeted by those who would deny rights to women and to the enslaved. In Northern Indiana in 1858 Truth faced rumours, started by anti-abolitionists, that she was a man. Calling the smearers out, she said she'd nursed many white babies 'to the exclusion of her own offspring'. Then she bared her bosom to the entire meeting room, saying (according to the correspondent who wrote up the event) that 'it was not to her shame that she uncovered her breast before them, but to their shame'. Truth (a new name this woman born Isabella Baumfree chose for herself) had a way with words, backed up by the reality of her hard-working body. She's famous for supposedly asking 'ain't I a woman' in a speech at the Woman's Rights Convention in Ohio in May 1851, a question which demanded to know why the courtesies extended to white women by men who would prefer them frail and delicate didn't apply to her.

But, as with many things in the surprising history of women's words in English, that famous quotation isn't quite what it seems. That question comes not from Sojourner Truth herself but from a re-creation of her speech written twelve years later by a white abolitionist, Frances Barker Gage.[6] In the more accurate transcription overseen by Truth and published in the *Anti-Slavery Bugle* a month after her Ohio speech, she didn't ask 'ain't I a woman?' but made a more mysterious statement. The labour she'd done as an enslaved woman was the match of anyone's and thus, showing off first her wits and then her muscles to her audience, she claimed equality in tersely peculiar syntax. 'I am a woman's rights', she said. *I am as entitled to a woman's rights as anyone else* was perhaps what she meant, or maybe something like *I'm living proof of how much every one of us deserves our rights*. Whether we speak our English as a mother tongue or, like Truth herself who spoke only Dutch until she was nine, have acquired it as a language later in life, I can think of no finer phrase, no better set of women's words, to have at your disposal: *I am a woman's rights*.

After Words

Old words, like many sorts of antique bits and bobs, seem quaintest without any of their original provenance. Easy to coo over a vintage object on a shelf if you're not so worried about its history. I've found plenty of remarkable and quirky terms in the English language of past centuries. But many of them, one way or another, started out in the service of sexist theories of women's supposed 'inferiority', of women's purported 'suitability' for a life of restriction and restraint. *Hic mulier*, that grammatically masculine woman who speaks in the pamphlet written about cross-dressing in the 1620s, says that she hasn't become some monstrous freak by going freely out and about in the world dressed in practical clothes. She's just a person 'with a mind busied, and a heart full of reasonable and devout cogitations', someone with a lively brain and a character devoted to good and rational purposes. Most of us, I think, would rather be just like her, busying our minds and hearts with the limitless horizons of our language's potential.

So despite these past words' retro charms, I wouldn't ever swap them for my equal rights. It's easy to forget how closely how the world-which-once-was snaps at our heels. I come from a teacherly, bookish family which shares my delight in words and memorable turns of phrase. My maternal grandmother, a schoolteacher, couldn't continue her career because of the bar which stopped married women carrying on their teaching jobs. She'd have liked to go to university (and the school to which she'd won a scholarship thought she had the brains to do it) but that was judged too expensive and too great a leap in life for a farmer's daughter, no matter how clever. When my mum passed her eleven-plus, the exam which determined your educational fate in England and Wales from the mid-1940s to the end of the 1960s, some girls with higher marks were displaced in favour of boys with lower marks so as to arrive at equal numbers of boys and girls heading to the more academic grammar schools. She too gave up her teaching job after I was born. And though women have been formally admitted to my university for a century, the Oxford college where I fell in until-death-do-us-part love with the English language and its literature first enrolled women as students fewer than twenty years before I arrived with my notebooks and sharpened pencils. My daughter and her friends might think such inequalities are ancient history, but they're not so very distant.

Yet today's teenagers and students probably don't feel blithely unconcerned about their right to equal treatment. They're all too aware that important rights can't be taken for granted, not least the right to an abortion which, as recent developments in the United States show, can be lost as well as gained. While sexism is much easier to denounce these days, in practice society's different treatment of men and women is a juggernaut which is hard to stop. Pressures on girls and women to conform to confining ideas of femininity in appearance seem to me to be getting stronger, not weaker. The cataclysm of testimonies of sexual harassment and sexual assault shared on Britain's Everyone's Invited website lays bare the rape culture in which girls grow up. And, if they have families when they are older, girls and young women might find certain problems intractable, and the deep ruts of women's historical oppression still easy to find. Having voyaged through many centuries of words, it's no surprise to me that time and progress don't always go onward in unison, step by step, ankles tied together for a race. The status quo fights hard to stay in place. As one restriction is escaped, another springs up to hold us back.

So we should be always on our guard, even as we're delighted about the progress we've made. We're speaking out about the many and varied consequences of living in a gendered society, as well as the realities of a life cycle lived in a female body. It seems that almost nothing is off limits. The Georgian and Victorian prudishness which curbed certain words and subjects might seem ridiculous in our much more no-filter era. But, despite this outpouring of truth-telling, inhibitions still tug at our sleeves. Alongside speaking out, there's plenty of infighting about the right way to speak. In recent years, when some topics relevant to a majority of women have been addressed, the words *woman* and *women* themselves have sometimes been avoided in favour of circumlocutions which go the long way round. In these instances vocabulary keeps a tight close-up on the issue under consideration – *those who menstruate*, say, or *pregnant people* – so as to avoid making broader observations about what generally (but not always) unites those in question.

It feels as though there are more rules to follow and more conventions to attend to when discussing women's lives. Such *verbal hygiene* (Professor Deborah Cameron's name for attempts to clean up language like this to make it match specific ideals or values) shows that the writer or speaker in question knows that common experiences which many women share won't impact every woman. It also acknowledges that some who are affected by the subject matter under discussion don't wish to be categorised as women. Some of us find this verbal purification unproblematic and helpfully precise, an inclusive sign of progress. Some of us prefer the gender-additive language of *women and* ... as a workable compromise.

Some activists shame those who won't adjust their vocabulary to make these explicit acknowledgements. Others challenge those who select this way of speaking, complaining that gender-inclusive wording doesn't come cost-free. Gender neutrality in wording, they argue, obscures social reality. If we write or talk about generic *people* or *individuals*, the explanation of how and why one particular subset of humans faces these particular challenges connectedly and systematically is left unsaid. This language activism usually arrives top down rather than being requested by those concerned or tested for its acceptability and usefulness. Choices made about women's words are now proxies for bigger arguments and many of us fear the consequences of choices which might meet with disapproval. Taking into account patriarchy's habit of urging women to be quiet and of caricaturing those women who do speak up or out as gossipy, frivolous, hysterical, dull or bitchy, it seems regressive to stifle women's words, however progressive the motivation. Each woman must have the terms of her own choosing.

So, though it's foolish to romanticise this waltzing around with the dancing fossils of our language, these elderly ancestors might feel inspiring in their less-than-perfect, ever-changing, I-wouldn't-start-from-here haphazardness. And the first women's words often have a just-right quality, neither too euphemistic nor too technical. Before English was fully established as a language of learning and knowledge, its vocabulary was more freestyle, extemporary and off-the-cuff. Such English finds its way onto the page as translators reached into everyday speech to find equivalents for French or Latin terms. For all the obvious sexism of English's first one thousand years, there was less agreement about what kind of language was unacceptable for public use.

Once decorum and modesty became society's guiding virtues,

what could be said and heard in public became more limited. Discussion of many subjects was steered up the high road of formal language, whether technical terminology or roundabout euphemisms. With earlier words fading out of fashion, spaces opened up which would eventually be filled in with whatever informal phrases you could grub up in the grotty back alleys of slang. Neither of these ways of talking necessarily work in women's interests. Technical terms, removed from everyday speech, don't feel especially comfortable while slang brings with it the risk of shame, the feeling that things named by dirty words are themselves taboo. We can't start again from scratch, or paddle back upstream to reinstate long-lost words, but we might try to imitate early English's plainspokenness where we can.

Feminists have long been suspicious of *Man Made Language*, as it was called in the title of Dale Spender's 1980 book, given men's historic domination of the institutions which construct our society's knowledge and thus for the most part control how the world is named and discussed. But we might feel also that English is ours to bend to our will. The vocabulary of English has always in some senses belonged to women, and not solely because your mother tongue was generally learned from your female carers. Women, largely excluded from more specialist education, were the perfect target market for dictionaries (and were also the perfect excuse for lexicographers to publish dictionaries that men might also need). The first monolingual English dictionary, Robert Cawdrey's *Table Alphabetical* published in 1604, was dedicated to five aristocratic sisters. Cawdrey pitched this wordbook as being for 'the benefit and helpe of Ladies, Gentlewomen, or any other unskilfull persons'. *Unskilfull* here means lacking in knowledge rather than hopelessly clumsy or inept. John Bulloker's 1616 *English Expositor* was the second-ever dictionary of English, dedicated to a countess and intended, as he says in his introduction, for use by 'greatest Ladies and studious Gentlewomen'. Thomas Blount's 1656 *Glossographia*, a dictionary of new and tricky words, was created, he said, for 'the more-knowing women, and the less-knowing men'. Though we weren't the first makers of dictionaries, we were their intended readers. A woman *more-knowing* about her own life and experience than any man could be, then or now, might thus feel entitled to everything in English vocabulary's rich and rampageous history.

By the middle of the eighteenth century, English was, for good or ill, sometimes said to be entirely women's responsibility. Samuel Johnson, who'd undertaken an eight-year project to create an authoritative record of English vocabulary, makes language itself female in the preface to his 1755 dictionary. He rewrites that strange Bible verse about interbreeding between women and angels in the Book of Genesis. While the things and ideas which words name are the 'sons of heaven', words are 'the daughters of the earth'. He means that words and women and nature are changeable, organic, in need of cultivation and management. As Johnson was preparing his dictionary, his patron Philip Stanhope, 4th Earl of Chesterfield, published a couple of think-pieces in a weekly magazine. He welcomed Johnson's plan to impose some order on English because it was, he quipped, now in a 'state of anarchy'. For this he blames his 'fair countrywomen', the women who speak English in an unruly, ungoverned way. With just-joking sexism, he points out that women jumble up their sentences, invent words and make mistakes because of their lack of education.

Despite the disarray he says they've caused in English's stock of words, Chesterfield nonetheless calls women 'the enrichers, the patronesses, and the harmonizers of our language'. Women drove the variety in English's vocabulary and sponsored its growth. How exactly we harmonised it, given what he says is our supposed fondness for many different ways of spelling or pronouncing a word, I'm not so sure. But the vernacular, Chesterfield says, 'is indisputably the more immediate province of the fair sex: there they shine, there they excel'. Women are directly responsible for the territory of English. With his tongue bulging in his cheek, he means by this that we're chatterboxes, we talk too much, but why don't we take him at his word and accept the compliments? As their presence as dedicatees shows, women had been the buyers and readers of the first English dictionaries. Much of English's ever-widening medieval and Early Modern vocabulary came into being as writers sought to meet the needs of far broader audiences than the narrow elite of educated men who could already read Latin, French and other foreign languages. Women made up the majority of this growing demand to learn about every subject under the sun in the mother tongue.

So in one way it's our language to do with what we want. In 1715, a self-taught scholar from Newcastle-upon-Tyne, Elizabeth Elstob, published the first grammar of the Anglo-Saxon language written in English rather than the more usual Latin of male academics.[1] Living as her clerical brother's housekeeper and drawing on his academic contacts, Elstob had the freedom to transcribe manuscripts and to edit and translate some of the earliest English texts. Her grammar found its way to the desk of Thomas Jefferson, third president of the United States, who used it to decipher ancient legal terminology which he came across in his studies. Praising Elstob's achievement and countering anyone who might disapprove of her endeavours, the clergyman-academic George Hickes pointed out that 'the Language that we speak is our Mother-Tongue; And who so proper to play the Critics in this as the Females?' Who better to be the experts in the oldest versions of English than women? I like his line of thinking. Who so proper to criticise, reconstruct and rearrange this mother (and now often other) tongue but we ourselves?

Acknowledgements

This book could not have been written without the painstaking labours and industry of many lexicographers, those patient souls who undertake the endless task of compiling and updating a dictionary's testimony of a language. The etymologies and histories of the words discussed in this book are recorded in the *Dictionary of Old English*, the *Middle English Dictionary* and the *Oxford English Dictionary*, as well as in dictionaries of the other languages from which English borrows some of its words. I have discovered many historical words and definitions through the Lexicons of Early Modern English project edited by Ian Lancashire (leme.library.utoronto.ca) which brings together dictionaries, wordbooks and glossaries from the fifteenth to the eighteenth centuries. Chasing language and ideas across a millennium of English speech and writing has taken me to the articles and books of many historians and literary scholars. I'm indebted to the knowledge and insight provided by each of those fellow academics on their particular specialist subjects.

As an academic writer venturing for the first time into trade publishing, I am very grateful for the wise counsels of my agent, Caroline Hardman, and her co-agent Sarah Levitt, as well as for the many necessary interventions of my editors Sarah Savitt, Clare Gordon and Allison Lorentzen. I'm not sure what collective noun could best describe this group of marvellous women – a *brilliance*, perhaps, or a *wondrel* (a lovely medieval term to name something extraordinary). Whatever the right word might be, I could not have written *Mother Tongue* without them.

Notes

Introduction: Women's Words

1. Dwight Bolinger, *Language, the Loaded Weapon: The Use and Abuse of Language Today* (Longman, 1980), p. 103.

Chapter One: Cors: Words for Female Anatomy

1. Alison Stone, *An Introduction to Feminist Philosophy* (Polity, 2007), pp. 43–6.
2. Katharine Park, 'Cadden, Laqueur, and the "One-Sex Body"', *Medieval Feminist Forum*, 46 (2010), pp. 96–100.
3. Janet Adelman, 'Making Defect Perfection: Shakespeare and the One-Sex Model', in *Enacting Gender on the English Renaissance Stage*, ed. Viviana Comensoli and Anne Russell (University of Illinois Press, 1999), pp. 23–52.
4. The Labia Library can be found at www.labialibrary.org.au and the Vulva Gallery at www.thevulvagallery.com.
5. www.beautifulcervix.com
6. Professor Helen King has led the way in countering these misconceptions. See her chapter 'Once upon a Text: Hysteria from Hippocrates', in *Hysteria Beyond Freud*, ed. Sander L. Gilman (University of California Press, 1993), as well as her books *Hippocrates' Woman: Reading the Female Body in Ancient Greece* (Routledge, 1998) and *Hippocrates Now* (Bloomsbury Academic, 2019).
7. Heather Meek, 'Of Wandering Wombs and Wrongs of Women: Evolving Conceptions of Hysteria in the Age of Reason', *English Studies in Canada*, 35 (2009), pp. 105–28 (at p. 107).

8. Leslie Lockett, *Anglo-Saxon Psychologies in the Vernacular and Latin Traditions* (University of Toronto Press, 2011).

Chapter Two: Flux: Menstrual Language

1. Research commissioned by the period tracking app Clue found in an analysis of 7.5 million cycles that the menstrual cycle does not sync with the phases of the moon (https://helloclue.com/articles/cycle-a-z/myth-moon-phases-menstruation).
2. Monica H. Green, *The Trotula: An English Translation of the Medieval Compendium of Women's Medicine* (University of Pennsylvania Press, 2002), p. 21.
3. womena.dk/how-many-women-menstruate
4. Sara Read, '"Thy righteousness is but a menstrual clout": Sanitary Practices and Prejudice in Early Modern England', *Early Modern Women: An Interdisciplinary Journal*, 3 (2008), pp. 1–25.
5. Patricia Crawford, 'Attitudes to Menstruation in Seventeenth-Century England', *Past and Present*, 91 (1981), pp. 47–73 (pp. 49, 58).

Chapter Three: Lust: Sex and its Terms

1. Recent research by Thorsteinn Vilhjalmsson has unpacked the early history of the *tribade*: 'The Tribadic Tradition: The Reception of an Ancient Discourse on Female Homosexuality' (MA thesis, University of Bristol, 2015).
2. See Peter Cryle and Alison Moore, *Frigidity: An Intellectual History* (Palgrave Macmillan, 2011).

Chapter Four: Matrix: The Womb's Words

1. Sophia M. Connell, *Aristotle on Female Animals: A Study of the Generation of Animals* (Cambridge University Press, 2016), p. 282.
2. Mary E. Fissell, 'Remaking the Maternal Body in England, 1680–1730', *Journal of the History of Sexuality*, 26 (2017), pp. 114–39.
3. Jennifer L. Morgan, *Laboring Women: Reproduction and Gender in New World Slavery* (University of Pennsylvania Press, 2004), Chapter 3.
4. As cited in Ruth Perry, 'Colonizing the Breast: Sexuality and Maternity in Eighteenth-Century England', *Journal of the History of Sexuality*, 2 (1991), pp. 204–34.
5. Allison Muri, 'Imagining Reproduction: The Politics of Reproduction, Technology and the Woman Machine', *Journal of Medical Humanities*, 31

(2009), pp. 53–67. See also Nick Hopwood's chapter on 'The Keywords "Generation" and "Reproduction"', in *Reproduction: Antiquity to the Present Day*, ed. Nick Hopwood, Rebecca Flemming and Lauren Kassell (Cambridge University Press, 2018), pp. 287–304.

6. As cited by Maryanne Kowaleski, 'Singlewomen in Medieval and Early Modern Europe', in *Singlewomen in the European Past, 1250–1800*, ed. Judith M. Bennett and Amy M. Froide (University of Pennsylvania Press, 1999), pp. 38–81 (at p. 46).

7. Amy M. Froide, *Never Married: Singlewomen in Early Modern England* (Oxford University Press, 2005), p. 3.

8. Jennifer Evans, *Aphrodisiacs, Fertility, and Medicine in Early Modern England* (Cambridge University Press, 2014), pp. 63–6.

9. Daphna Oren-Magidor, *Infertility in Early Modern England* (Palgrave Macmillan, 2017), pp. 1, 165.

10. nursingclio.org/2020/10/06/pregnancy-and-miscarriage-on-social-media-new-metaphors-to-make-miscarriages-easier-to-talk-about-and-easier-to-bear

11. This paragraph is indebted to the discussion of this subject by Monica H. Green, 'Gendering the History of Women's Healthcare', *Gender & History*, 20 (2008), pp. 487–518.

12. Zubin Mistry's book *Abortion in the Early Middle Ages, c. 500–900* (York Medieval Press, 2015) gives a history of the Church's early attitudes to abortion.

13. Wolfgang P. Müller, *The Criminalization of Abortion in the West: Its Origins in Medieval Law* (Cornell University Press, 2016), pp. 66–75.

14. Carla Spivack, 'To "Bring Down the Flowers": The Cultural Context of Abortion Law in Early Modern England', *William & Mary Journal of Race, Gender, and Social Justice*, 14 (2007), pp. 107–51.

15. Shulamith Shahar, *Childhood in the Middle Ages* (Routledge, 1990), p. 35.

16. Joyce E. Chaplin, *Subject Matter: Technology, the Body, and Science on the Anglo-American Frontier, 1500–1676* (Harvard University Press, 2001), pp. 263–4.

17. Monica H. Green unpacks the many problems with this narrative in her article 'Gendering the History of Women's Healthcare', *Gender & History*, 20 (2008), pp. 487–518 (pp. 489–98).

18. psyche.co/ideas/philosophy-can-explain-what-kind-of-achievement-it-is-to-give-birth

Chapter Five: Nurse: The Language of Care

1. Londa Schiebinger, 'Why Mammals are Called Mammals: Gender Politics

in Eighteenth-Century Natural History', *American Historical Review*, 98 (1993), pp. 382–411.

2. Jennifer L. Morgan, *Laboring Women: Reproduction and Gender in New World Slavery* (University of Pennsylvania Press, 2004), Chapter 1.

Chapter Six: Industry: Working Words

1. Jane Humphries and Jacob Weisdorf, 'The Wages of Women in England, 1260–1850', *Journal of Economic History*, 75 (2015), pp. 405–47.

2. Jane Whittle and Mark Hailwood, 'The Gender Division of Labour in Early Modern England', *Economic History Review*, 73 (2020), pp. 3–32.

3. Cordelia Beattie, *Medieval Single Women: The Politics of Social Classification in Late Medieval England* (Oxford University Press, 2007), Chapter 5.

4. Ruth Mazo Karras, *Common Women: Prostitution and Sexuality in Medieval England* (Oxford University Press, 1996), p. 48.

5. Amy Louise Erickson, 'Mistresses and Marriage: Or, A Short History of the Mrs', *History Workshop Journal*, 78 (2014), pp. 39–57.

6. On the dangers of overstating the benefits of *sole merchant* status for women, see a blogpost by the legal historian Professor Sara M. Butler: legalhistorymiscellany.com/2019/02/08/femme-sole-status-a-failed-feminist-dream.

7. Cordelia Beattie, 'Married Women, Contracts and Coverture in Late Medieval England', in *Married Women and the Law in Premodern Northwest Europe*, ed. Cordelia Beattie and Matthew Frank Stevens (Boydell & Brewer, 2013), pp. 133–54.

8. Alexandra Shepard, *Accounting for Oneself: Worth, Status, and the Social Order in Early Modern England* (Oxford University Press, 2015).

Chapter Seven: Ghyrles and Hags: Words for Ages and Stages

1. Daria Izdebska, 'Weapon-Boys and Once-Maidens: A Study of Old English Vocabulary for Stages of Life', in *Medieval English Life Courses: Cultural-Historical Perspectives*, ed. Thijs Porck and Harriet Soper (Brill, 2022), pp. 47–89.

2. Joyce Hill, 'Childhood in the Lives of Anglo-Saxon Saints', in *Childhood and Adolescence in Anglo-Saxon Literary Culture*, ed. Susan Irvine and Winfried Rudolf (University of Toronto Press, 2018), pp. 139–61.

3. Jennifer Higginbotham, *The Girlhood of Shakespeare's Sisters: Gender, Transgression, Adolescence* (Edinburgh University Press, 2013), Chapter 2.

4. Amy M. Froide, *Never Married: Singlewomen in Early Modern England* (Oxford University Press, 2005), p. 2.

5. Froide, *Never Married: Singlewomen in Early Modern England*, Chapter 6.
6. Michael Stolberg, 'A Woman's Hell? Medical Perceptions of Menopause in Preindustrial Europe', *Bulletin of the History of Medicine*, 73 (1999), pp. 404–28.
7. Malcolm Gaskill, 'Witchcraft Trials in England', in *The Oxford Handbook of Witchcraft in Early Modern Europe and Colonial America*, ed. Brian P. Levack (Oxford University Press, 2013), pp. 283–98 (at p. 284).

Chapter Eight: Fors: Naming Male Violence

1. Sara M. Butler, *The Language of Abuse: Marital Violence in Later Medieval England* (Brill, 2001), Introduction and Chapters 2 and 5.
2. Corinne Saunders has untangled the history of Anglo-Saxon and medieval rape laws in her article 'The Medieval Law of Rape', *King's Law Journal*, 11 (2000), pp. 19–48, and her book *Rape and Ravishment in the Literature of Medieval England* (Boydell & Brewer, 2001). See also Caroline Dunn, *Stolen Women in Medieval England: Rape, Abduction and Adultery, 1100–1500* (Cambridge University Press, 2013).
3. For full details of this new discovery, see the special issue on 'The Case of Geoffrey Chaucer and Cecily Chaumpaigne', guest edited by Sebastian Sobecki and Euan Roger, of *The Chaucer Review*, 57:4 (2022).
4. Helen Barker, *Rape in Early Modern England: Law, History and Criticism* (Palgrave Macmillan, 2021), pp. 89–119.
5. Marilyn Frye, *The Politics of Reality: Essays in Feminist Theory* (Crossing Press, 1983), pp. 4–5.

Chapter Nine: Custom and Tyranny: Finding Feminism's Vocabulary

1. Simone de Beauvoir, *The Second Sex*, trans. Constance Borde and Sheila Malovany-Chevallier (Vintage Classics, 2011), p. 16.
2. Interview of Beauvoir by Susan J. Brison in Rome on 7 September 1976. Transcribed and translated in the *Cambridge Companion to Simone de Beauvoir*, ed. Claudia Card (Cambridge University Press, 2003), p. 192.
3. Judith Wellman, *The Road to Seneca Falls: Elizabeth Cady Stanton and the First Woman's Rights Convention* (University of Illinois Press, 2004), pp. 200–1.
4. sallyroeschwagner.com/f/ reaction-to-ny-times-opinion-piece-how-the-suffrage-movement-be
5. Lisa Tetrault tells the story of this mythification in her book *The Myth*

of *Seneca Falls: Memory and the Women's Suffrage Movement, 1848–1898* (University of North Carolina Press, 2014).

6. To compare the two versions of the speeches, see Leslie Podell's Sojourner Truth Project website (www.thesojournertruthproject.com) which builds on the historical research of Princeton University's Professor Nell Irvin Painter.

After Words

1. These details are drawn from an article by Yvonne Seale, 'The First Female Anglo-Saxonist', *History Today*, www.historytoday.com/first-female-anglo-saxonist

Index